The Archaeology and Epigraphy of Indus Writing

Bryan K. Wells

with technical appendices by

Andreas Fuls

Archaeopress Archaeology

Archaeopress
First and Second Floors
13-14 Market Square
Bicester OX26 6AD

www.archaeopress.com

ISBN 978 1 78491 046 4
ISBN 978 1 78491 047 1 (e-Pdf)

© Archaeopress and B K Wells 2015

Front cover image: Great Bath as seen from the Stupa of Mohenjo-daro, Pakistan. Photograph taken by the author in 1999.

All rights reserved. No part of this book may be reproduced, stored in retrieval system, or transmitted, in any form or by any means, electronic, mechanical, photocopying or otherwise, without the prior written permission of the copyright owners.

This book is available direct from Archaeopress or from our website www.archaeopress.com

Dedication

This book is dedicated to:

David H. Kelley who has led the way. Mentor, friend and colleague, Dave's open mind and heart serve as a model of humanity and intellect for future generations of scholars. His years of dedicated work and insightful analysis inspirer us all to try harder. His pioneering research is echoed in this book. Thank you Dave from all of us.

DAVID HUMISTON KELLEY
APRIL 1, 1924 TO MAY 19, 2011
(PHOTO: NOVEMBER 2003 UNIVERSITY OF CALGARY, CALGARY, ALBERTA)

Contents

Dedication

List of Figures iii

List of Tables vi

Acknowledgements vii

Preface viii

Introduction 1

Chapter 1: The Indus Valley Script 4

Chapter 2: The Indus Sign List 13

Chapter 3: Patterns of Sign Use and the Syntactic Structure of Indus Texts 23

Chapter 4: Tablets, Pots and the Volumetric System of Harappa 55

Chapter 5: Numerals in the Indus Script and their Uses 66

Chapter 6: Proto-Dravidian and the Indus Script 77

Appendix I: Automated Segmentation Of Indus Texts 100

Appendix II: Positional Analysis of Indus Signs 119

Appendix III: Classifying Undeciphered Writing Systems 134

Literature Cited 141

List of figures

Figure 1.1 Map of some major archaeological sites discussed in the text. 4
Figure 1.2 Chronological table showing approximate temporal relationships between the Indus Valley and Mesopotamia. 5
Figure 1.3 Various types of intaglio seals: a) Square, b) Rectangular, c) Circular, d) Cylinder. 6
Figure 1.4 Examples of seal impressions use as closures. 8
Figure 1.5 Text on the back of DK12145/M-0426. 8
Figure 1.6 Possible pen nib M-2129. 9
Figure 1.7 Bas relief and Incised miniature tablets from Harappa, and a Copper tablet from Mohenjo-daro . 9
Figure 1.8 Inscribed post –firing text (H-2336); Pre-firing seal impressions on ceramic vessel 10
Figure 1.9 Miscellaneous inscribed artifacts from various sites and periods. 11
Figure 2.1 Flowchart of the method used to define indus graphemes. 13
Figure 2.2 Methods of sign elaboration and construction. 14
Figure 2.3 The five largest allographic sets of Indus signs. 15
Figure 2.4 Graphemic vs. allographic variations of signs 155, 156 and 158. 16
Figure 2.5 Overlapping contexts of signs 18
Figure 2.6 An Indus Sign List. 19
Figure 3.1 Continuum of text clasification of Indus texts by sign distribution and clustering. 23
Figure 3.2 Deviation of text types from expected random frequency of occurrences 24
Figure 3.3 Elements of the Patterned text M-0393. 24
Figure 3.4 Text M-0647 showing "conjunctive" sign 741 and frequency of pairing. 25
Figure 3.5 Graphemes based on sign 740 with infixed numbers. 25
Figure 3.6 Examples of signs 920/320 in Initial and Terminal clusters 26
Figure 3.7 Percentage of ICTM by their positions in txts from right (1) to left (10)................... 27
Figure 3.8 ICTM by one sign initial clusters. 27
Figure 3.9 Distribution of sign 1, 2, and 60 in long (6+ signs) Patterned texts 28
Figure 3.10 Structural analysis of IC from text M-0355 29
Figure 3.11 Segmentation "tree" of text M-0355.. 30
Figure 3.12 Graph showing the solo and IC percentage for 11 common signs found in ICs................. 31
Figure 3.13 Distribution of sign 550 in long Patterned texts 31
Figure 3.14 Distribution of sign 817 in long Patterned texts 31
Figure 3.15 Percentage of Set 1 and 2 ICs pairing with ICTMs in long Patterned texts 32
Figure 3.16 The most common ICTM-Constant combinations in ICs................................. 33
Figure 3.17 ICs with sign 220 right-adjacent to ICTMs that employ Semi-variable. 34
Figure 3.18 Contexts of sign 368 right adjacent to ICTMs 35
Figure 3.19 Long ICs with 002 as ICTM. Frequency of collocation given between signs. 35
Figure 3.20 Fish signs used in Indus writing. 36
Figure 3.21 Sign 220 plus number clusters in medial contexts... 37
Figure 3.22 The five most common fish sign in the normal order in fish sign clusters. 37
Figure 3.23 Pairing of fish signs in long Patterned texts 38
Figure 3.24 Collocations of fish signs with signs 798 and 803 39
Figure 3.25 Affixing patters for signs 100-415 Bonded Cluster (BC). 40
Figure 3.26 Affixing paradigms for sign 590+ phytomorphic signs as Bonded Clusters................. 41
Figure 3.27 Affixing paradigms for the 033/705 Bonded Cluster. 42
Figure 3.28 Contexts of Set 17 signs initial and terminal contexts pairing with sign 350 i. 43
Figure 3.29 Well known terminal cluster in strings which could be mistaken for Post Terminals. 43
Figure 3.30 DK.E, E2475 showing the list of three BCs... 44
Figure 3.31 Sign 740 solo example from Diamabad (Dmd-1). 44
Figure 3.32 Comparison of a Patterned (top) and Complex (bottom) text in terms of sign correlations ... 46
Figure 3.33 Comparison of Pure texts (H98-3491, top) and Hybrid Complex (Nd-1, bottom). 47
Figure 3.34 Segmentation trees for H98-3491 and Nd-1.. 48
Figure 3.35 All of the complete texts using the 920-140 pair. 49
Figure 3.36 The Dholavira signboard 50

Figure 3.37 Text with related structures to the Dholavira signboard. 50
Figure 3.38 H-006 with the partially rotated sign 625/850. 51
Figure 3.39 The longest Indus text on a single surface (M-0314). 54
Figure 4.1. Possible depiction of a Viiii tree offering on M-0478. 56
Figure 4.2. Examples of artifacts bearing V+# texts. 57
Figure 4.3. Tabulation of tablets with V+# texts found at Harappa, Pakistan 58
Figure 4.4. Miniature tablets with V+# texts by mound at Harappa. 58
Figure 4.5 Purana Qila pots *in situ* after Vats (1940: Vol. II, Plate 23a). 59
Figure 4.6. The Purana Qila pots from Harappa with V+# texts and an example from Kalibangan. 60
Figure 4.7 All non-Harappan examples of V+# texts 63
Figure 5.1. Basic Indus Script Stroke Numerals 66
Figure 5.2. Economic texts from three ancient writing systems compared to the Indus script 67
Figure 5.3. Contexts of signs 031 and 032 with numeric syllabic examples 71
Figure 5.4. Inscribed ceramics with matching inscriptions to tablets (from Harappa). 72
Figure 5.5. Associations of "fish" signs and numeral signs. 73
Figure 5.6. Numeral signs associated with sign 740 74
Figure 5.7 Examples of sign 900 as a numeral in positional notation 75
Figure 5.8. Various Contexts of Sign 055 76
Figure 6.1 Copper tablet artifacts from Mohenjo-daro with the 'hare eating grass' replacement set 84
Figure 6.2. Some examples of sign 820 in various contexts. 85
Figure 6.3 Contexts of 740 and 820 using the same bonded cluster. 86
Figure 6.4 Positional analysis of sign 820 in Patterned, Long Complex and Short Segment texts texts. ... 87
Figure 6.5. Some examples of 740 and 752 pairing in texts. 88
Figure 6.7. Bas-relief miniature tablet H-182 with drummer and tiger. 89
Figure 6.6. Possible reading of M-30. 89
Figure 6.8. The Dholavira signboard with photo reversed to reflect reading order 90
Figure 6.9. Segmentation tree for the Dholavira Signboard 91
Figure 6.10. Other text containing the Dholavira toponym. 92
Figure 6.11. Suggested readings for Dholavira signboard signs. 92
Figure 6.12. H-176 with the sign sequence 861+740 reading 'cow at the city'. 93
Figure 6.13. Examples of the various contexts of sign 821. 93
Figure 6.14. The distribution of sign 798 in all complete text in which it occurs. 94
Figure 6.15. The Mohenjo-daro bangle pot with seal impression and reconstructed bangles. 94
Figure 6.16. The Mohenjo-daro bangle pot text. 95
Figure 6.17. Evidence for 575 as a syllable sign. 96
Figure 6.18. Various contexts of sign 575. 96
Figure 6.19 Possible relationship between signs and images on M-1919. 97
Figure 6.20. Proposed values for some Indus signs. 98
Figure 6.21 Proto-Dravidian verb endings and associated signs 98
Figure AI.1 Segmentation of H-026 102
Figure AI.2 Segmentation tree using the z-score method 103
Figure AI.3 Logarithmic influence of initial sign frequency) on the connectivity 105
Figure AI.4 Example of a) highly structured text, b) less structured text, both 8 signs long. 110
Figure AI.5 Step by step process of segmentation and final Multivariate Segmentation tree 112
Figure AI.6 Segmentation tree of H-026. Compare segmentation results to figure AI.1 113
Figure AI.7 Mean tree index, mean connectivity and its standard deviation for different text classes ... 113
Figure AI.8 Relationship of mean connectivity to its standard deviation (std) by text class 114
Figure AI.9 Mean tree index and mean connectivity for different artefact types 114
Figure AII.1. Normalization of sign positions for different text length 122
Figure AII.2. Initial signs 190, 853, and 880. 123
Figure AII.3. Positional histograms of Post-Terminal signs. 126
Figure AII.4. Signs with an almost constant positional distribution. 126
Figure AII.5. Signs with a constant but with low frequency in the initial position 127
Figure AII.6. Signs with an Early-Medial positional distribution. 127
Figure AII.7. Signs 741 and 742 have a Mid-Medial distribution. 127
Figure AII.8. Signs with a Late-Medial sign distribution. 128
Figure AII.9. Histograms of sign 590 for different text classes 130

Figure AII.10. Histogram of sign 550 with two maxima at position 1 and 8 in various text classes. 131
Figure AII.11. Positional histogram of signs in the text +740-540-002-820+ (seal M-1088)..................... 133
Figure AIII.1: Rank versus number of signs with the same frequency in a double-logarithmic scale 136
Figure AIII.2: Relationship between exponent G of sign frequency curve and mean word length 137
Figure AIII.3: Modified power law (MPL) of Indus signs results in exponent G = -1.347 (R^2 = 0.991). 139

List of Tables

Table 4.1. Measurements of the Purana Qila vessels with radius and volume calculations 61
Table 4.2. Summary of the estimated units of the Harappa volumetric system........................ 62
Table 5.1. Right-adjacent collocations of Short-Linear Stroke signs. 69
Table 5.2. Right-adjacent collocations of short stacked stroke signs. 70
Table 5.3. Right adjacent collocations of long linear stroke signs.. 72
Table 6.1 The proto-Dravidian number system. 83
Table AI.1 Segmentation parameter and their effect on the connectivity between signs. 109
Table AII.1. Frequency of text lengths in the reduced text corpus of complete inscriptions.... 120
Table AII.2. Positional histograms of Initial sign and graphically similar signs.......................... 124
Table AII.3. Positional histograms of Terminal marker and graphically similar signs............... 125
Table AII.4 Comparison of signs and their doubled graphem... 128
Table AII.5. Comparison of signs and their mirrors. 129

Acknowledgements

The research summarized here was undertaken in Chennai, India in 2009. The many interesting and enthusiastic researchers and visitors at the Institute of Mathematical Science in Chennai all contributed critique, assistance, comments and ideas from a thoughtful and considerate perspective (usually over a cup of coffee).

I would like to thank Dr. Richard Meadow of Harvard University and the HARP project for sharing their unpublished photographs with me and for giving copyright permission for the figures in the book.

Thanks to Dr. Andreas Fuls (Technical University of Berlin) for his many insightful comments and corrections. His help in this research was crucial to its success as much of the analysis was performed using analytical techniques and software developed by him (Appendix I-III).

Many thanks to Mr. Chandrashankar Subramanian of the Indus Research Centre for his many helpful suggestions and especially comments and corrections in Chapter 6.

The author wishes to especially thank the Archaeo-Astronomy Programme of Sir Jamsetji Tata Trust for facilitating his visit to India.

I would like to thank Mayank Vahia for his detailed comments on the early drafts of Chapter 4 and his many suggestions and corrections, which have improved this book immensely.

Thanks are also due to the Institute of Mathematical Sciences (Chennai) for providing a home for this research in India and the PRISM project at the Institute of Mathematical Sciences for financial support.

Monetary and logistical support from the Roja Matahi Library and Dr. I. Mahadevan was indispensable in the research and writing of this book.

Preface

This book summarizes the research undertaken at the Institute of Mathematical Science, Chennai, India in 2009. The goal of this research was to define the relationship between the signs in Indus texts. More specifically to define the morphological processes used in combining the signs into texts. The electronic corpus and sign list developed at Harvard University (Wells 2006 and 2011) was expanded to include all of the HARP texts from material obtained from Richard Meadow (HARP director). This resulted in a online database annotating 3903 artifacts with 4794 texts and 17650 examples of 695 signs. The online database is imbedded in an interactive analytical program written and managed by Dr. Andreas Fuls of the Technical Universitat, Berlin. The analytical software uses new analytical methods developed by myself, Dr. Fuls and by Sinha *et al* (2010 and 2011). These techniques of sign and text analysis were essential to the research presented here (see Appendixes).

The Indus script has been the subject of some controversy of late. This controversy centers on the issue of whether or not the Indus script is really writing, or if they are magical symbols. It is my opinion that the Indus script is a writing system similar to other old world systems of writing in use in adjacent areas during the Bronze Age. The idea that this is not writing is based on misinformation and ill intent. There is no data to support this claim (Wells 2011) and it is only the controversy that keeps this idea in print. The structural analysis offered here demonstrates beyond doubt that the Indus signs are arranged in particular orders (syntax) and cluster in ways that can only be explained if it is a system of writing (affixing). Definable syntagmatic and paradigmatic units (Chapter 3) are irrefutable characteristics of language base writing.

Structural analysis is a method (Kelley 1976) that compares texts with overlapping but different sign sequences to discover how the elements combine in relation to each other. The interchangeable parts are called replacement set and have been used to good effect to define verbal affixing, allographic variation and polyvalence in several ancient scripts (especially Linear B and Classic Maya; Kober 1942, 1945, 1946 and 1948, and Kelley 1973). I use this method in the analysis of text segments.

Bigger issues of regional variations or multiple languages in the Indus script need further work, but without chronological control it is unlikely we will ever understand the developmental characteristics of Indus writing. There are marked regional differences in sign uses and artifact inventories. Future research should focus on defining these regional differences in text structure.

This study is based on all Indus texts, but wherever possible the analysis focused on the bulk of texts that come from Mohenjo-daro and Harappa; with other sites used in a supporting role. Further care was taken not to mix the corpus into a monolithic unit, as it is demonstrably affected by spatial and temporal variation (Wells 2011).

One further point needs stressing: If the bulk of the texts result in sign associations or patterns of sign use, these results are not nullified by a small sample of texts that do not fit the pattern. Not that these texts are eliminated from analysis, but rather integrated as outliers often are, as separate entities. We cannot know the sources of these variations (spatial, chronological or linguistic). This is especially true of unprovenanced artifacts and those from minor peripheral sites.

The decipherment of the Indus script has had a checkered past. Of 100+ decipherments of the Indus script none has gained widespread acceptance. The reason for this is that they are in the main poorly conceive and idiosyncratic. Often only the decipherer can "make it work". The reputation as a fringe academic comes as an automatic consequence of working in this field. This results in extreme skepticism regarding any readings of signs and texts. This colorful history has served to discourage professional academics from pursuing decipherment as anything other than a hobby. The result of this is that the basic research such as regional studies and mathematical analysis has been lacking until very recently. The disinterest of qualified linguists is likely the biggest obstacle to decipherment. In most circles working on the Indus script is the kiss of death for an academic career. For this reason I hesitated to add Chapter 6 to this book, but as this sort of analysis is the first step toward decipherment, it is necessary to pursue these ideas. Chapter 6 offers several possible interpretations of Indus signs based on contextual clues. While the data collection and analysis of the corpus is necessary and important, the search for clues to specific readings is likewise an important component of decipherment. The hope is that both approaches are mutually complementary. The positional analysis and syntax of the root language must agree with the reading generated through the analysis of specific contexts. In this sense "context" refers to both the epigraphic and archaeological context of the inscription.

 It is my hope that the readings in this chapter (6) will stir others to action. I look forward to the critique, which I hope goes beyond the usual out-of-hand dismissal of all epigraphic work on the Indus script as a waste of time. The idea that the Indus script is beyond decipherment and all work in that direction is "fringe" or a waste of resources makes no contribution to our understanding. It is the easy way out. It underestimates human ingenuity and the power of inter-disciplinary cooperation.

The Indus script is a difficult problem, but not beyond hope. This analysis has used an expanded database and sign list, interactive analytical software, and new analytical techniques developed in Germany and India to define detailed structures and sign associations in Indus texts. This level of international and interdisciplinary cooperation is necessary if we are to make progress towards decipherment. We have never had so much data relating to the characteristics of Indus writing, nor has there been a time when so much technology can be brought to bear on this problem.

I believe that we need to focus future research on the structural detail given in Chapter 3 in order to identify the underlying language of the Indus script. This work falls to linguists. There are several important characteristics of Indus writing that the identification of the root language may be possible, or at least we can eliminate some of the candidate languages from consideration. I hope that interested researchers will take the material offered in this book as a challenge to step up both the quality and quantity of research into Indus writing. We are at a point in the history of research into Indus writing where online resources and data exchange are available to everyone with a home computer and an internet connection. It is my hope that they will all participate.

Introduction

Epigraphy is the study of ancient writing systems with the specific goal of decipherment. Just as "archaeology is anthropology or it is nothing" (Binford 1962), epigraphy is archaeology or it is nothing. The study of ancient writing systems has no meaning without its cultural, historical and geographic contexts. As archaeologists we are interested in artifact contexts, not just for their esthetic beauty, monetary value or political significance, but for what they can tell us about the lives of ancient people. The use of writing tells us much about the level of literacy and sophistication of social interaction, but if we can read their writing we can get at the details of social, cultural, political and economic behavior that cannot be had any other way. One basic mistake made by most researchers studying the Indus script is that they treat the corpus as homogenous, without geographic, chronological or functional differences. This is demonstrably untrue (Wells 2011). As epigraphers we are often working with fragmentary remains of people long dead. In the case of the Indus script it was last written 4000 years ago (2600 – 1900 BC). There are no known direct descendants of the Indus people, and their language is likewise unknown. General facts about Indus culture and writing are limited and many past conjectures in the literature have become imbedded in dogma as truths. For example: The Indus texts are all names; the texts are too short to have syntax; or the Indus script cannot be deciphered (fill in your own reason(s)). What is wrong with these statements is that they are not completely accurate. If we look at the corpus of Indus texts we find that 1644 texts have 7 or more signs. Further, these text comprise about half of the signs in the corpus. That is to say that half the corpus is being ignored by those who say the texts are 4-5 signs long and therefore too short to have syntax.

An examination of ancient writing systems shows that at its most basic level written communication requires a minimum of two signs. Most often this takes the form of numbers and noun pairs or noun plus verb. For example, proto-Sumerian texts from early deposits at Uruk are often Number+Noun pairs (10+goats etc., see Chapter 5). Longer texts are most often lists of Number+Noun pairs. More extreme examples such as the Dresden codex Eclipse Warning Table (Post-Classic Maya), contains Verb+Noun pairs. Not just once but all 59 entries annotating the Lunar Node. These are logo-syllabic scripts, as is the Indus script. The minimum number of signs required to express the full Subject-Object-Verb construction in a logo-syllabic writing system is 3 signs. The average text length in the Indus corpus is ≈ 4.5 signs. This is sometimes argued to be evidence that the texts are simply names. We need to cast off the limiting assumptions of the 20th Century research that has been so unproductive and begin to look at Indus writing as a problem that needs to be analyzed systematically. This analysis begins with creating a corpus and sign list (Wells 2011). The next step is to look at the structure of the texts and sign relationships. This book focuses on the analysis of the structure of Indus texts. Further, all archaeological data regarding artifact types and function should be factored into the analytical process.

The one fact that most Indus scholars would agree on is that the texts are read from right to left. It has been shown that Indus writing is most likely a logo-syllabic system (Wells 2011), but many of the details of sign use remain poorly understood. The purpose of epigraphy is to give these long dead people a voice. Whatever the texts say they will give details of ancient life that cannot be had with a pick and shovel, or in the laboratory.

Most successful decipherments come as a result of interdisciplinary academic cooperation often over several generations. Decipherment is cooperative and cumulative. There are, of course, individual brilliance and insight along the way, but much of the work of decipherment is building on the work of our mentors and colleagues filtered through critical analysis.

The best history of past research is Possehl (1996). Major contributions to our understanding of the Indus script have also been made by Knorosov (1968 and 1970), Mahadevan (1970, 1977, 1982 and 1986), and Parpola (1970 and 1994). This book is base on the techniques and methodology of these researchers and especially David H. Kelley (Kelley 1976) who made a significant contribution to the decipherment of Classic Maya writing.

It is my belief that the less we know about a writing system, the more we must turn to contextual data. By contextual data I mean historical, linguistic and archaeological data. The Indus artifacts with inscriptions also contain iconographic elements. The images can be quite cryptic, but there are repeating themes and symbols. As can be expected the iconography varies by site and artifact type (Wells 2011). The link between images and texts is not transparent in every case. There are some cases where a link between image and text can be posited (Chapter 6). The arguments for each example need to be analyzed separately. Also demonstrated in this study (Wells 2011) was the fact that sign inventories differ by site and artifact type. When the frequency of signs that occur at both Mohenjo-daro and Harappa are compared, it can be seen that certain signs are more common from one site or the other. The same can be said for artifact types. For example sign 400 E occurs in 442 Indus texts. Of these 358 come from Harappa, while only 79 come from Mohenjo-daro. Of the 358 examples from Harappa, 325 are found on various types of miniature tablets.

Chapter 1 is an overview of the Indus civilization and types of artifacts with writing on them. This is not an exhaustive treatment, but rather a summary of the variety and scope of this material.

Chapter 2 gives the Indus sign list used in this analysis. Sign lists of this type (of an undeciphered script) are from necessity works in progress. A more detailed account of the analytical process of sign definition is given elsewhere (Wells 2011).

Chapter 3 is a detailed examination of the structure of Indus texts. This detailed analysis focuses on the variations in the organization of Indus texts. The syntax of Indus texts and the relationship and uses of important signs is given in detail.

Chapter 4 deals directly with the subject matter of the script. One set of inscribed artifacts from Harappa gives the key to understanding one specific type of text.

Chapter 5 looks closely at stroke (numeral) signs and their epigraphic contexts. This chapter also deals with the problems of polyvalence and allographic variations.

Chapter 6 gives several cases where we may have clues to the meaning of some Indus signs. These suggestions are not a decipherment *per se*, but language-independent values based on linguistic and archaeological contexts. These results are discussed in terms of their implications for a Dravidian decipherment. This chapter looks closely at the morphological process of Dravidian words and Dravidian syntax, and compares these to Indus texts to see if they are similar enough to suggest that Indus writing is based on these paradigms.

Chapter 1

The Indus Valley Script

Introduction

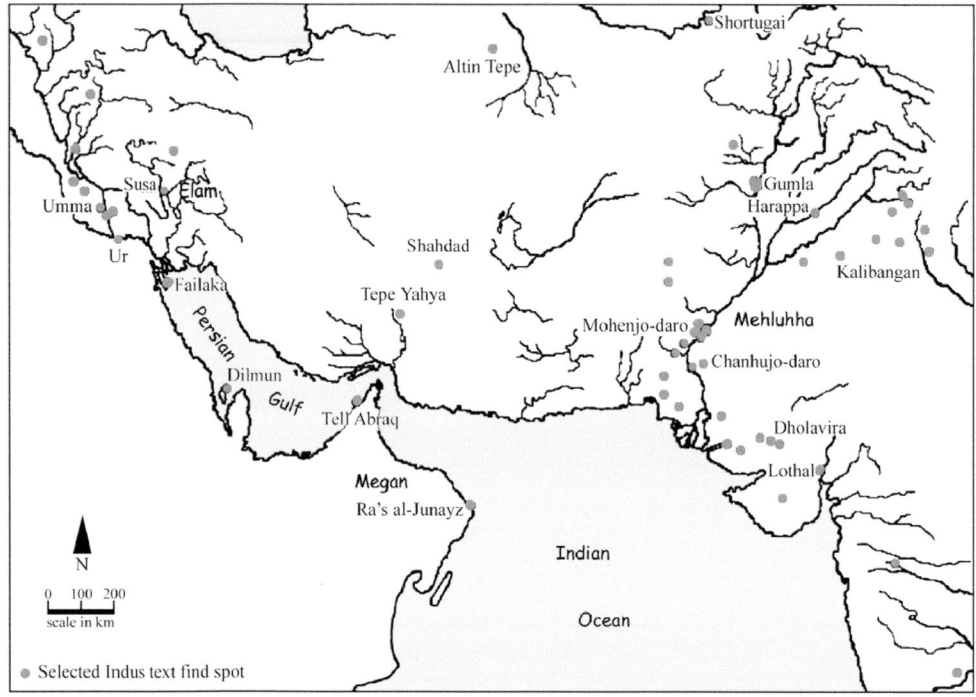

FIGURE 1.1 MAP OF SOME MAJOR ARCHAEOLOGICAL SITES DISCUSSED IN THE TEXT.

The Indus Valley Civilization (IVC) is known from archaeological sites across modern Pakistan and northwestern India (Figure 1.1). Historically this area was a mosaic of cultural and linguistic groups. There is no reason to believe that the Indus people were homogenous.

Trade between the IVC and adjacent areas is well documented (Ratnigar 1982), although many more details are known today. Trade routes along the west coast of India and down the Ganges river from Kanlibagan were likely in existence, but they are not documented. The same might be true for the coast of Oman given well-known currents and trade winds. The trade routes to Mesopotamia and Dilmun are known with certainty from artifacts in both areas.

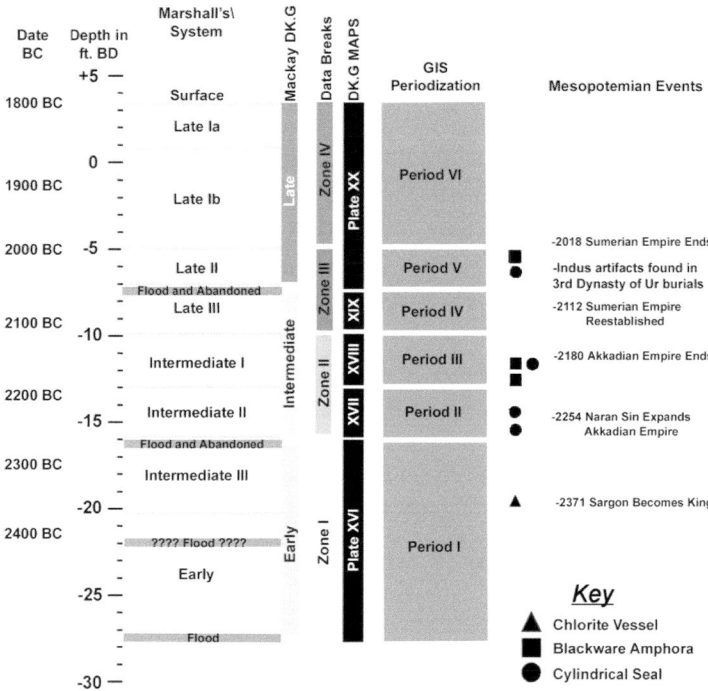

FIGURE 1.2 CHRONOLOGICAL TABLE SHOWING APPROXIMATE TEMPORAL RELATIONSHIPS BETWEEN THE INDUS VALLEY AND MESOPOTAMIA.

The Bronze Age sites of the IVC date to ca. 2600-1900 BC (Figure 1.2). From the artifacts recovered at these sites and others in Mesopotamia we know that the IVC traded with adjacent areas for raw materials and finished products. Trade was both by land and water (river and ocean). Inscribed Indus style seals, lapis Lazuli, copper/bronze ingots and carnelian beads are the best documented of these trade items. Exotic woods and animals are both mentioned in Sargonic texts as coming from Meluhha, most likely the IVC (Parpola 1994, Parpola *et al* 1977). These connections can be used to date the deposits at Mohenjo-daro, Dk.G (Figure 1.2). The presence of Mesopotamian style seals and Indus trade-wares (Blackware amphora) show the strength of these relationships. From Sargonic texts we can say that the Indus (Meluhhan) traders were in Mesopotamia. The records of the Isin-Larsa period also attests to a colony of Meluhhans at Lagash at this time (Parpola *et al* 1977). At Mohenjo-daro there are Mesopotamian style seals found in Intermediate II and I periods but not in the Late III period. Then again in the Late II there is a Mesopotamian style seal found. Following the Intermediate I there is a decrease in the amount of inscribed material at Mohenjo-daro. The link between Indus and Mesopotamia is evident in the grave goods from the Third Dynasty of Ur (III) royal cemetery, where many Indus beads and one Indus seal were found (Woolley 1954). Mohenjo-daro reached it peak during the Sargonic period (2300-2100 BC).

The Indus script is not directly relate to other Old World writing systems in Elam or Mesopotamia. That is, there are no direct borrowings of signs into the Indus script. The Indus script is related thematically to Elamite and appears to use many of the same strategies for sign elaboration and construction. In detail, there is no overlap. Indus signs are noticeably different in the shapes they employ. The similarities lie in the pattern of infixing signs and numbers in enclosures, and are more thematically similar than copied. The Indus script seems unrelated to the regional inventories of potters' marks, beyond the expected shared inventory of graphic universals (Wells 2011). While Cuneiform and Egyptian have long developmental histories and were adopted and adapted by subsequent cultures, the Indus system comes into and falls out of use suddenly, in archaeological terms. The IVC reached its peak about the same time as the Akkadian Empire of Sargon the Great, and ended about the same time as the Third Dynasty of Ur (2600 – 2000 BC). As these were major trading partners, their collapse would have had a devastating effect on the IVC. Other factors were also likely at play such as climate (especially drought), the changing course of the Indus River and seismic activity.

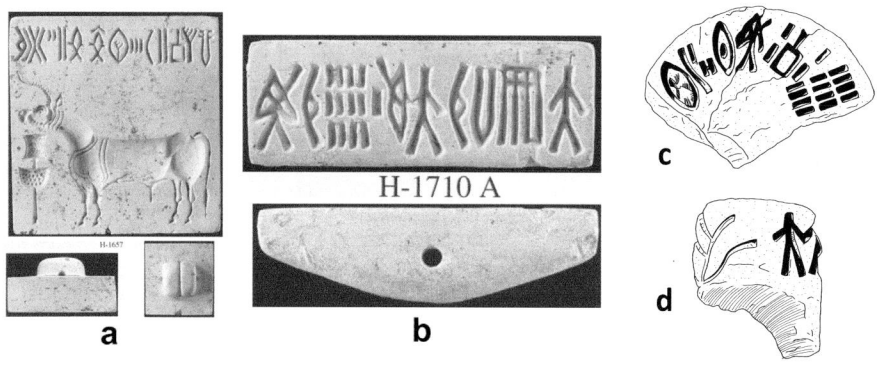

FIGURE 1.3 VARIOUS TYPES OF INTAGLIO SEALS: A) SQUARE, B) RECTANGULAR, C) CIRCULAR, D) CYLINDER. (A AND B COURTESY OF HARP)

The archaeology of the IVC is not well known because of the poor quality of the excavations, both historic and modern. The origins of IVC are poorly understood, with arguments surrounding whether there was a pre or proto Indus culture. In either case urbanism comes to the Indus Valley suddenly about the same time as evidence for rice cultivation in Pakistan. This avenue of research needs further work.

The Indus script presents a special problem to decipherment for several very good reasons:

1. The exact use of the artifacts is unknown in many cases.
2. The root language of the script is unknown.
3. The texts are short (mean = 5 signs) and found on small artifact (most ≈ 1 inch^2 or less).

4. The details of the mechanics of the script are not completely understood.
5. The complete corpus of texts is not widely available.
6. There are no bilingual texts.

About the only fact that most researchers can agree on is that the texts are read from right to left in their normal reading order.

This situation has left many researchers frustrated and discouraged. There are many Indus scholars who believe that a decipherment of the Indus script is not possible. In my opinion a full decipherment of every sign is unlikely as about 30% of the signs occur only once. However, a partial decipherment may be possible given recent improvements in the corpus and computer technology. The first steps towards decipherment have been made (Wells 2011). An extensive database of Indus texts is available online as is software specifically written to manage and display the Indus texts. These improvements allow the display and analysis of hundreds of texts at once. Further the methods of decipherment have been improving over time, and the recent advancements in our understanding of Egyptian and Classic Maya writing have shown that decipherment is a process of successive approximations, with scholars contributing unique perspectives derived from there various fields of study.

Inscribed Indus Artifacts

Inscribed Indus artifacts can be divided into 13 broad types: Seals (3), seal impressions (1) (Tags), miniature tablets (3), ceramics (4) and a miscellaneous category containing various inscribed items (1). There is a great deal of variety within each class, with seals, tablets and ceramics as the most numerous. Each of these classes will be treated in tern below. For details of the artifacts and their texts and iconography see Wells 2011. It is important to keep in mind that artifact types vary both by site and over time.

Intaglio Seals

In all there are 1979 intaglio seals of various types in the corpus of Indus texts. Seals are carved in negative-mirror image (intaglio). Of these 1560 are square seals, 335 are rectangular and 84 are of other types (Figure 1.3). There are 1280 seals from Mohenjo-daro, 414 from Harappa and 185 from all other sites. Seals are seldom larger than 1 in^2 and the average text is about 4-5 signs long. Circular seals are in the Dilmun style, while the cylinder seals are similar to Mesopotamian examples. In both these cases the inscriptions have Indus signs, but with unusual sign sequences. But seals are only half the story. Seals by definition are used to make impressions (Tags).

Seal Impressions

Tags are impressions of one or more intaglio seals (Figure 1.4). There are 121 tags with texts. They are sometimes confused with bas-relief miniature tablets. There are two

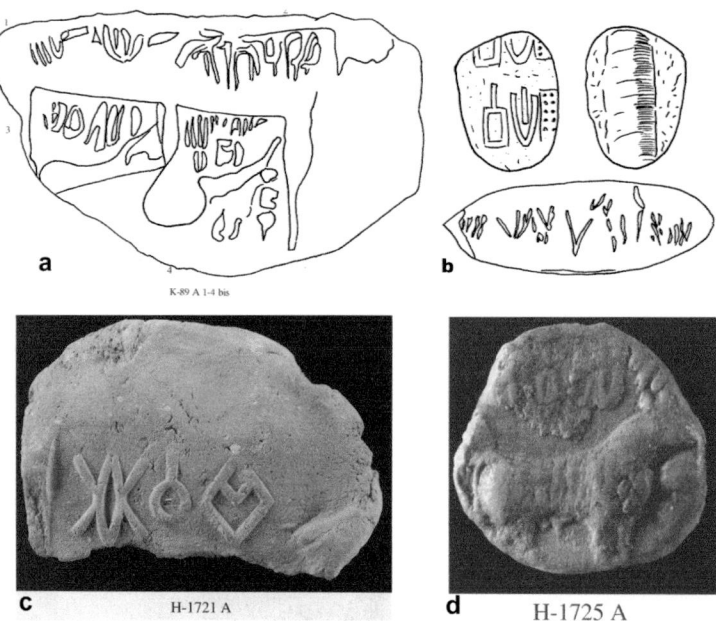

FIGURE 1.4 EXAMPLES OF SEAL IMPRESSIONS USE AS CLOSURES. A) K-89, MULTIPLE SEAL IMPRESSIONS; B) M-0426, MULTIPLE IMPRESSIONS WITH IMPRESSION OF WRITING ON REVERSE; C) H-1721, SINGLE IMPRESSION; D) H-1725, SINGLE IMPRESSION ON JAR STOPPER. (C AND D COURTESY OF HARP)

FIGURE 1.5 TEXT ON THE BACK OF DK12145/M-0426.

differences between them: 1) tags are made by attaching a ball of clay to a shipment, box or door and impress it with one or more seals. The manufacture of bas-relief miniature tablets is more complicated and discussed below. Further, bas tablets are made of fine pastes (Faince) and are mold made. Care must be taken not to confuse tags and bas-relief tablets.

Not all seals and tags have texts, containing instead only iconography. Seal impressions are very important as one was found in Mesopotamia. Another example from Mohenjo-daro (DK12145, M-0426) was found sealing a large ceramic vessel use to fire (oxygen reduced) ceramics and glazed stoneware bangles. So while relatively rare – surviving only when fired by accident in antiquity – tags give us a good deal of information about Seal use and resource management in the Indus Valley.One additional tag of interest comes from Mohenjo-daro and is unique, having the impression of an inscription on the attachment side of the tag

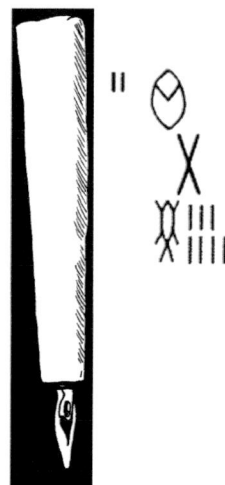

(Figure 1.4 and 1.5). This text was written on a doweling used as a closure. It was written with a pen or fine brush (Figure 1.6). The top of the text (the diagnostic bits) is off the top of the tag.

While practical in antiquity (i.e. both the written text and the tag texts would have been legible in its original closure), it means we cannot reconstruct much of the original text.

In terms of insights into why the Indus people wrote, tags make a considerable contribution. Further study of the tag texts is needed. One problem is that of the 121 tags: 67 come from Lothal, 16 from Kalibangan, 15 from Mohenjo-daro and 11 from Harappa. That is to say that the sites with the most seals have the fewest surviving examples of tags. This is an example of how the harsh environment of the Indus valley limits the corpus of texts.

FIGURE 1.6 POSSIBLE PEN NIB M-2129.

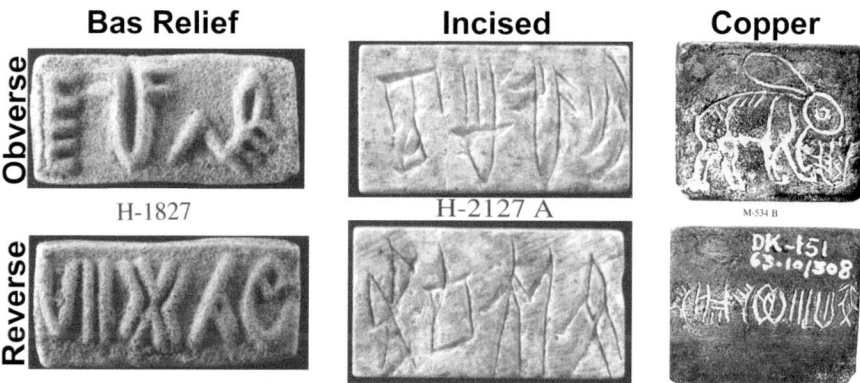

FIGURE 1.7 BAS RELIEF (H-1827) AND INCISED (H-2127) MINIATURE TABLETS FROM HARAPPA, AND (M-0534) A COPPER TABLET FROM MOHENJO-DARO (C AND D COURTESY OF HARP)

Miniature Tablets

There are three types of miniature tablets (n = 1281): bas-relief (665). Incised (440) and copper (176) (Figure 1.7).

This artifact group is far more complex in terms of variation in shape and material. The defining characteristic of tablets is that they are meant to be read directly, and not to impress the text.

Bas-relief tablets are made from fine pastes. Formed in a mold and fired in a kiln. There is a wide variety of colors and shapes. Bas-relief tablets most often contain iconography, but examples of tablets with only either imagery or texts are both common. The study of these artifacts is an immense undertaking, only partially completed in this work. We will look closely at the tablets and ceramics from Harappa, which can be shown to use a system of volumetric measures (Chapter 4).

The incised tablets are mostly steatite and can be carve very roughly (ad hoc). These artifacts rarely have iconography. It has been shown (Meadow et al 1999) that Incised tablets are chronologically late at Harappa.

The Copper tablets, which come solely from Mohenjo-daro, have unusual sign sequences when compared to other artifact types. Their examination is limited here but future research is planned. One set of tablets is examined in detail, leading to several suggested identifications of sign values.

One final point with regard to tablets in general is that there are often many duplicates. This is logical for the mold-made bas-relief tablets, but is also true for incised and copper tablets that are incised one at a time. That is, they were incised individually with identical texts and iconography.

Ceramics

The various types of texts found on Indus pottery are discussed in detail elsewhere (Wells 2011). There are four general classes of ceramic texts (408): Graffiti (342) can be incised pre or post-firing, but must consist of a series of signs in a recognizable text (Figure 1.8). For this reason potters' marks are not dealt with here. Ceramics impressed

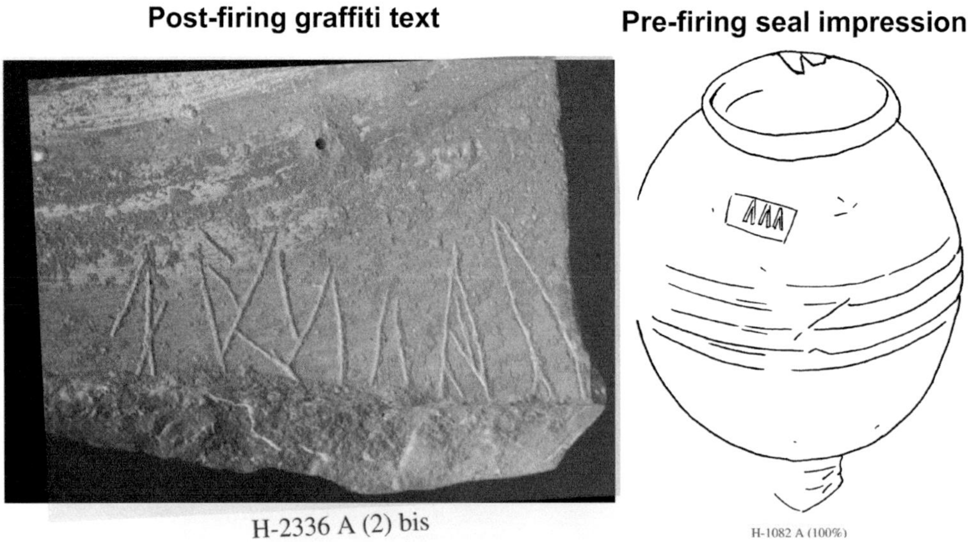

FIGURE 1.8 INSCRIBED POST –FIRING TEXT (H-2336); PRE-FIRING SEAL IMPRESSIONS ON CERAMIC VESSEL (POINTED-BOTTOM GOBLETS, H-1082) (COURTESY OF HARP)

with seals (59) are most common at Harappa (41). Graffiti texts vary greatly in detail – placement of the text, the number of signs and the type of ceramic.

The majority of these texts were inscribed post-firing, but rare examples are incised pre-firing. There is a fine line between graffiti texts and potters' marks, and the classification must precede one artifact at a time. The practice of classifying all pre-firing texts as potters' marks is inadequate given the complexity of the inventory of graffiti texts. Further study will focus on the classification of these texts based on their sign sequences and inventories (Chapter 3). The most similar classes of pottery texts are the painted and graffiti. Seal impressions on pottery often consist of one or two signs although longer text are attested.

These seal impressions never contain iconography. They are most common on Pointed-base goblet (Figure 1.8 right). Interestingly, the pointed-base goblets with seal texts are found at both Harappa and Mohenjo-daro, but there is no overlap in texts.

Miscellaneous Inscribed Artifacts

Another interesting artifact type is comprised of Miscellaneous artifacts (Figure 1.9). They consist of copper tools and rods, ivory rods, spindle-whorls, pottery cones, a figurine and other objects whose function in antiquity remains cryptic. One notable item in this class is the Dholavira signboard (Chapters 3 and 6). This is another class of artifact that deserves detailed analysis and will receive more attention in future research. These texts are often unique, and as will be seen below, repeated texts are very important. This is especially true for the copper artifacts from the DkG copper hoard and the Dholavira signboard.

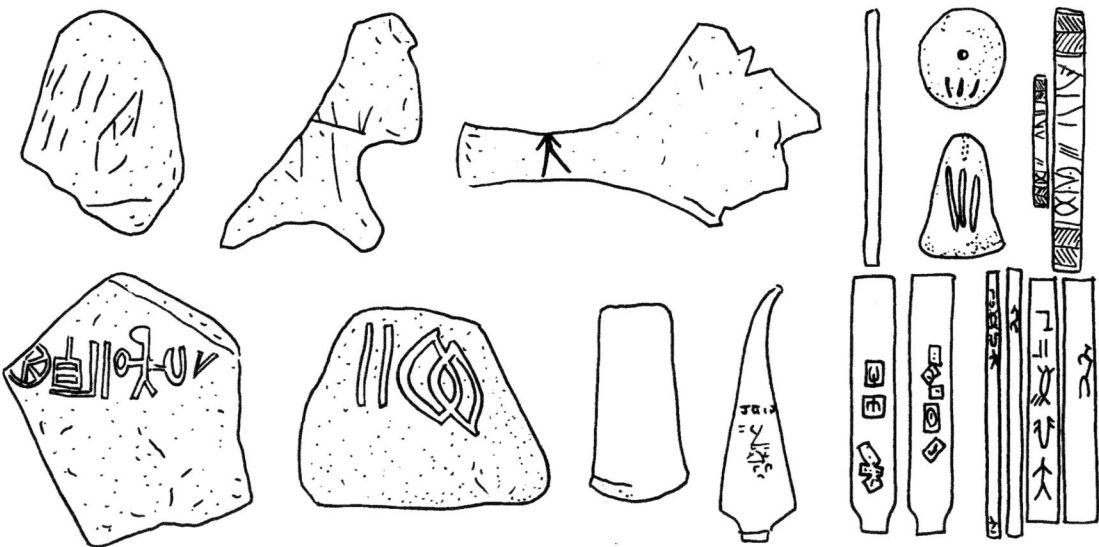

FIGURE 1.9 MISCELLANEOUS INSCRIBED ARTIFACTS FROM VARIOUS SITES AND PERIODS.

One interesting fact is that no inscribed artifacts have ever been found in a burial. The single exception being the Square Indus seal found by Wooley at Ur (1934). This artifact was found in the shaft fill of a royal tomb. The point being that the most important information about Indus texts is archaeological. Epigraphic analysis must begin with a clear understanding of the artifact origin and type. Regional variations in the corpus of Indus inscriptions point to difference in social organization between all Indus site, but especially between Mohenjo-daro and Harappa. As these are the two largest donors to the database they have a disproportional influence on analysis. Regional variations in the distributions of inscribed artifacts can lead to interesting subsets of the whole corpus (Chapter 4).

Finally, There is far more variation in the classification system than given here (Wells 2011). The point being made by this chapter is that care must be taken to look at the artifacts and their context in conjunction with their epigraphic or linguistic character.

Chapter 2

The Indus Sign List

One challenging aspect of studying the Indus script is the creation of a working sign list. As the Indus script is mostly a mystery, a sign list (of necessity) must initially be based on visual similarities between sign graphs. In epigraphy, a grapheme (from the Greek: "write") is the fundamental unit in written language. Graphemes include alphabetic letters, Chinese characters, numerals, punctuation marks, and all the individual symbols of any of the world's writing systems. An allograph is the variation in how letters and other graphemes are written.

The sign list used here (Wells 2011) was constructed using a uniform method. This method begins with signs that have similar graphs. This starting point is critical in that it must be very detailed. Using the 3903 inscribed artifacts found at Indus sites, 4794 texts can be defined. Of these 3723 texts are complete. In all there are 17650 legible Indus sign graphs, grouped into 694 signs (graphemes) using the method as given in Figure 2.1.

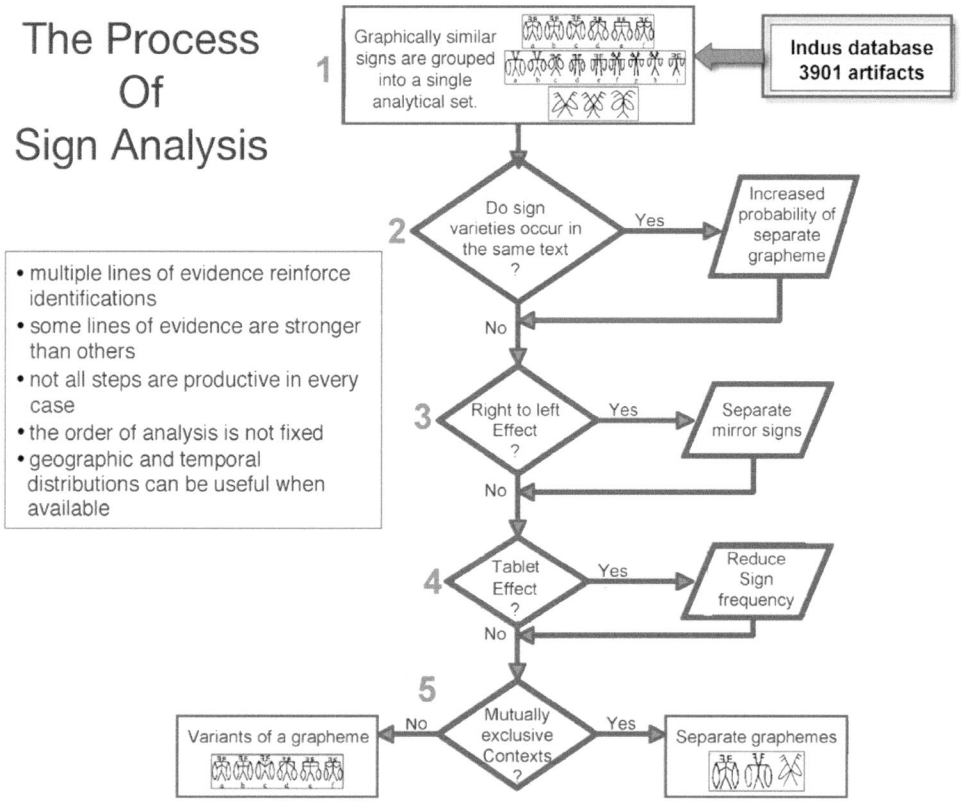

FIGURE 2.1 FLOWCHART OF THE METHOD USED TO DEFINE INDUS GRAPHEMES.

The Indus sign list must begin with the most detailed accounting of all sign variations (Wells 1998). Several consecutive sign lists began with 950 signs and as problem areas are defined they are analyzed separately. Figure 2.2 lists the ways in which signs are elaborated.

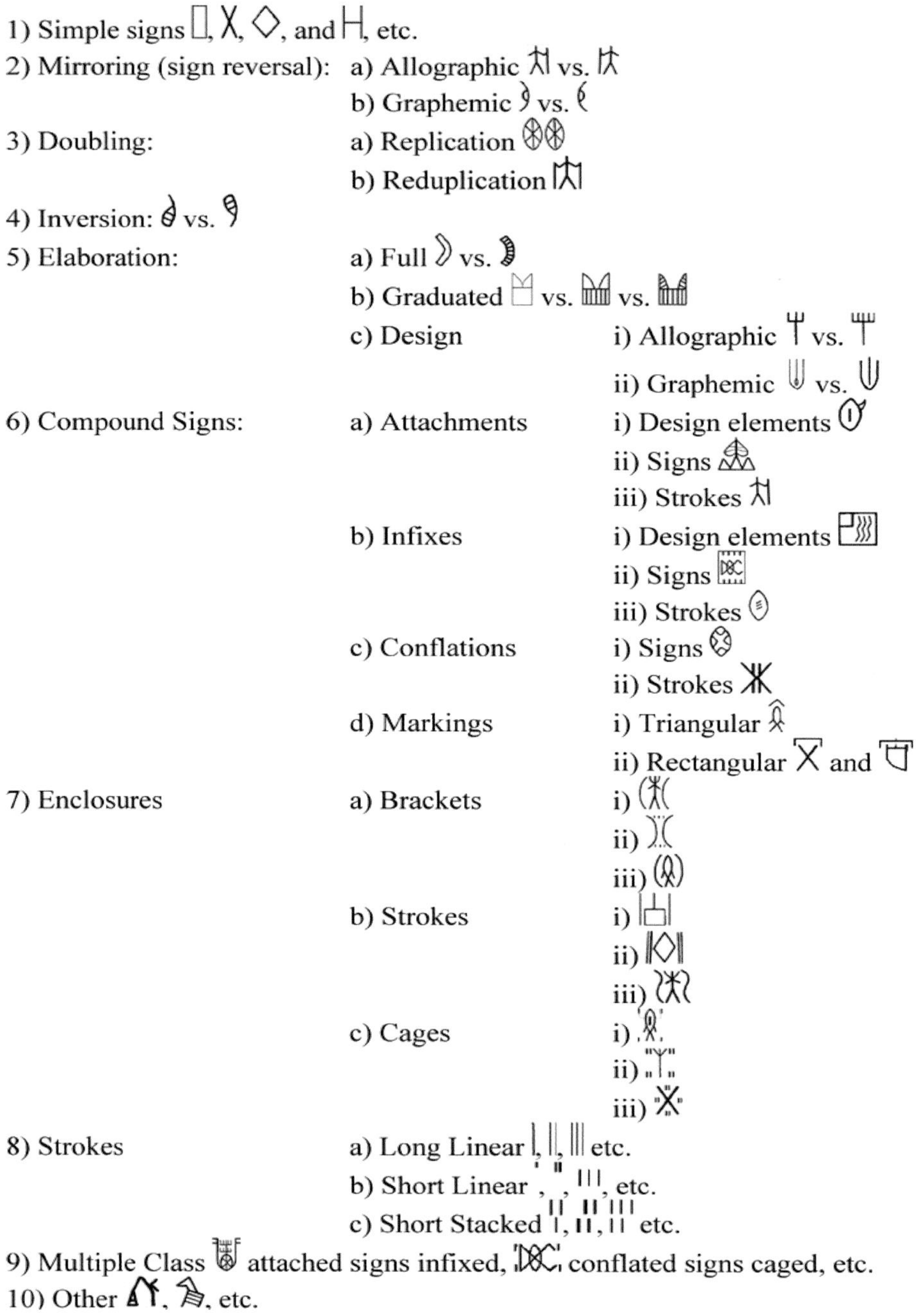

1) Simple signs ⌷, X, ◇, and H, etc.
2) Mirroring (sign reversal): a) Allographic ⋔ vs. ⋔
                                   b) Graphemic ꝯ vs. ꜫ
3) Doubling: a) Replication ⊛⊛
                b) Reduplication ⋔
4) Inversion: ꝯ vs. ꝯ
5) Elaboration: a) Full ⟩ vs. ⟩
                    b) Graduated ⌂ vs. ⋈ vs. ⋈
                    c) Design i) Allographic Ṫ vs. Ṫ
                                 ii) Graphemic ⋓ vs. ⋓
6) Compound Signs: a) Attachments i) Design elements ♂
                                          ii) Signs ⛰
                                          iii) Strokes ⋔
                       b) Infixes i) Design elements ⌸
                                 ii) Signs ⌸
                                 iii) Strokes ⌬
                       c) Conflations i) Signs ⊛
                                     ii) Strokes ⋇
                       d) Markings i) Triangular ⌂
                                   ii) Rectangular X and ⊓
7) Enclosures a) Brackets i) ⟮X⟯
                              ii))(
                              iii) ⟮⊛⟯
               b) Strokes i) ⌸
                              ii) |⊙|
                              iii) ⟮⋔⟯
               c) Cages i) ⌂
                            ii) "ˈYˈ"
                            iii) ⋇
8) Strokes a) Long Linear |, ||, ||| etc.
               b) Short Linear ʼ , ʼʼ , ʼʼʼ , etc.
               c) Short Stacked ꞈ, ꞉, ⋮ etc.
9) Multiple Class ⛰ attached signs infixed, ⌸ conflated signs caged, etc.
10) Other ⋔, ⛰, etc.

FIGURE 2.2 METHODS OF SIGN ELABORATION AND CONSTRUCTION.

The most common sign Old 288/New 740 ⋃⋃⋃⋃⋃⋃ initially had 6 varieties. A close examination of these texts showed that all variations occurred interchangeably and their sign graphs inter-grade between variants. This is good evidence that the variations are stylistic rather than semantic. Further evidence comes from the excavations at Mohenjo-daro, DK.G (Mackay 1938). Here the signs have a mutually exclusive chronological distributions, as styles of sign 740 fall in and out of fashion. In the end all varieties are subsumed under Graph 740 and are represented by the standard sign ⋃. The process of analysis is applied to each set of graphically similar signs (Wells 2011). Variants are represented by a standard graph. This allows the texts to be compared for parallel structures in a way not possible using the photography alone.

Some Indus signs are composed using a set of well-understood mechanisms — conflations and additions of a fixed inventory of signs and design elements (Figure 2.2). Additionally, signs can be inverted, mirrored and doubled. Signs can be combined in ways that cannot be easily deconstructed. (Figure 2.3). We can say that these complex signs are sign clusters, of independent signs or that they are elaborations of basic sign using well-known design elements.

So while Indus signs are complex, they follow a set of rules for their construction that is limited. One important problem area are cases where variations in sign distributions are ambiguous. Thes signs are kept separate, but are grouped into allogrphic sets (Figure 2.3).

In the Indus script one sign dominates the compound and gives it its form. For example, ⋏ compounds with 22 other signs, but in all circumstances ⋏ dominates the pairing. For example, one never finds ⊕, nor ⋓.

Some elements – ⋎, ⋎ and ⋎ – are commonly found as minor elements in compound signs. For example, signs ⫼, ⫼, ⋔, ⋔, ⋔, ⋔, ⊕, ⊕ and ⋓ to list just a few.

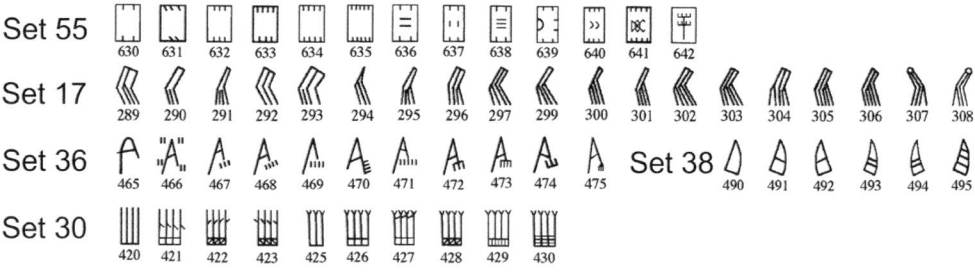

FIGURE 2.3 THE FIVE LARGEST ALLOGRAPHIC SETS OF INDUS SIGNS.

In addition to 2 sign compounds, there are 3 sign compounds (⟨sign⟩ and ⟨sign⟩), 4 sign compounds (⟨sign⟩ and ⟨sign⟩), and five sign compounds (⟨sign⟩). Some compounds seem to form sequences: ⟨signs⟩, or related set: ⟨signs⟩, and ⟨sign⟩. The signs most often used as subsidiary signs in compounds are ⟨sign⟩, ⟨sign⟩, ⟨sign⟩, and ⟨sign⟩. Not all relationships between compounds and constituent elements of compounds are as transparent as those discussed above. Compound signs are found in all parts of Indus texts, and once compounded the distributions of these signs are no longer related to those of their constituent signs. Compounding signals a shift in semantic values of the constituent signs. In other cases these are clusters of graphemes. The best example of conflated signs is as follows:

M-0036 ⟨signs⟩ This square seal has an initial cluster (read right to left) of three signs. When compared to Dk7997 ⟨signs⟩ similar signs appear conflated to form sign 768, but with the sign elements in reverse order, perhaps to make it fit in a cramped space (as visible in the photography). These signs are all in the initial cluster, but are they graphemic equivalents? They are syntactic equivalents and take sign 002 as an affix.

One interesting feature of sign lists is that some signs cannot be exactly defined because of either their low frequency or enigmatic contexts. In this first case signs occur infrequently, but extant examples have minor variations in designs that may or may not be signaling graphemic change. The second circumstance occurs when the design of signs have systematic variations that cannot be discarded without definitive contextual information demonstrating they are not separate graphemes. These signs are kept separate until the issues surrounding their identification can be resolved. This has the effect of increasing the number of signs in the list, but the option of collapsing them into one sign (for the sake of convenience) is unacceptable, as we may loose valuable functional and graphemic information critical to understanding the Indus script.

The Indus sign list given here was developed over 25 years and it is still a work in progress. This is a necessary because the conflation of different signs creates false relations between signs and looses legitimate relationships between signs.

For example, Mahadevan's (1977) sign #15 is often described as the ligature of three graphic elements: ⟨sign⟩ + ⟨sign⟩ + ⟨sign⟩. The first two are common Indus signs, while ⟨sign⟩ never occurs as an individual sign. Mahadevan lists nine varieties for his sign #15 and Parpola (1994) lists 27 varieties in his sign 4 (Figure 2.4; Wells 2011).

Some of these signs are obviously separate graphemes. Through the analysis of their contexts the remaining examples can be grouped into four separate graphemes: Sign

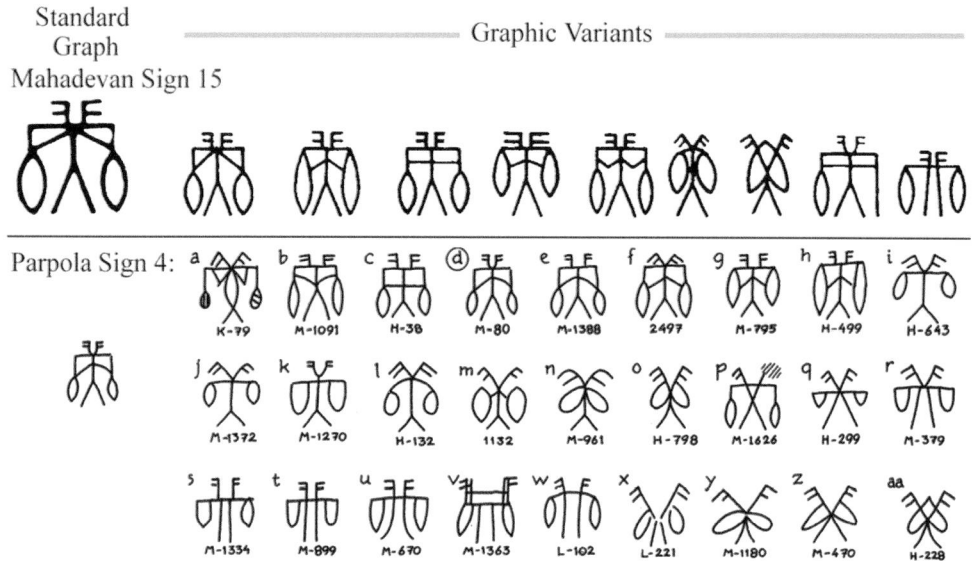

FIGURE 2.4 GRAPHEMIC VS. ALLOGRAPHIC VARIATIONS OF SIGNS 155, 156 AND 158.

156 - those with arms and a carrying pole; Sign 155 - those with no arms, but which have a carrying pole; and sign 158 - those with neither arms nor carrying pole. The final group are those varieties that are completely unique (Parpola's sign 4v and Mahadevan's). Sign 153 is a separate grapheme despite Parpola's list.

Sign 156 has six unique contexts including adjacency to stroke signs and sign 176. Signs 158 and 155 share some contexts, as do signs 156 and 155, but signs 156 and 158 share no contexts (Figure 2.5).

The context most relevant to these signs (155, 156 and 158) is the sequence: that occurs five times at Mohenjo-daro and 17 times at Harappa, with signs 155 and 158 co-varying, and signs 467 to 468 occurring in most cases. Sign 156 never occurs in this context. The most constant element in this sign cluster is the middle sign (806). Sign 806 is never replaced by sign 803 and therefore signs 806 and 803 are not allographs as Parpola (1994:17) suggests. Likewise signs 390 and 407 must be separate graphemes, as their ligature forms are separate graphemes.

Sign 156 , sign 155 , and sign 158 are commonly represented by the sign 156 graph, and in Parpola's (1994) sign list sign 806 and sign 803 are also represented by the sign 803 graph. This results in being represented as in Parpola's

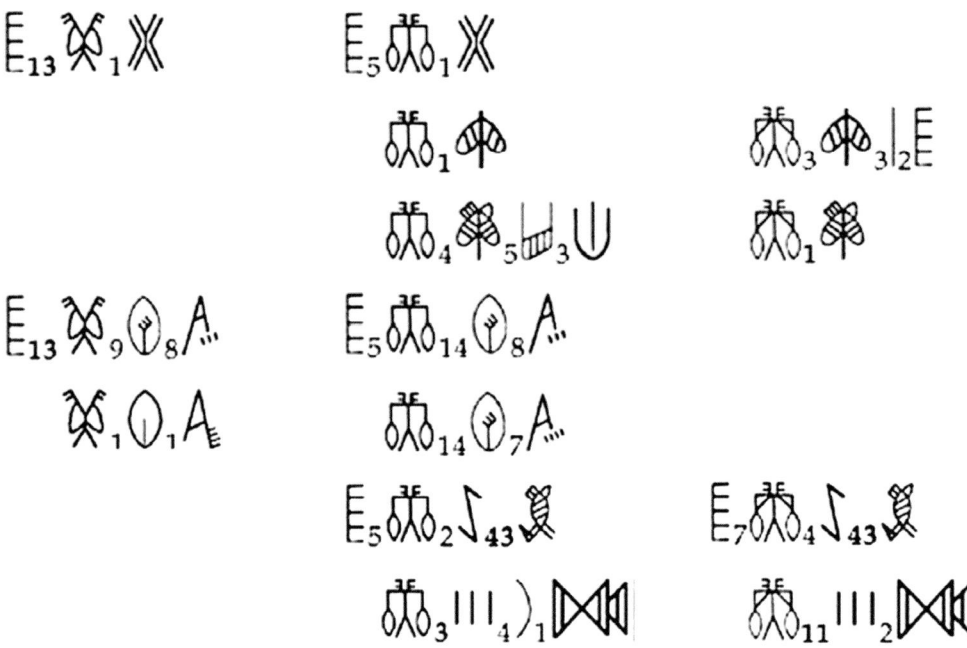

FIGURE 2.5 OVERLAPPING CONTEXTS OF SIGNS 155, 156 AND 158 WITH PAIR FREQUENCY GIVEN BETWEEN SIGN GRAPHS.

system. The relationship between ⚭ and ◉ is lost, and a relationship between ⚭ and ⚲ is fabricated where none exists. This cautionary tale demonstrates the folly of defining graphemes based on graphic similarity alone. Further, to separate these signs after they have been conflated is no simple task. The lesson then is to maintain separate signs until it is certain that they are allographs. This example also demonstrates how a single context can be used to identify several graphemes, and how inadequate terse sign lists based solely on graphic similarity are.

Wells (2011) has examined this issue in detail. This analysis has led to the sign list in Figure 2.6. The sign list is a work in progress, allographic sets being still under study. For this reason as much detail as possible is preserved for each sign. Low frequency signs can often be successfully analyzed if the contexts are especially telling. Unfortunately, the other extreme also exists. Sign behavior can be very complicated and care must be taken with the reduction of signs in a sign list.

The sign list given here is the best approximation possible with the data at hand.

Using 3903 inscribed artifacts, 4794 texts can be defined. There are 17650 legible Indus sign graphs in the corpus. Detailed analysis results in 694 signs.

THE INDUS SIGN LIST   19

FIGURE 2.6 AN INDUS SIGN LIST

20 THE ARCHAEOLOGY AND EPIGRAPHY OF INDUS WRITING

FIGURE 2.6 AN INDUS SIGN LIST (CONTINUED)

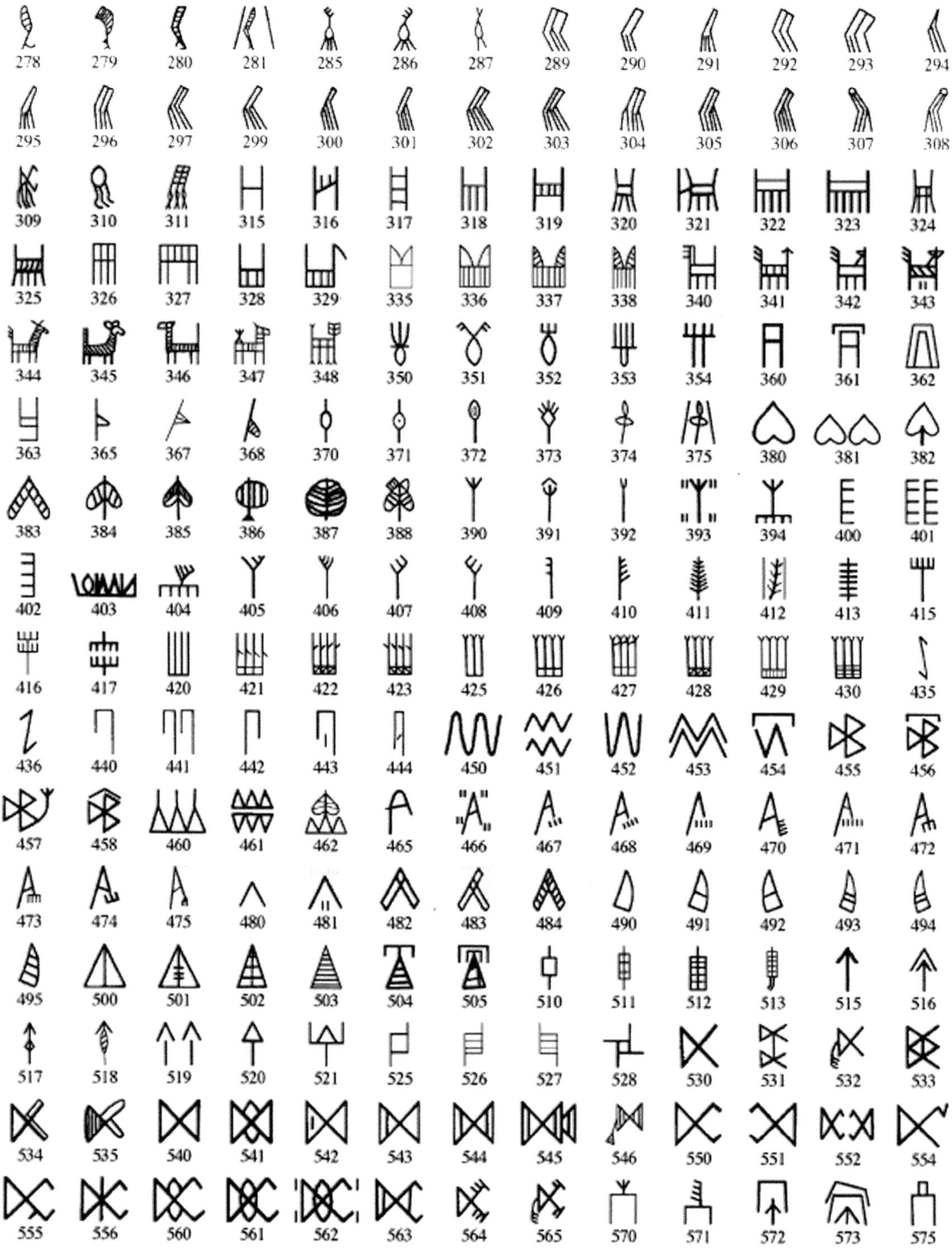

FIGURE 2.6 AN INDUS SIGN LIST (CONTINUED)

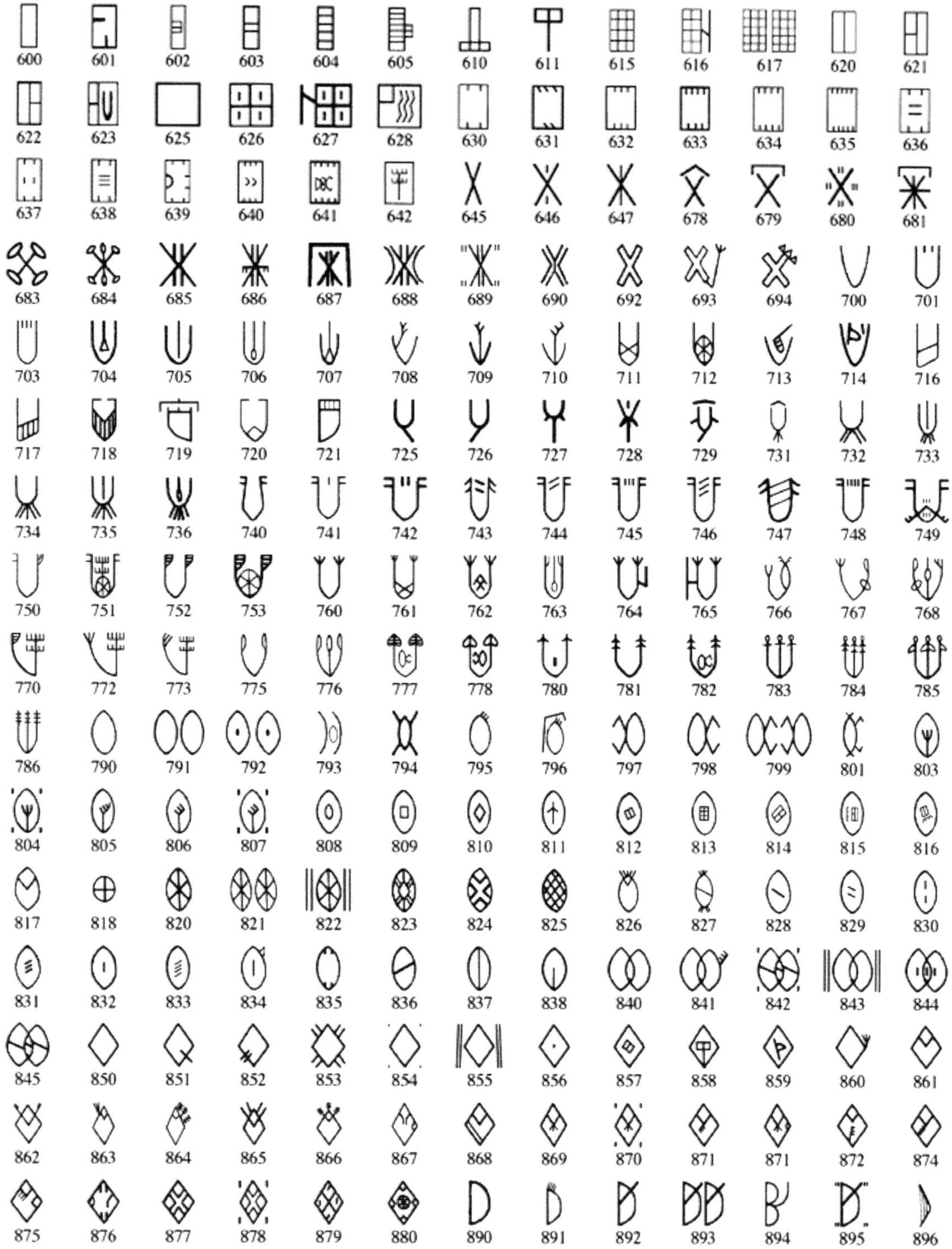

FIGURE 2.6 AN INDUS SIGN LIST (CONTINUED)

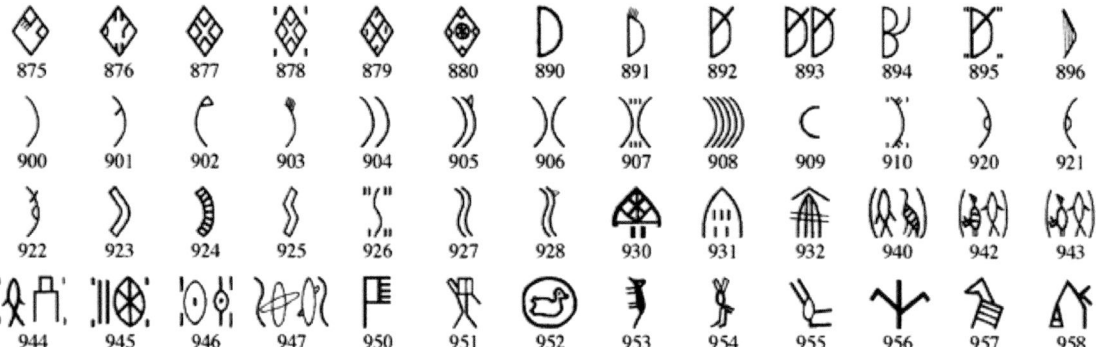

Chapter 3

Patterns of Sign Use and the Syntactic Structure of Indus Texts

Classifying Indus Texts

As seen in Chapter 1, one method of classifying texts is by artifact type. It was suggested by Steve Bonta (Pers. Com. 2002) that perhaps the texts could be classified by their sign inventories and sign sequences. As it turns out, this is a very powerful tool for the analysis of the texts (Figure 3.1). A close examination of Indus texts reveals that many of them are highly formulaic (Wells 2011), others are less so. This study is based on complete texts only. Fragmentary texts are used in a supplementary way. The differences in text types are structural and systematic. It has been demonstrated (Wells 2011) that, for complete texts that could be classified, the vast majority of Indus texts could be classified as

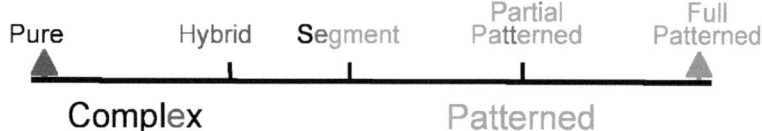

FIGURE 3.1 CONTINUUM OF TEXT CLASIFICATION OF INDUS TEXTS BY SIGN DISTRIBUTION AND CLUSTERING.

one of three broad classes: Complex, Pattered and Noun + Number texts. The Noun + Number texts are common in ancient economic texts where tallies are given. They are a special case and discussed in detail in Chapters 4 and 5. The subject of this chapter is the sign distributions of Patterned and Complex texts. Segment texts consist of one of the three syntactic elements identifiable in Patterned texts. Partial Patterned texts consist of two of the three syntactic elements of full Patterned texts. Hybrid Complex texts have one element of patterned text but with additional sign strings that are not in their "normal" sequence found in Patterned texts. Pure Complex texts have none of the three syntactic elements of Pattern texts.

As Figure 3.2 demonstrates, text types are not randomly distributed by site. This departure from random is bimodal. Especially obvious is the presence of 700+# texts (a special case of the Noun+Number class) at Harappa and multiple segments from Mohenjo-daro.

The most obvious feature of this graph is that text types are not uniform, but rather there is a great deal of variability. The 700+# texts are more common at Harappa because there is a set of artifact types that use a system of measurement whose values are expressed using 700+# texts. The texts at Mohenjo-daro are longer types. These differences are reflecting underlying regional variation in artifact use and subject matter. There is no

24   THE ARCHAEOLOGY AND EPIGRAPHY OF INDUS WRITING

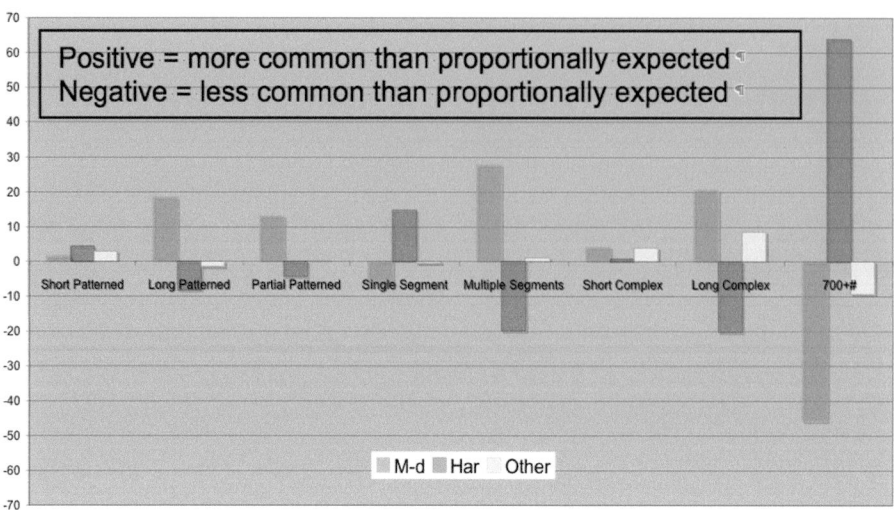

FIGURE 3.2 DEVIATION OF TEXT TYPES FROM EXPECTED RANDOM FREQUENCY OF OCCURRENCES

evidence that the corpus contains more than one script, and Complex texts are the only possibility for a second language. If they are syllabic spelling in a second language then Hybrid-Complex texts must be linguistically mixed texts. This idea is difficult to test and would be a unique circumstance in ancient writing systems.

Patterned Texts (n = 1095)

The simplest place to begin this discussion of text type is with the Patterned texts, which can then be used as a baseline for comparison to other text types. Patterned texts consist of three fields (Initial, Medial and Terminal). There is variation in the exact configuration and sign inventory between fields that makes the pattern of sign use evident.

What all Patterned texts share is that their signs are arranged in three fields. The following example illustrates this structure (Figure 3.3):

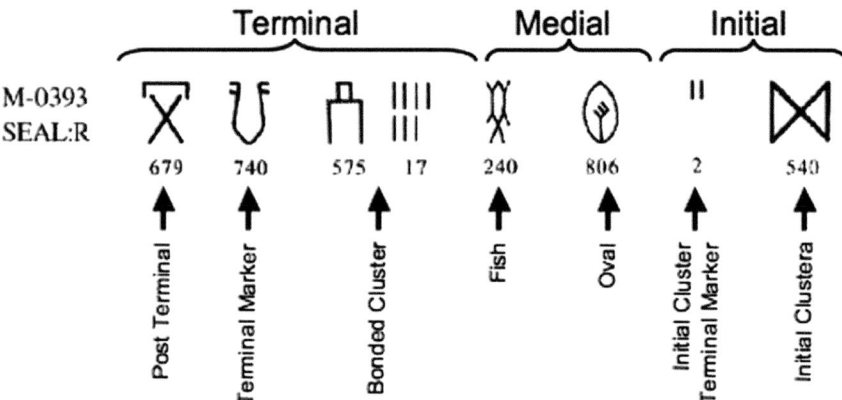

FIGURE 3.3 ELEMENTS OF THE PATTERNED text M-0393.

Within each field there is a fixed inventory of signs and sub-elements. Especially restricted are Initial Cluster Terminal Markers (ICTMs) and Terminal Markers (TMs). In the following discussion each field will be discusses in turn. Fish signs are the most common medial signs, but other signs are also used in this field. Typical medial signs include signs whose design is oval shaped and numerals. When occurring in medial contexts the order of these signs can vary. In fact the order of signs in both initial and terminal clusters is more fixed than in medial clusters.

There is one set of signs that occur regularly between initial and medial clusters (Figure 3.4).

FIGURE 3.4 TEXT M-0647 SHOWING "CONJUNCTIVE" SIGN 741 AND FREQUENCY OF PAIRING.

Graph	⊔	⊔	⊔	⊔	⊔	⊔	⊔
Number	740	741	742	745	746	747	748
Frequency	1696	200	37	34	6	7	3

FIGURE 3.5 GRAPHEMES BASED ON SIGN 740 WITH INFIXED NUMBERS.

These signs consist of sign 740 (the most common Indus sign) with an infixed number (1-4; Figure 3.5). In their typical contexts these signs occur between the Initial and Terminal clusters (i.e. there is often no medial clusters). There are several cases of 741 occurring in patterned texts (n=21).

But examples of 741 occurring with Fish signs are rare (n=2). The most common context finds 741 etc. separating Initial and Medial clusters. They are therefore referred to here as a conjunctive signs. That is, they are not part of either initial, medial or terminal clusters *per se*, but rather are associated with the initial clusters when contextually appropriate. One epigraphic feature of conjunctive signs is that they are less frequent the more marked they are. Here I suggest that these conjunctive signs function in a similar way in initial clusters to 740 in terminal clusters. We can say that because of two texts from Mohenjo-daro (M-1350 and M-0111; Figure 3.6) contain the same sign pair with 742 following in one case (M-1350 and 740 following in the other (M-0111).

Signs 920/320  pair 13 times in the corpus, with 12 of these in terminal clusters and M-1350 being the only example with these signs in an initial cluster. While the function and reading of sign 740 and related signs (Figure 3.5) are unknown, we can see that their

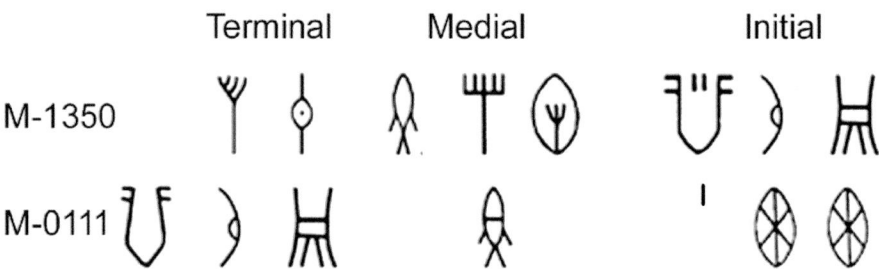

FIGURE 3.6 EXAMPLES OF SIGNS 920/320 IN INITIAL AND TERMINAL CLUSTERS

distributions depend on the nature of their markings. Because conjunctive signs are not well understood, and because of their position between Initial and Medial cluster, they are considered a special case in terms of delineating the syntactic boundaries of Indus texts.

Initial Clusters

In its simplest form an Initial Cluster consists of two signs, an initial sign and an ICTM. There are only three ICTMs used in Indus texts: Sign 060 ″, Sign 001 ′, Sign 002 ″. Here it is important to remember that in many languages there are unmarked case (i.e. genitive) and so this system may have an "invisible" fourth case that is unmarked.

The uses of signs 001 and 002 is more complicated as these signs are polyvalent. That is, they have more than one value or function. The subject of ICTMs is returned to later in this discussion.

Polyvalent contexts of signs 001 and 002

Sign 001 and sign 002 are found is a variety of contexts that show they cannot have a unitary value or function. It is suggested here that these contexts can be interpreted as syllabic, numerical, word divider and ICTM uses (Wells 2011). In these cases the semantic and phonetic values may vary as in other scripts where polyvalence occurs (Maya, Sumerian, Egyptian, etc). We cannot be sure what any of the values of these signs are, but we can say that their contexts preclude interpretations of homogeneity.

For a detailed description of the evidence for the polyvalence of signs 001 and 002 see Wells (2011). The focus here is on their contexts as Initial Cluster Terminal Markers (ICTM).

What is interesting is that sign 060 does not have any other contexts (Figure 3.7). This suggests that 001 and 002 were in existence when the specialized context was created for which no existing sign could be co-opted and sign 060 was created for this context. The unique character of sign 060 is further evident in its distribution in texts, where it is never found left of the 4th position (Figure 3.7). In design it resembles sign 002 with

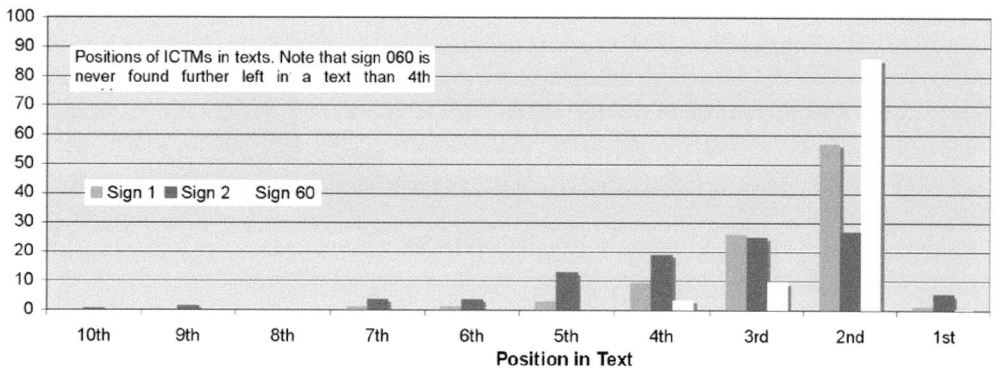

FIGURE 3.7 PERCENTAGE OF ICTM BY THEIR POSITIONS IN TXTS FROM RIGHT (1) TO LEFT (10)

an extended right element. Their function and semantic values are unknown. What is known is that they represent three states of the same item. The fact that 001 and 002 were co-opted, suggests a connection between the phonetic values of the numbers 1 and 2 and the phonetic alterations to sign 740.

In their tersest form initial clusters consist of two signs: an initial sign followed by an ICTM. There are six signs that are most commonly used as main signs in these two sign constructions. Not all of these signs pair with every ICTM. In fact, their combinations are very restrictive (Figure 3.8). The possibility that ICTMs are grammatical elements seems likely (case, mode, tense, gender, clitics and post-positions are all possible). While their exact value is a mystery, the relationship between these groups of signs is clear.

FIGURE 3.8 ICTM BY ONE SIGN INITIAL CLUSTERS.

Sign #	Graph	001	002	060
817		*	143	*
861		*	113	*
820		14	77	26
692		4	1	40
920		1	*	55
550		1	*	24

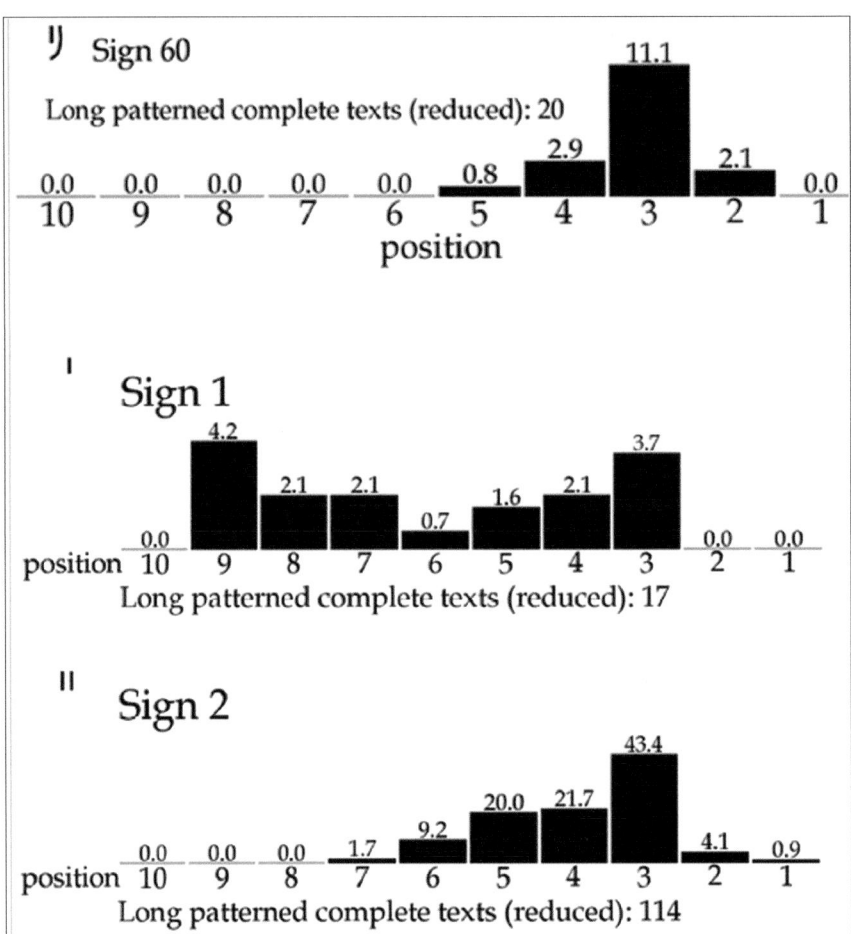

FIGURE 3.9 DISTRIBUTION OF SIGN 1, 2, AND 60 IN LONG (6+ SIGNS) PATTERNED TEXTS

If we examine in detail the distribution of these signs in Patterned texts we can see variations in sign behavior. This analytical technique was developed by Fuls (2010:35-37) and elaborated on in Appendix 2. It can be seen that sign 60 has the restricted ICTM context (Figure 3.8), while signs 2 and 1 have more varied and complex distribution (Figure 3.9).

Whatever else one sign ICs are, they are certainly logographs. We know that sign 060 is not polyvalent because it has only one context. Consequently, it is unlikely that 060 has a syllabic value. It may not have an audible value at all if it turns out to be a determinative. Signs 001 and 002 have unique distributions, although 002 and 060 are far more similar than either is to sign 001. One interpretation of the Sign 001 graph is that it has two distinct and common contexts. This is the case as the following texts demonstrate:

In this text (H-008) sign 2 is an ICTM and 001 is a post-terminal or word divider with ⧻ being a logograph in the second case. Further, the sign sequence (H-026) where 001 is in the familiar ICTM context. It is unclear if these two contexts have the same reading or are functional equivalents.

There are examples of Multiple Segment texts where two terminal clusters are separated by sign 001 (H-027): . These two terminal clusters are examined in detail in the discussion of terminal clusters. These contexts verify that sign 001 is polyvalent. The question for linguists is, "In which proto-language does the word for the number 1 have a second function in the marking of verbs or nouns"? The third function, of dividing Indus words, may not have a verbal expression (i.e. determinatives).

In their more lengthy and complex forms Initial Clusters accrete using several strategies. One pattern has a constant sign right adjacent to the ICTM, including many of the one sign ICs. This cluster is preceded by 1-4 additional signs. Some long introductory phrases precede the most common one sign initial clusters (discussed above). In the following example (Figure 3.10) sign 861, that is most often a single sign initial cluster, is prefixed by four signs. The text elements and sign usage left of sign 861 is typical of long patterned texts, but with a double Bonded Cluster (Figure 3.10).

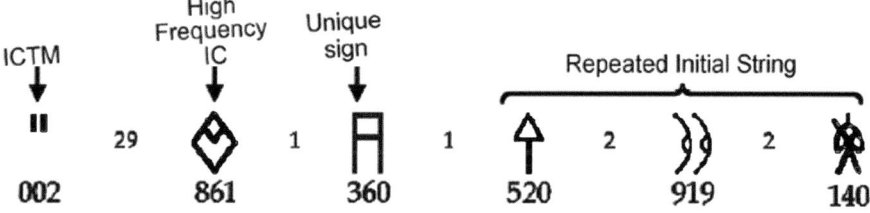

FIGURE 3.10 STRUCTURAL ANALYSIS OF IC FROM TEXT M-0355

This type of analysis was pioneered by Sinha *et al* (2010) at the Institute of Mathematical Science (Chennai, India). Under the direction of Prof. R. Balasubramanian significant resources have been directed to the study of the mathematical relationships between Indus signs and their consequences for defining elements of Indus syntax. In Figure 3.11 the thickness of the pair connections measures the how highly correlated the sign pair is in the corpus. The dendritic connectors are constructed from most common to least common pairs. The database is "reduced" for these purposes. Reduction is a process where identical texts, from the same artifact type and from the same site are reduced to a frequency of 1 for the purposes of calculations. The sign frequency can be compared to pair frequency to establish sign relationships. For example, because sign 877 occurs 22 times in the full database and in Figure 3.11(reduced) only 4 are used, we can see it is often in duplicate texts. Note too that of these four texts all are paired with sign 740 left adjacent. The most highly correlated pair of signs are the ubiquitous sign pair

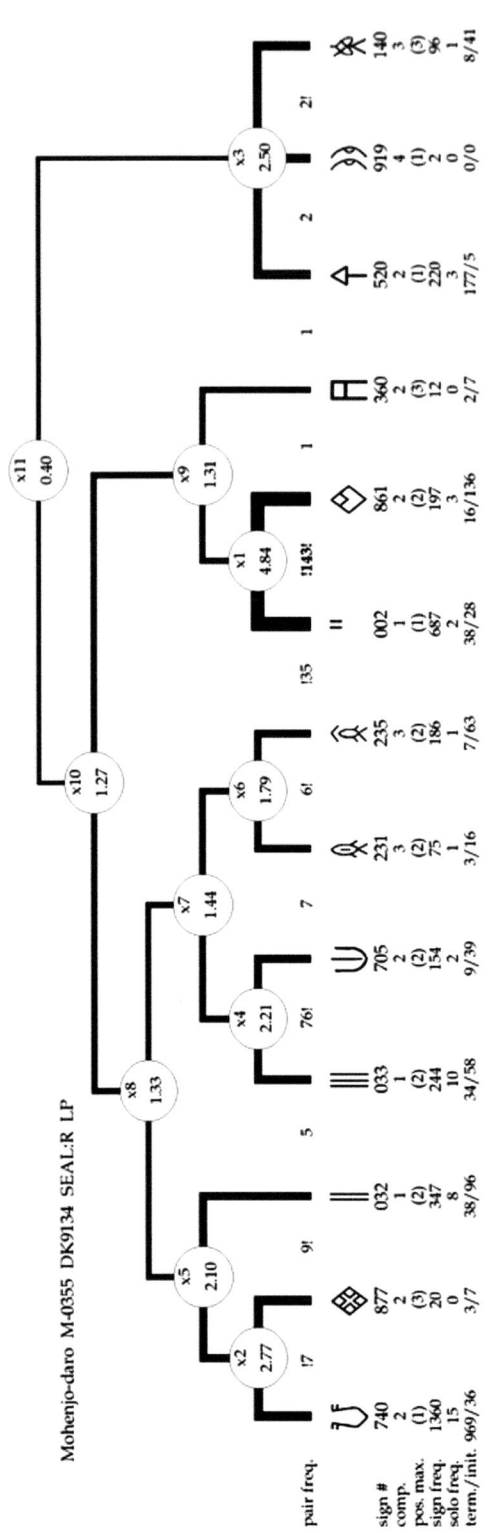

FIGURE 3.11 SEGMENTATION "TREE" OF TEXT M-0355

002/861. Also of interest are the introductory four signs. Of these four signs, three occur one other time, but the forth sign is replaced by sign 032 ‖.

By tracking the high frequency single sign ICs, and recognizing the patterns of IC construction (by prefixing signs) we can define this context. These signs have a unique place in the study of ICs. Here referred to as Set 1 initial signs (signs: 817, 861, 820, 692 and 920; Figure 3.12). They are most frequently found in IC and very often are the only sign right adjacent to ICTMs.

They are not the only sign to occur right adjacent of ICTMs. Further examination of the corpus shows other signs also often occur right adjacent to ICTMs. In this discussion they are referred to as Set 2 initial signs (signs: 220, 031, 390, 368 and 595). Figure 3.12 compares the frequency of these signs in initial clusters, and how often they are the only sign in the initial cluster (Solo IC).

Set 1 has a good deal of variation in the percentage of N used in ICs. Why does this happen? Some signs (550 in Figure 3.13) are also frequently terminal and without medial contexts except in Complex texts. This is contrasted by Sign 817 (Figure 3.14) that is most commonly found in initial contexts.

These variations in distribution clearly differentiate between single use signs (60 and 817) and multiple

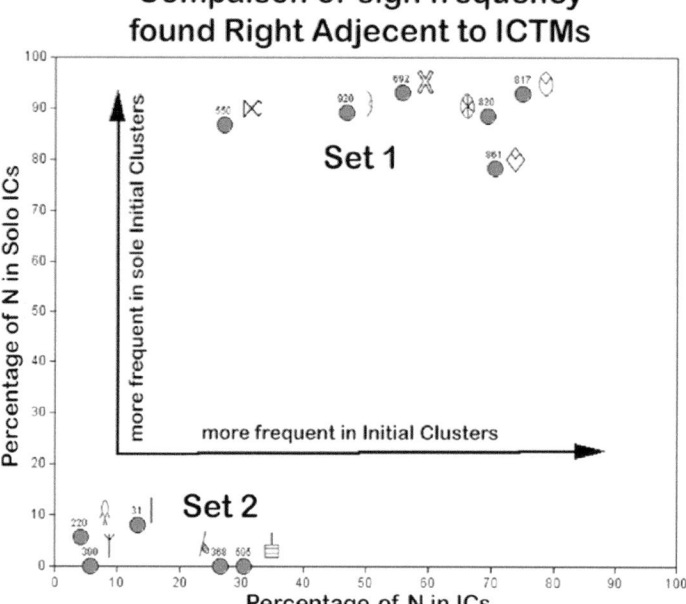

FIGURE 3.12 GRAPH SHOWING THE SOLO AND IC PERCENTAGE FOR 11 COMMON SIGNS FOUND IN ICs

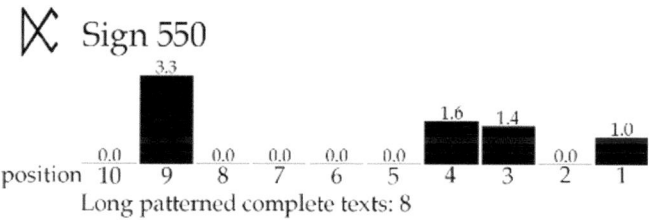

FIGURE 3.13 DISTRIBUTION OF SIGN 550 IN LONG PATTERNED TEXTS

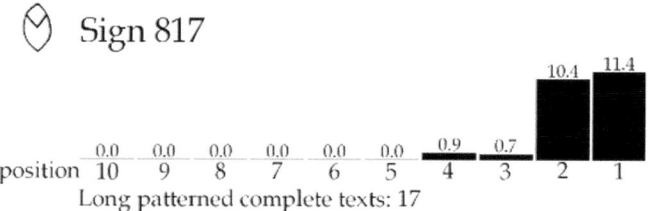

FIGURE 3.14 DISTRIBUTION OF SIGN 817 IN LONG PATTERNED TEXTS

use signs (1, 2 and 550). There are several possible reasons for these variations in sign use: (1) Single position signs may be logographs, and therefore are bound by syntax. Further, they are not polyvalent. (2) Signs that occur in multiple positions are most likely syllabic or polyvalent logographs. In their polyvalent contexts the logograph may take on a syllabic, numeric or second meaning. As a syllabic sign it may function as a word building sign or phonetic complement. Polyvalent logographic signs may be functioning as determinatives. Signs with multiple uses or meanings are common in all logo-syllabic scripts.

In general Set 1, in addition to being frequent IC signs also occur solo in ICs. The single exception to this is sign 692, which does not have a really exceptional high proportion of sign occurrences in ICs. This is the factor that distinguishes Set 1 from Set 2. The only reasonable explanation is that it is not a solely logograph, but rather polyvalent or syllabic. The lowest scoring Set 1 sign in terms of how frequently it is found in Initial Clusters is sign 550. This sign's distribution is polarized between its initial and semi-terminal contexts. As will be seen in the discussion of terminal sign clusters, sign 550 is a part of a frequent terminal pair. These two signs with polarized use seem to point to distinct, but restricted usage. Sign 920 is likewise polyvalent, but because neither one has significant medial presence they are unlikely to be syllabic signs. If we examine the characteristics of these signs we can see that most of the signs are right adjacent to predominately one or other of the ICTM. Only signs 861 and 817 pair with sign 002 alone. All other signs pair with at least two ICTM. I will suggest based on Figure 3.15 that signs 861, 817, 820, 920, 550 and 692 are logographs and signs 390, 031, 220, 368 and 595 are syllabic signs. Further, signs 920, 550 and 892 pair mostly with sign 060, sign 595 most often pairs with sign 001.

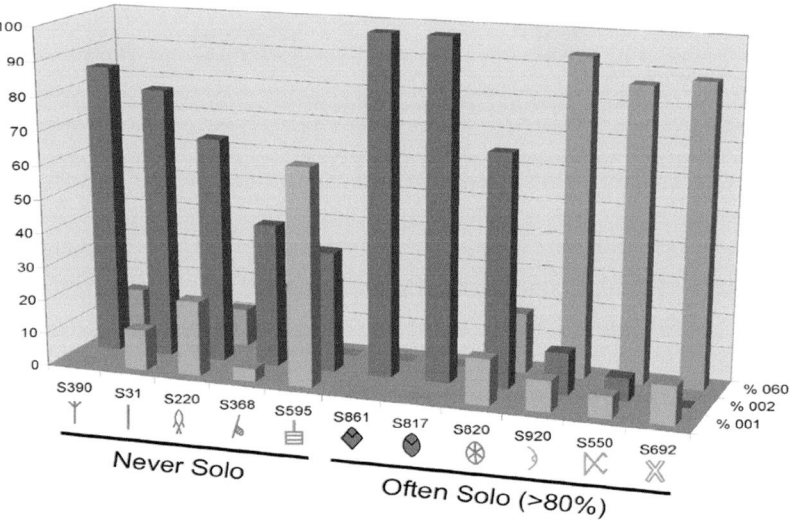

FIGURE 3.15 PERCENTAGE OF SET 1 AND 2 ICS PAIRING WITH ICTMS IN LONG PATTERNED TEXTS

Summary of Initial Cluster Forms

It is clear from the data presented here that Initial Clusters can vary widely in length (from two signs to six signs). Further, not all signs are used in initial clusters. As demonstrated elsewhere (Wells 2011) signs with a frequency of <6 (singletons and low frequency signs) are most often initial signs, most often on square seals, and most of these are from Mohenjo-daro. This results in a good deal of variety in initial cluster sign inventories between sites. What is important here is that there is also a good deal of overlap between sites.

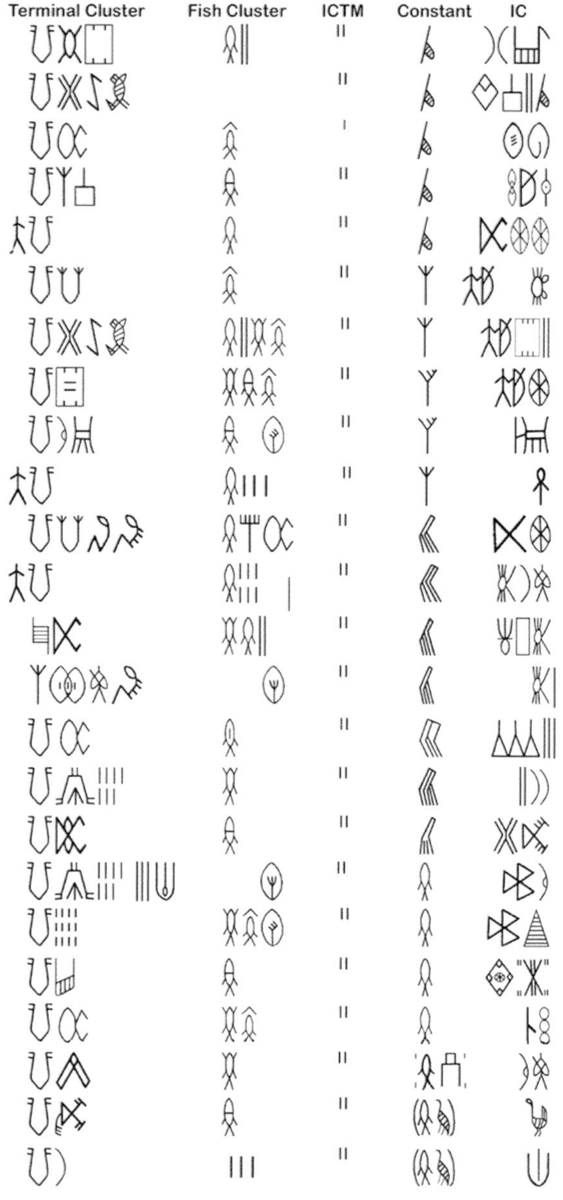

Regardless of complications, Initial Clusters seem to be limited to the *ICTM + 1 sign* (solo) form), the *sign cluster + solo IC sign + ICTM* form and the *sign cluster + ICTM* form. Initial clusters using this last form are very frequently limited in the signs that can occur right adjacent to the ICTM. These signs (*constants* in Figure 3.16 and 3.17 also pair very frequently with a limited number of signs right adjacent to the constant (semi-variables). In most cases there is an initial sign right adjacent to the semi-variable. These look to me like

FIGURE 3.16 THE MOST COMMON ICTM-CONSTANT COMBINATIONS IN ICS.

syllabic spellings of the functional equivalents of one sign ICs. Of the 18 occurrences of 220+ICTM, 7 also use Fish sign left of the ICTM. It is interesting that none of these medial clusters use sign 220 and only sign 220 is used in Initial Clusters.

The most vexing problem is: "What is the subject matter of ICs?" If we use the proto-Dravidian syntactic model they would be names. But I am unaware of any structure of proto-Dravidian (p-D) that could account for the tripartite affixing of ICTMs as case markers,

34 THE ARCHAEOLOGY AND EPIGRAPHY OF INDUS WRITING

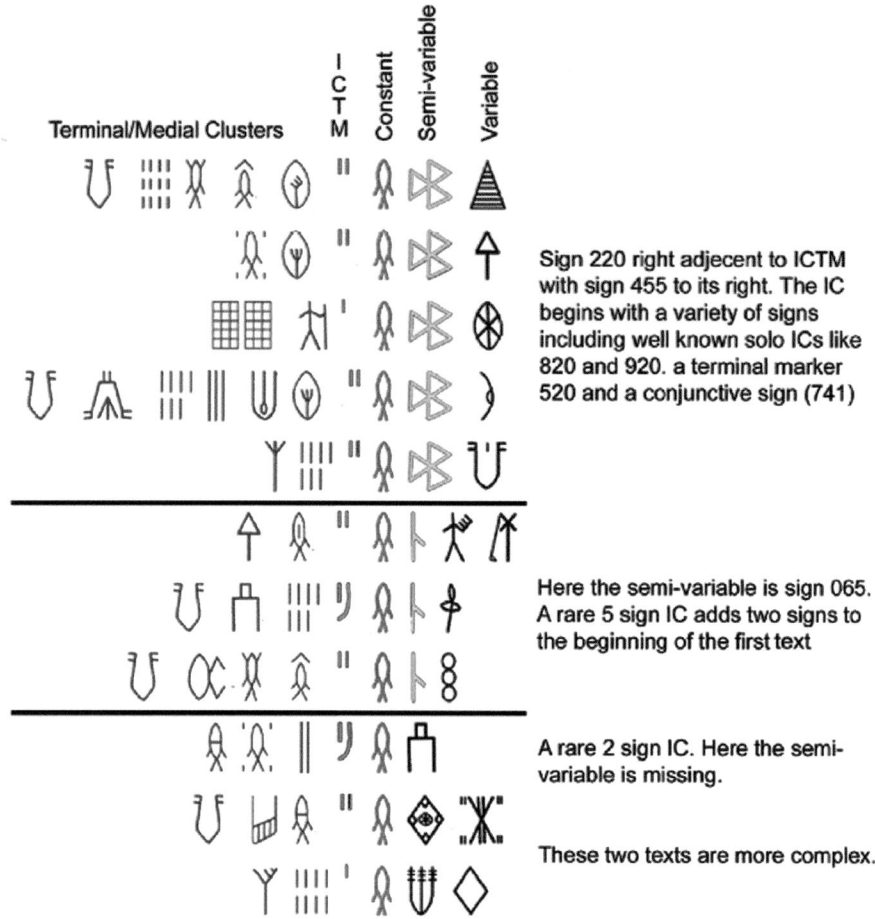

FIGURE 3.17 ICs WITH SIGN 220 RIGHT-ADJACENT TO ICTMs THAT EMPLOY SEMI-VARIABLE.

clitics or postpositions. One possibility is that the constants are the names of professions (Figure 3.16 and 3.17). They could also be honorific endings or titles, if ICs are nominal.

While we have no certain identification of ICs or ICTMs as linguistic units, we can say that ICs have structure that should be recognizable element in the Indus language. Two telling features of Initial Cluster construction can be seen in Figure 3.18. The contexts of sign 368 right adjacent to ICTMs clearly show that: 1) Sign 368 is infixed between sign 60 and 817; 2) The final text show the 368/817 pair without an ICTM (i.e. ∅ case). From this I would infer that both infixing and a four part marking system.

While the one sign (logographic) ICs are the most common form, and prefixed sign clusters are the rarest form, it is the third type from which we can learn the most about the structure of the Indus Language. We know that the first word or phrase has three possible endings (001, 002 and 060) and perhaps a fourth [∅] case (i.e. unmarked). This last case is hard to demonstrate. The unmarked case would mean that ICs have 4 possible states

FIGURE 3.18 CONTEXTS OF SIGN 368 RIGHT ADJACENT TO ICTMS WITH ∅ CASE IDENTIFIED FROM INITIAL CLUSTER CONTEXTS IN THE LAST EXAMPLE.

and are normally 1-5 signs + 1 of 4 endings (ICTM). These constants are most likely secondary endings, special infixed adjectives or syllabic signs. Initial clusters can take a variety of forms, but these forms follow rules of sign association that implies that IC are describing limited subject matter.

As demonstrated earlier, initial clusters take a variety of forms. There simplest form is the one sign with an ICTM. This simple form can take prefixed signs (1-4). A third set consists of a sign right adjacent to the ICTM prefaced by 1-3 signs (Figure 3.19). The final form consists of 2 or more signs that do not match the other criteria.

Medial Clusters

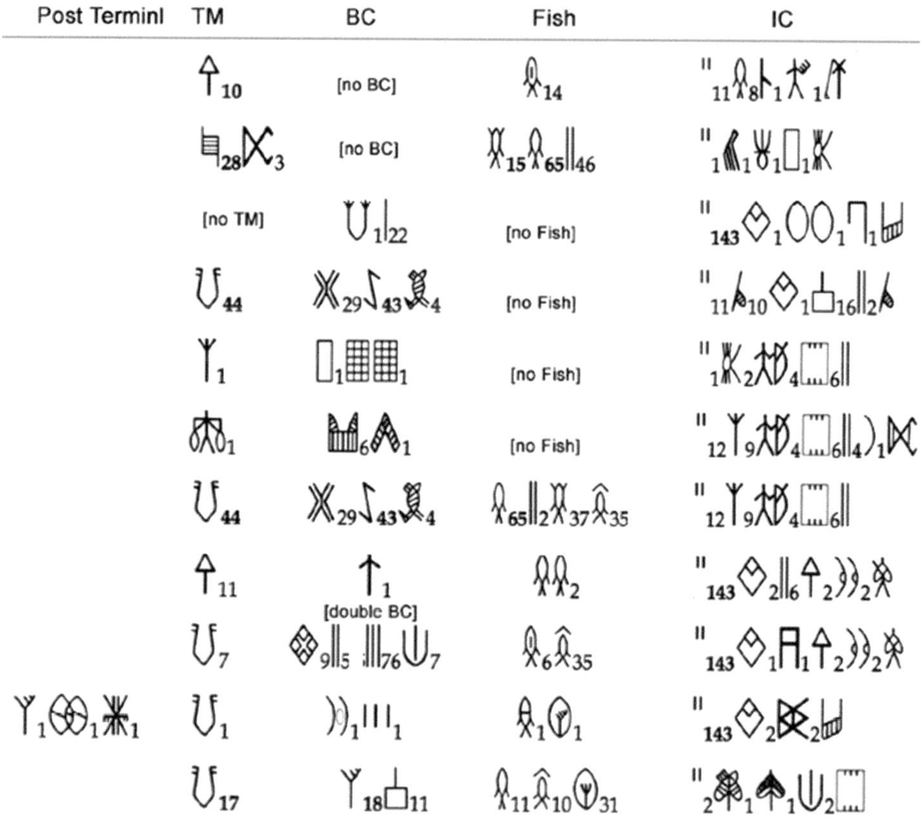

FIGURE 3.19 LONG ICS WITH 002 AS ICTM. FREQUENCY OF COLLOCATION GIVEN BETWEEN SIGNS.

Medial clusters in patterned texts can take a variety of forms, but the constituents are primarily Fish and certain Oval signs. This can be somewhat confusing because the same Ovals and Fish signs occur elsewhere and in a variety of contexts. As shown in the discussion of initial clusters, sign 220 (the basic Fish sign) is attested in initial clusters. More complex Fish signs (more marked) can be found as terminal signs. For example, sign 226, 241, 232, 236 and 234 (Figure 3.20). The basic Fish sign (220) is elaborated to create a variety of more complex (marked) signs.

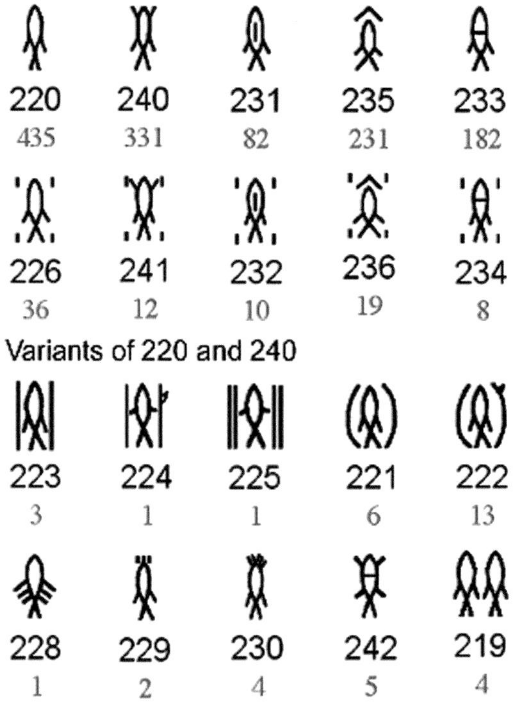

FIGURE 3.20 FISH SIGNS USED IN INDUS WRITING.

Fish signs in medial clusters often pair with numbers (Wells 2011). These contexts have a good deal of variety (Figure 3.21). In this figure we can see the variety of initial and terminal clusters framing sign 220. Numerals are discussed in Chapter 4. Sign 220 collocated with all varieties of numerals as well as with other fish sign.

Fish signs also have a preferred order in medial clusters when more than one is written. That is, they most often (but not always) are found in a certain order (Figure 3.22).

Fish signs occur in clusters and with numerals, especially sign 220. They have a significant number of occurrences in non-patterned text, which will be outlined in the discussion of Complex texts that follows. In patterned text sign 220 is most frequently

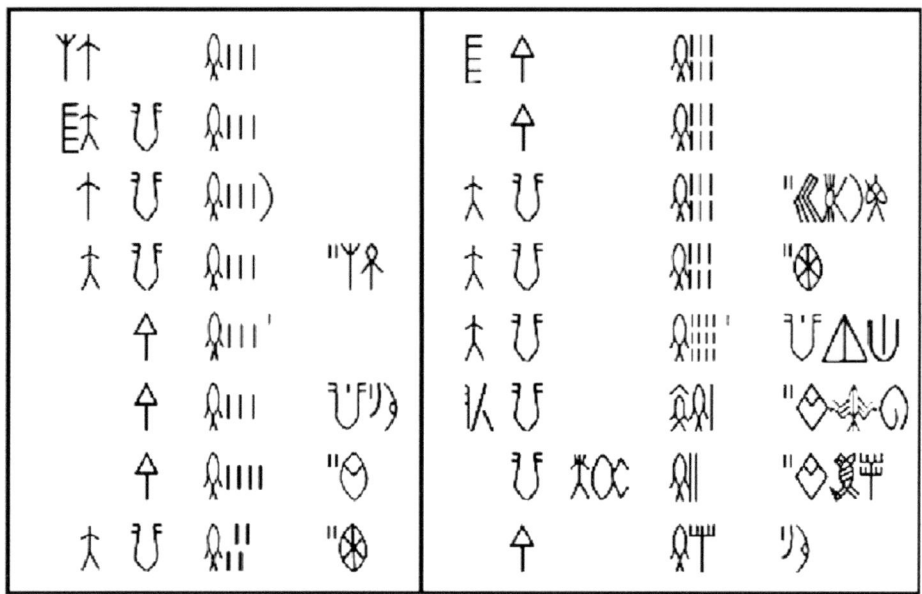

FIGURE 3.21 SIGN 220 PLUS NUMBER CLUSTERS IN MEDIAL CONTEXTS

FIGURE 3.22 THE FIVE MOST COMMON FISH SIGN IN THE NORMAL ORDER IN FISH SIGN CLUSTERS (RIGHT TO LEFT).

found in medial clusters. This fact is likely linked to the highly formulaic nature of these texts that may result from a limited subject matter.

As stated earlier fish signs occur together in patterned sets. These pairings are not uniform and all pairings are not equally frequent. As Figure 3.23 shows, the sequences of (right to left): 240/235, 240/220 and 233/245 all pair 20 times or more and 8 of 25 cells in the table are pairs with a frequency of 10 or more. The implication being that some combinations are far more common than expected. With 5x5 matrix and a sample of 200 pairs, we can expect that each cell would score 8 pairs. With 17 of 25 scores = 8 or less and 8 cell with greater than expected frequency, the distribution of this table is not what is expected given the laws of probability. It would be foolish to offer serious explanations of these sign pairs without some more information regarding the function of the artifacts on which these texts are inscribed, or some inkling of the subject matter of the texts.

Bonta (1995) has suggested that: because fish signs occur together and collocated with either other fish signs or with numbers, fish sign are likely metrological. Regardless of interpretations of fish signs, they still remain enigmatic. For example, in this discussion of Patterned texts sign 220 is shown to have contexts in initial and medial clusters, and

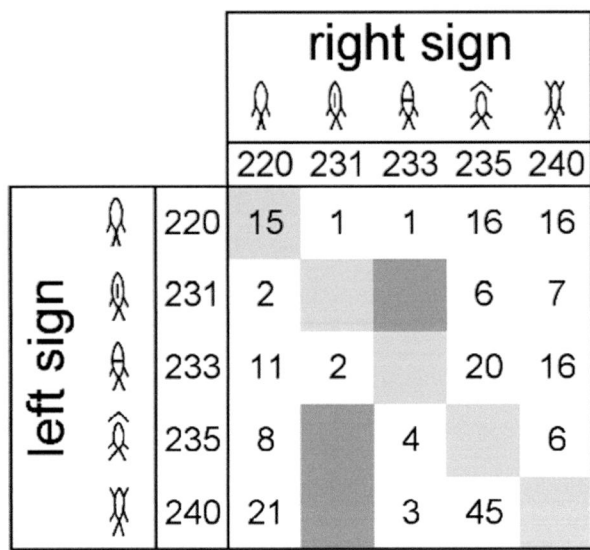

FIGURE 3.23 PAIRING OF FISH SIGNS IN LONG PATTERNED TEXTS

as will be shown below they can occur as terminal signs. In medial contexts this sign either collocated with other fish signs and with numerals, or with a limited number of oval signs. It is important to realize that only sign 220 occurs in the initial cluster context, while other fish signs are mostly restricted to medial contexts.

Other common medial signs

Medial clusters can be complex, with combinations of fish signs with other signs (mostly numerals and ovals). The two most common signs found in medial clusters collocating with fish signs are signs 803 and 798. The two signs occur with fish signs in medial clusters 51 and 61 times, respectively. There are however differences in how they collocate with fish signs. As Figure 3.24 shows sign 803 occurs before fish signs 86% of the time, while sign 798 occurs after fish signs 82% of the time.

Sign 803 is found 40% of the time in medial clusters collocating with fish signs. Of the 51 texts with sign 803 and fish signs, 86% (44) are prefixing (right adjacent) to fish signs (Figure 3.24). This is contrasted by the 61 texts in which sign 798 is post-fixing fish signs 82% of the time. Sign 798 may be functioning as part of (or all of) a Bonded Cluster (discussed below). That is, the syntactic break could be between sign 798 and their associated fish signs when 798 follows fish signs. Each case needs individual consideration. Both sign 803 and 798 occur in terminal clusters as Bonded Clusters. In short the relationship between these signs is complimentary. As Figure 3.24 shows, both signs occur with all fish signs in some way, but it is clear that certain combinations are more common (especially 789 right of 220/415). Prefix or postfix being a function of the overall context. The use of 798 in Bonded Clusters as part of a terminal cluster adds to the confusion.

Graph	Sign #	n=	With Fish	Significant Pairs	% W Fish
ψ	803	128	51	740/803=17 798/803=7	39.84

Graph	Sign #	Sign n=	Left of 803	Right of 803	% Left	% Right
	233	182	13	2	7.14	1.10
	220	435	3	4	0.69	0.92
	231	82	1		1.22	
	240	331	6		1.81	
	235	231	10	1	4.33	0.43
	220/032	65	6		9.23	
	220/415	62	5		8.06	
			44	7		
	% l/r		86.27	13.73		

Graph	Sign #	n=	With Fish	Significant Pairs	% W Fish
∝	798	128	61	740/798=38 798/803=7	47.66

Graph	Sign #	Sign n=	Left of 798	Right of 798	% Left	% Right
	233	182	4	6	2.20	3.30
	220	435	5	5	1.15	1.15
	231	82	5		6.10	0.00
	240	331	3	15	0.91	4.53
	235	231	3	2	1.30	0.87
	220/032	65		4		6.15
	220/415	62		18		29.03
			20	50		
	% l/r		32.79	81.97		

FIGURE 3.24 COLLOCATIONS OF FISH SIGNS WITH SIGNS 798 AND 803

Terminal Clusters

The third element of Patterned texts is the terminal cluster. Like initial clusters and their associated ICTMs, terminal clusters have a fixed set of Terminal Markers (Figure 3.25).

These markers are prefaced with signs and sign clusters (Bonded Clusters). While Bonded Clusters can get quite complex, they most often occur as one or two signs. A third component of terminal clusters are the Post-Terminal signs. Post-Terminal signs do not occur in all examples, but rather are restricted in frequency and sign inventory. TMs are likewise restricted in the signs used and pairings with Post-Terminals. These variations in combination of elements to form terminal clusters are highly patterned and suggest an underlying linguistic motivation. The Terminal Cluster, like all aspects of the Indus Script, are complex and their distributions are such that TCs range from one sign (C-10): ⏃𖣂𖣂‖"⊘ to 5 signs (H-020): ⏃𖣂⁂𖣂⊙"𖣂. The most common Post-Terminals (left adjacent to a Terminal Marker) are sign 400 Ɛ and 90 𐤀, but other signs can also act as affixes depending on the Bonded Cluster (Figure 3.26). Bonded Clusters are defined here as one or more signs that occur repeatedly in Patterned and Segment texts in a variety of contexts.

Affixing patterns vary between bonded clusters. For example, signs 100-415 pair in 37 texts 𐤇₃₇ 𝍮. Figure 3.26 shows examples of each affixing pattern for this BC. Holding

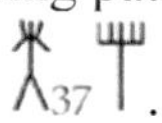

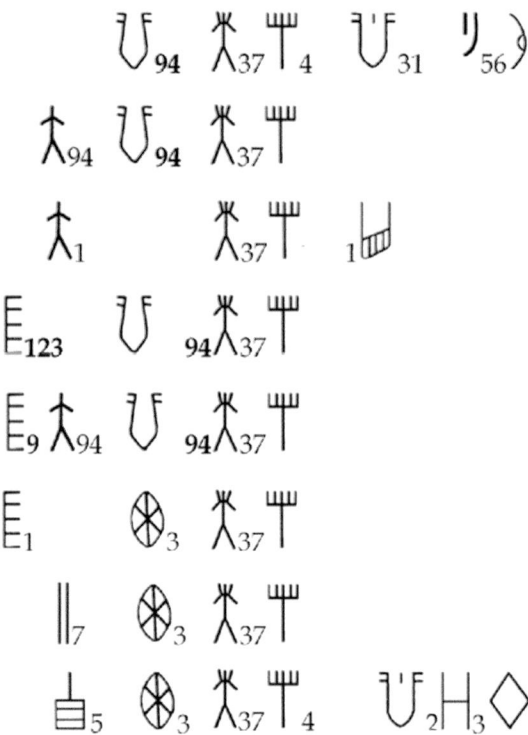

FIGURE 3.25 AFFIXING PATTERNS FOR SIGNS 100-415 BONDED CLUSTER (BC).

the 100-415 pair constant it can be seen that TMs and PTs vary from text to text. These variations in affixing patterns are not linked to variations in their associated texts. They, therefore, must be marking various states of the 100-415 pair. This BC is not the only one. The BC 100-415 takes two primary affixes, 740 and 820. Students of Indus writing will recognize that sign 740 is very often in this context, while 820 is found in several different context. The implication is that 740 (identified as a logograph) has only one function, while 820 is most likely a word building sign. The most common secondary affixes are signs 90 and 400. Sign 820 and sign 740 both take other secondary affixes, but not associated with the signs 100/415 BC. Note too that there are examples of BC without primary affixes (i.e. ∅ case). There are also examples of two secondary affixes (100 and 400) following a TM.

If we expand our consideration to other common BCs we find that there is both overlap and differences. One common cluster finds sign 033 pairing with 705 (Figure 3.27). Here the TMs 520 and 526+550 are most common, with sign 400 being the most common affix.

This pattern can be repeated for all recognizable BCs. The results show that Sign 740 is the most common TM and sign 400 is the most common affix. However sign 090 is

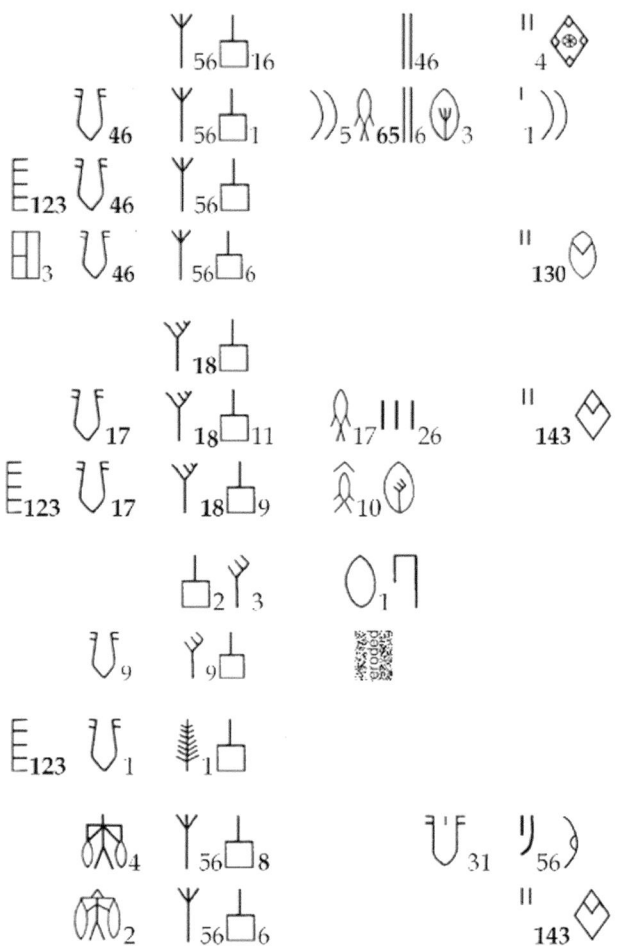

FIGURE 3.26 AFFIXING PARADIGMS FOR SIGN 590+ PHYTOMORPHIC SIGNS AS BONDED CLUSTERS

more wide spread, occurring with a greater variety of TMs. Additionally, the sign of Set 17 () fit a pattern noticed in other signs. They occur as PTs, BCs and Constants in ICs as shown by the following examples (Figure 3.28).

Set 17 is a group of signs with similar but unique sign graphs. It has been shown that variations in Set 17 sign forms are systematic. (Wells 2011). While their low frequency makes their analysis difficult, we can utilize their common pairing with sign 350 to compare related contexts. This examination demonstrates that this pair (Set 17+sign 350) can occur in initial clusters (ICs) and in terminal clusters. They take the affix sign 400 as though they are a TM (c.f. 526 etc. + 550 etc.), but as Figure 3.28 shows, Set

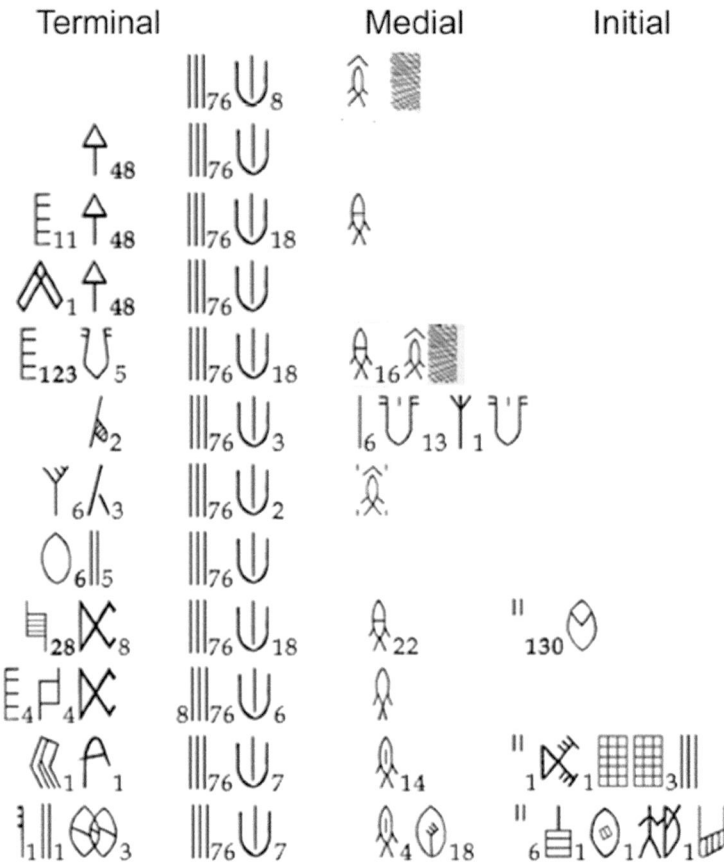

FIGURE 3.27 AFFIXING PARADIGMS FOR THE 033/705 BONDED CLUSTER. NUMBERS INDICATE THE FREQUENCY OF SIGN PAIRING.

17+sign 350 can behave as a TM. The impression given by these and other contexts demonstrate that both signs are word building elements, perhaps syllable signs.

Some affixed clusters are clearly not grammatical. For example, in Figure 3.29, a Multiple Segment text, the second terminal cluster could be interpreted as a Post Terminal sign cluster. Controlling for these cases removes some of the mystery of Indus text construction.

These texts contain two definable parts, each a stand-alone text found duplicated elsewhere in the corpus. We also know that BCs can occur in lists (Figure 3.30; Wells 20011).

Here we can see a series of three Bonded Clusters (BCs) preceded by a fish sign cluster and followed by the TM sign 740. An important implication of the identification of lists in the Indus texts is that only nouns or adjectives can be listed. This fact limits

PATTERNS OF SIGN USE AND THE SYNTACTIC STRUCTURE OF INDUS TEXTS   43

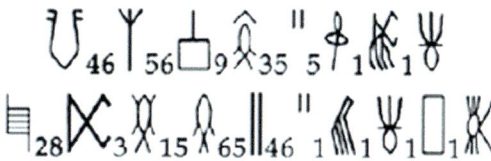

FIGURE 3.28 CONTEXTS OF SET 17 SIGNS INITIAL AND TERMINAL CONTEXTS PAIRING WITH SIGN 350 INCLUDING A TWO-LINE TEXT (BOTTOM).

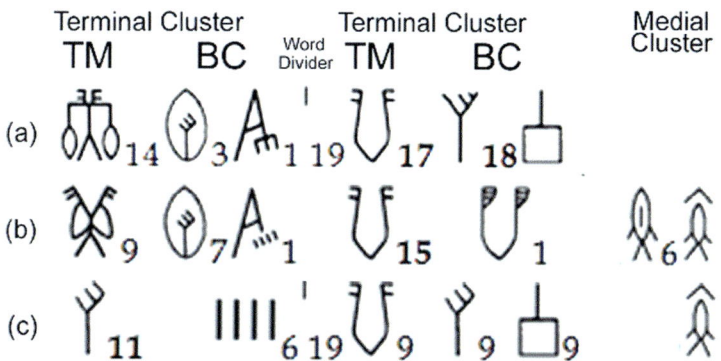

FIGURE 3.29 WELL KNOWN TERMINAL CLUSTER IN STRINGS WHICH COULD BE MISTAKEN FOR POST TERMINALS: (A) H-158 (B) H-058 (C) M-1320. ALL THREE ARE MULTIPLE SEGMENT TEXTS.

TM   BC3   BC2   BC1   Fish   Oval   IC

FIGURE 3.30 DK.E, E2475 SHOWING THE LIST OF THREE BCS.

Dmd-1 A

FIGURE 3.31 SIGN 740 SOLO EXAMPLE FROM DIAMABAD (DMD-1).

what sign 740's functions can be. We know it is a word sign because it occurs solo in about 1% (15) of its examples. But how certain is this identification? Upon close examination these examples can be shown to be fragmentary or unusual or damaged artifacts (Figure 3.31).

In common use, sign 740 is left adjacent (most often terminal) to one or more signs. Bonded clusters are common right adjacent elements, but ICTM with recognizable ICs occur too. For example, sign 60 occurs right adjacent to sign 740, frequently (104 times). In the case of M-0257, the text consists of IC+ICTM+TM+PT. That is, there is no BC or medial clusters. In Sktd-2, 740 is terminal but also initial. In this initial context 740 cannot be functioning as a TM (i.e. it is not terminal) and therefore must have a second function, or be syllabic. All other initial contexts of 740 consist of 740+PT. It would be unwise to place too much importance on Sktd-2. Surkotada is a relatively minor element of the corpus having only 2 seal text (complete) and 4 other fragmentary texts all painted on pottery. As sign 740 is the most common Indus sign (n=1696), and therefore its identifications is very important to any attempt at decipherment. Sign 740 is not alone in having multiple contexts. But what is the reason? As shown elsewhere, some signs (400) are more common at one site (80% from Harappa) and from specific artifact types (80% Form tablets). While sign 400 is most often a PT sign, it also occurs in medial and initial contexts in small numbers. These distributions can be best explained if signs are either syllabic or polyvalent or both.

These sorts of complications make structural analysis of Indus texts difficult, but they are the minority in the corpus. Using the Patterned texts as a template, these sorts of complications can be identified. Structural analysis shows that there are subsets of texts with similar structures. Patterned texts are used here to define the elements of Indus syntax. In turn Single Segment and Multiple Segment texts can be seen to be subsets of one or two syntactic elements used in Patterned texts (Figure 3.28). Single segments can be combined to form Patterned texts as the following example demonstrates:

M-0792, (square seal) ⟨signs⟩ can be recreated using other seals CH 1293 ⟨sign⟩, Ksr-2 ⟨signs⟩ and M-0825 ⟨signs⟩.

We can say with some confidence that sub-elements of syntax contain enough information to do there job as seals, but that more complex messages are used when necessary. This does not exhaust the variety of combinations used in Indus texts. There are Partial Patterned texts that contain any two of initial, medial and terminal clusters but in the same order (i.e. I+T, I+M and M+T).

Another text type defined elsewhere (Wells 2011) is sign 700+number texts are part of a larger set of noun + number texts that are dealt with in detail in Chapter 4. As with all aspects of the Indus script there are unique texts and a small number of texts (mostly unprovenienced or from peripheral sites) that do not fit any of these models of text organization. In this study these texts are referred to as Complex texts.

Complex Texts

Complex texts do not follow the method of sign cluster sequencing described in the sections above. Some of these texts do contain one element of Patterned texts, but often in a different order and always with sign sequences that cannot be easily segmented into separate syntactic elements. As described earlier, Sinha *et al* (2011) have developed a method for statistically defining sign relationships in terms of their frequency of pairing. A second method has been proposed by Andreas Fuls (Appendix I).

By comparing a Patterned text and a Complex text segmentation tree we can see that Patterned texts are highly organized while Complex texts are not (Figure 3.32).

While the Complex text in Figure 3.31 has some structure (an ICTM-001 and PT-400), it lacks the Fish+Oval and TM+BC that are clear in the Patterned text in the same figure. One feature of this Complex texts is that it is unique in the corpus. All sigh pairs have a frequency of one. Low frequency pairings is a characteristic of Complex texts.

Complex texts can contain some of the sign clusters found in Patterned texts, these texts are referred to as Hybrid Complex texts, while those texts without Patterned elements are referred to as Pure Complex texts Figure 3.33).

These texts can be compared in terms of their information content and degree of organization. The height of segmentation trees measures the degree of organization of a text. Texts with high scores for tree height are less organized than those with low tree height scores. Both texts have 9 signs, but H98-3491 scores 4, while Nd-1 scores 8 for tree height. In spite of the fact that Nd-1 (Figure 3.33, bottom) has a partial patterned

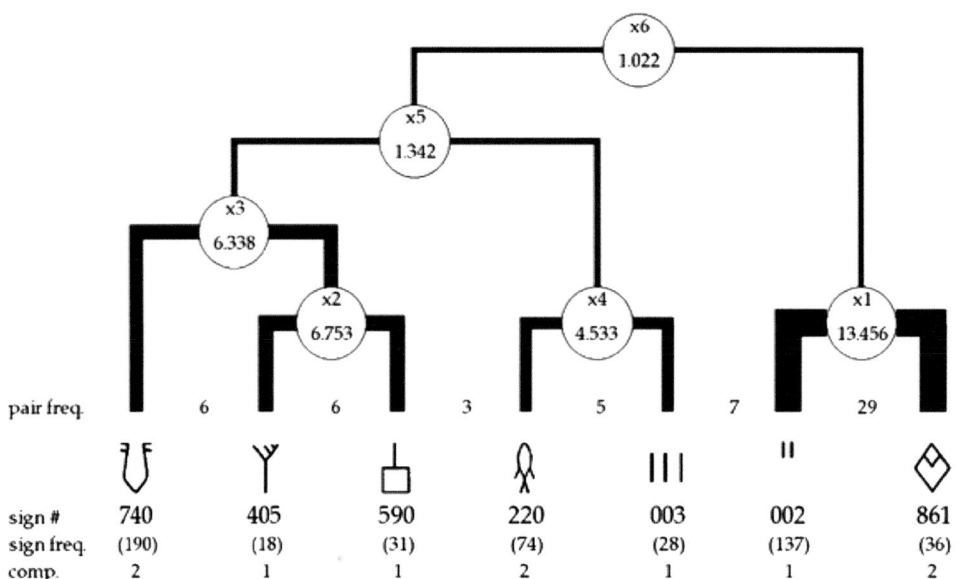

Harappa H-134 5436 SEAL:R LP
CompSum 10 CompMean 1.429
NodeSum 33.444 NodeMean 5.574 PairSum 36.606 PairMean 6.101
ID 1624 #Signs 7 tree height 4 index 0.57

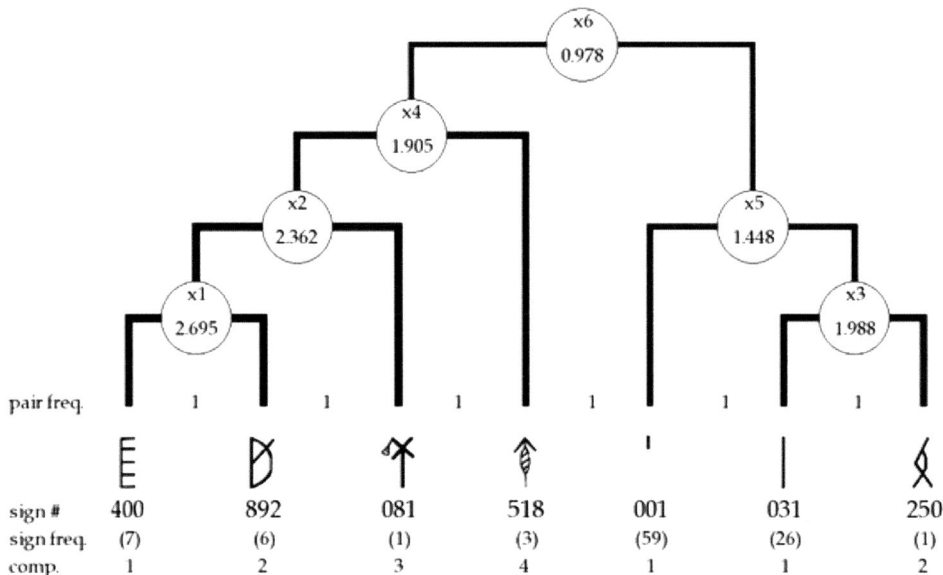

Mohenjo-daro - DK11245 SEAL:S LC
CompSum 14 CompMean 2.000
NodeSum 11.376 NodeMean 1.896 PairSum 12.818 PairMean 2.136
ID 3015 #Signs 7 tree height 4 index 0.57

FIGURE 3.32 COMPARISON OF A PATTERNED (TOP) AND COMPLEX (BOTTOM) TEXT IN TERMS OF SIGN CORRELATIONS

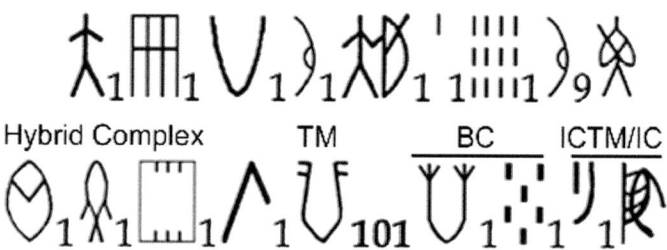

FIGURE 3.33 COMPARISON OF PURE TEXTS (H98-3491, TOP) AND HYBRID COMPLEX (ND-1, BOTTOM).

text imbedded in it, H98-3491 scores twice as high in terms of its overall organization. While counterintuitive this result points to the underlying organization of Pure Complex texts (Figure 3.33).

With a tree height of 4, H98-3491 is highly organized with 3 first level pairs. While there is a high correlation between sign 740-760 in Nd-1, the rest of the text is not highly correlated. Unlike the Patterned text in Figure 3.31 (top,H-134) with a mean node score of 5.574, Nd-1 (Figure 3.34, bottom) has a mean node score of 3.32. That is, Nd-1 has lower level of organization than the Patterned texts even though it has patterned elements in it. The Pure Complex text (Figure 3.34, top) is also more highly organized than Nd-1.

In Figure 3.35 contexts of the sign pair 920-140 demonstrate the extremes of sign usage. In text *a* this pair is in a typical Partial Pattern texts with an IC-ICTM BC-TM-PT. This is the only text in which this pair is a BC (M-1165). In all other contexts this pair is part of an IC. They are initial in both Complex and Patterned texts. What follows 920-140 in texts varies greatly from 2 to 6 signs.

The sign inventory of these text show some relationships (Figure 3.35). For example, texts *e* and *f* demonstrate a complex relationship between signs 220 and 575, and the function of enclosing short strokes. In *e* these sign are enclosed as a pair, but in *f* only 220 is enclosed (to form sign 226). The differences in sign arrangement suggest that in terminal rather than IC context this shift in placing the enclosures is grammatically necessary, perhaps because of the sign 002 affix in *e*'s IC, or the fact that sign 220 is terminal in *f*. Both are square seal texts from different areas at Mohenjo-daro. In Figure 3.35 texts *b, c, d, f, g* and *h* are all Complex texts. This figure also demonstrates the difficulty with segmenting Complex texts – they do not segment completely. In some texts there are well defined ICs (*d* and *e*) and in others well-known PTs are used (*b, d* and *h*). Regardless of these recognizable features, the majority of these texts have several unanalyzed sign clusters. This is the challenge of Complex texts. These patterns indicate that, while the basic principles of text construction are in use, the formulaic sign sequence of Patterned texts are replaced by less predictable sign sequences.

48 The Archaeology and Epigraphy of Indus Writing

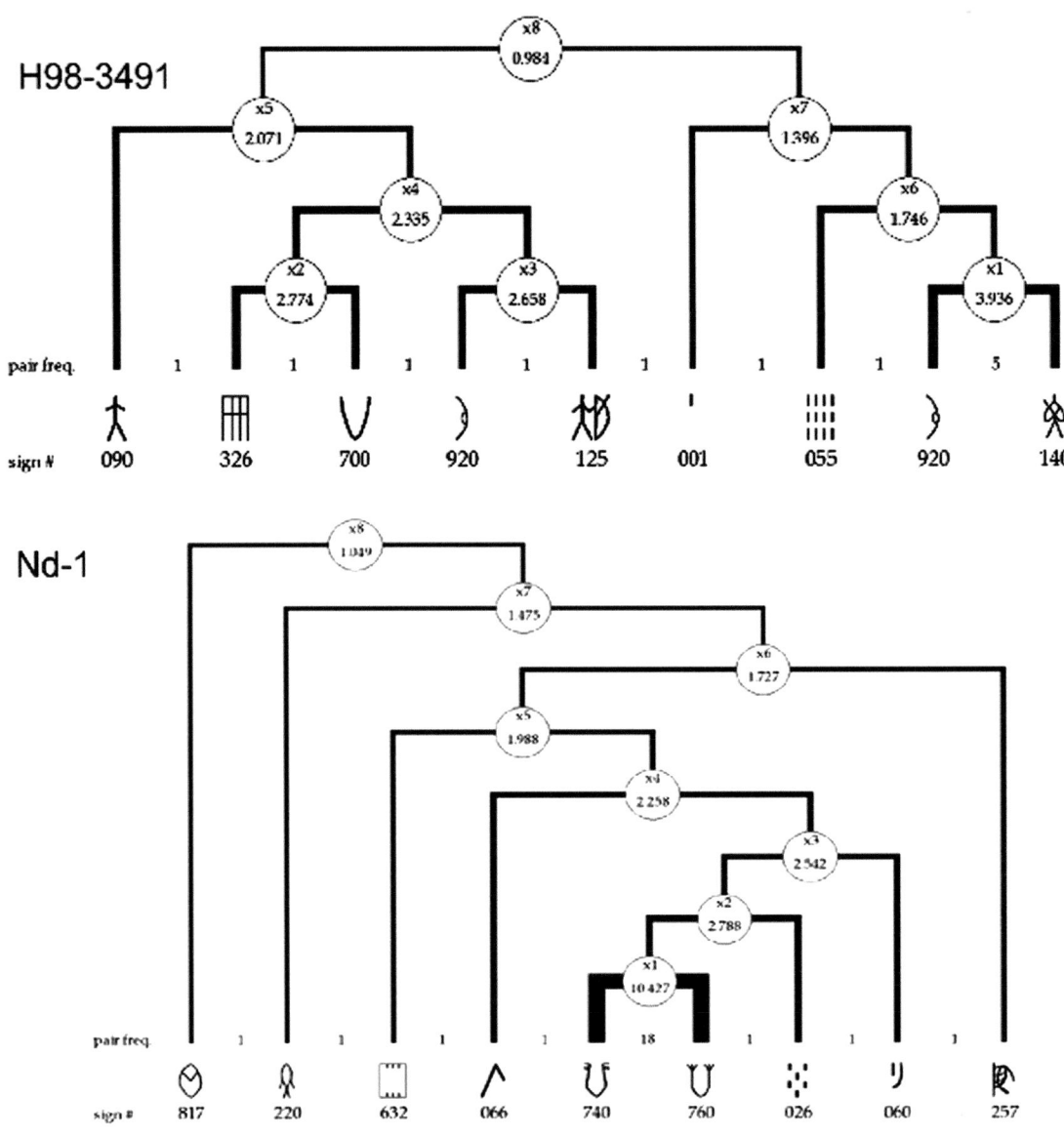

Figure 3.34 Segmentation trees for H98-3491 and Nd-1.

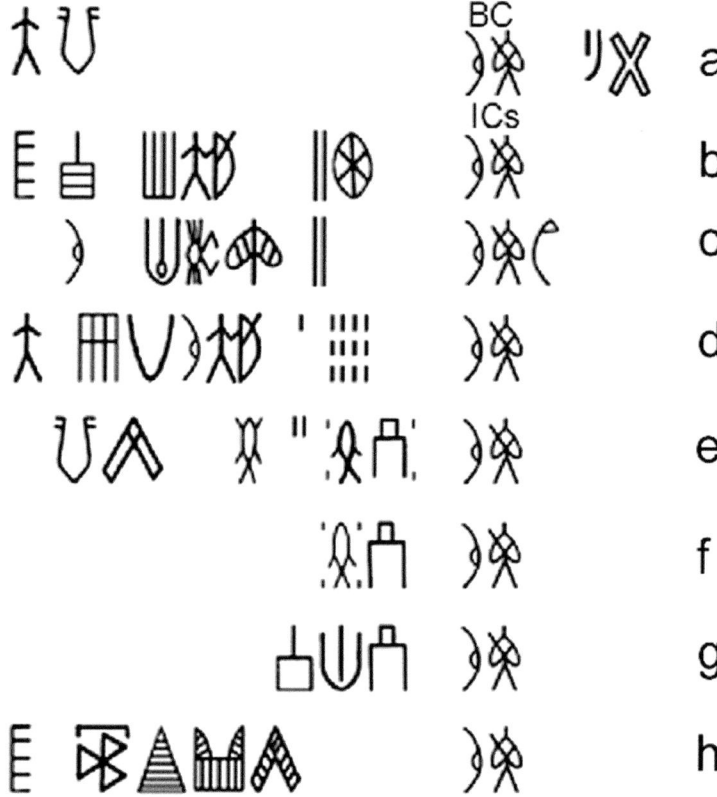

FIGURE 3.35 ALL OF THE COMPLETE TEXTS USING THE 920-140 PAIR.

The Dholavira Sign Board

One text that is unusual in the corpus is the Dholavira signboard. The Dholavira signboard consists of a series of steatite blocks arranged to form 30 cm high signs that were attached to a wooden backing. It has a relatively long text containing 10 signs (Figure 3.36). From the order of the signs we know the signboard fell face down and therefore the image in Figure 3.36 has been reversed to maintain the right to left reading order of Indus texts.

It has been suggested that the signboard hung over the entranceway of one of the gates of Dholavira. I would postulate that some of these signs could be spelling the ancient name of Dholavira. Further, if the signboard text contains the name of Dholavira, then the signs spelling the name of this important site should be repeated elsewhere in the Indus corpus. This is exactly what happens. The sign sequence is repeated on several artifacts (7) of different types (Figure 3.37). The repeating sign sequence has two elements: ∧◇ and ⊛⊛. This is known because ∧◇ occurs without ⊛⊛ and

FIGURE 3.36 THE DHOLAVIRA SIGNBOARD (PHOTO REVERSED TO MAINTAIN READING ORDER; COURTESY OF RAJESH RAO)

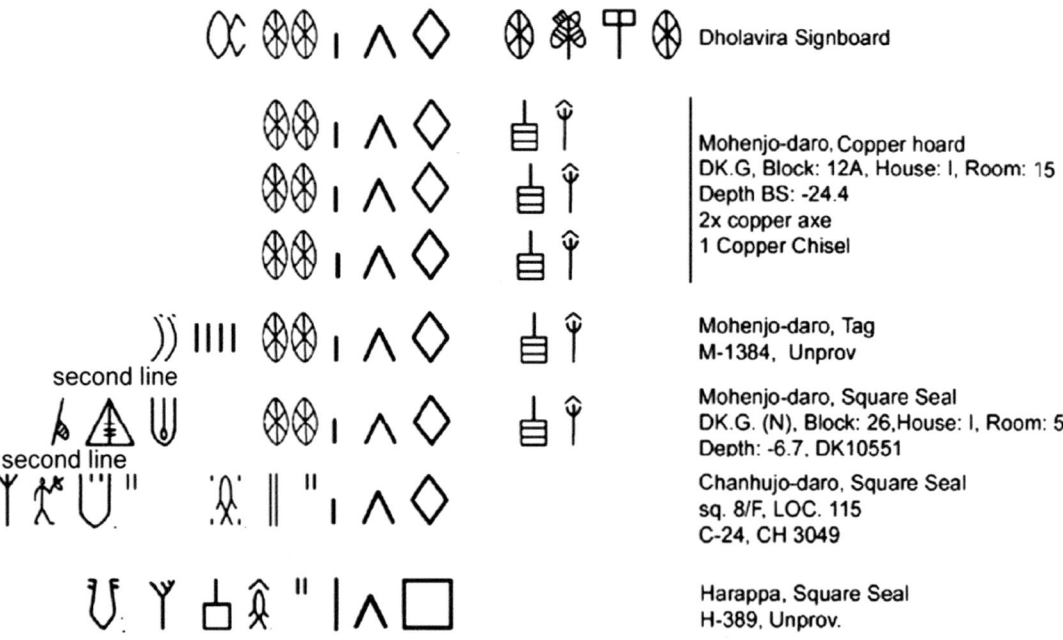

FIGURE 3.37 TEXT WITH RELATED STRUCTURES TO THE DHOLAVIRA SIGNBOARD.

vice versa. The identities of the other signs:  and the terminal sign ⌀ are not as clear, but there placement suggests that ⌀ is a word sign, either syllabic cluster (○+✕) or logograph (i.e. isolated at the end of the text), and ⊕❋⊤⊕ is a separate introductory phrase. The sign sequence ∧◇ may be 3 syllabic signs spelling Dholavira's ancient name. This small sample of texts is surprisingly informative.

The archaeology of the texts is interesting. Three of the 7 texts come from a copper hoard from Mohenjo-daro (GK.G, Block 12A). One is a copper/bronze chisel and two are copper/bronze axe heads. Found at a depth of -24.4 feet, they are from the Intermediate II phase and can be dated to about 22-2300 BC. All three copper tools and the only seal text with this sign sequence comes from Mohenjo-daro and all have the same two sign sequence prefacing the Dholavira toponymn. The tag from Mohenjo-daro also has this preface, but with a affix of two (numeral) signs. In these texts the toponym is medial.

The Dholavira place-name ⊗⊗ ∧ ◇ is a medial cluster in most cases. When it is not medial it is initial, but in these two examples sign 821 is replaced by sign 002. One explanation for this is that, in the medial position it is a toponym and in the initial position it is a name or title, requiring a shift in affixing. One interesting difference between the Southern (Chanhujo-daro) and the northern (Harappa) text is in the initial sign. There is one clue. Chanhujo-daro is very close to Mohenjo-daro (about 130 km south), while Harappa is not (about 350 km north). It is possible given these geographic locations that Harappa and Chanhujo-daro that they might share a language, while Mohenjo-dar and Chanhujo-daro most likely do. It seems likely that in the medial position this sign cluster is a toponymn, and in the initial position its most likely a name or title (he of Dholavira?). This situations is further complicated by the Harappan example being different from the other texts. The variations are informative. They suggest that the initial sign 850 is the equivalent of sign 625. It may be that sign 625 was the original form and that sign 850 resulting from rotation to save space. The third sign in the southern texts is intermediate in form between 001 and 031. It may be that the southern examples have shorted sign 031 to save space, or for esthetic reasons. The rotation of sign 625 to be sign 850 can be seen in Figure 3.38. In this text the half rotated sign is an intermediate form. This shift may be chronologically based or it may be that the northern style is sign 625 and the southern style is 850. We cannot know with the data at hand which of these suggestions

FIGURE 3.38 H-006 WITH THE PARTIALLY ROTATED SIGN 625/850.

is correct and, in fact, both could be operating, with the northern style being abandoned over time for the more space efficient southern style. Note that there are 7 examples of sign 850 from Harappa and all but one is clearly diamond shaped.

Assuming that this identification of the toponym and name are correct, this has implications for the root language of the script. This is the pattern you would expect for a Dravidian language. The analysis of these texts is returned to in Chapter 6.

Other Text Types

There are a series of text not yet discussed in detail. For example, there are 1717 texts that are damaged or too short (1-3 signs) to be classified. There are also a set of texts with numbers pairing with single signs to form either the entire inscription, or a complementary inscription (reverse) that need special consideration. These texts are discussed in the following Chapter (4).

Summary

We can see from this chapter that Indus texts are divisible into general categories based on sign sequence and the presence of "markers" (ICTMs, Fish, and TMs especially). The highly formulaic Patterned texts are the easiest to identify, as are many other types (i.e. 700+#, Segment texts). There are intermediate forms between classes (Partial Patterned and Hybrid Complex) and these can be more difficult to identify. This classification system can be useful in grouping the texts for analysis. The comparison of classes (especially Complex and Patterned) is useful, and shows that signs in Patterned texts pair in more predictable ways than other types. But why are these texts type so different. We know from examples in the Hieroglyphic Egyptian corpus that foreign words (mostly names) take more signs to write. They have to be spelled syllabically rather than with a logograph. The same is true for loan words. For example, Aztec god names in the Dresden codex are spelled syllabically. There are simply no word signs for these names and so they must be written one syllable at a time.. The sign sequences in these examples conform to the rules of spelling in the various systems of writing. This may explain the long introductory phrases in some ICs.

One feature of the Indus texts is that a complete text can have one to 17 signs. Several possibilities suggest themselves. First, short text could be abbreviations of long texts, where the original text is so repetitive that only mnemonics are necessary to cue the reader. Longer texts would then be explicit descriptions of contents (seals) or actions (tablets) that are not know from the context or by repetition. Tag texts can be anything from a symbol (swastika etc.) to long multiple impression texts. The longest tag text has four seal impressions with 17 signs. Some of the multiple seal impressions are simply the same seal being impressed multiple times. We can see that there is no easy solution to the definition of what comprises an Indus text.

When we have clear texts of any kind, we can analyze them with structural analysis and segmentation routines to define sub-elements. The most common structure is three-part with Initial, medial and terminal sign cluster. These are most likely subject-object-verb elements, not necessarily in that order. What we do know is that, in their fullest form these subunits consist of 1-5 signs, but on average about 3 signs per cluster. Often in Patterned texts the medial cluster or the BC is dropped. As the system of "affixing" terminal cluster was defined in this chapter by holding the BC fixed, texts without BCs were not considered in this analysis. It is likewise obvious that TMs without BCs are like a case without a stem. So if TMs are not case markers what are they? First, they must be words, either logographic or syllabically spelled. Second, they must be able to incorporate other morphological elements or stand-alone. Third, we know that the stem of the Dholavira toponymn takes different affixes when it is in the initial or medial positions. This could mean that the initial and medial positions are nouns. The terminal position should then be the verb. If so, then the TM could be the basic verb and BC are incorporated elements, possibly adverbial.

What I have tried to show in this chapter is that Indus texts are not a unified set. There are regional and temporal variations in texts types and sign usage. The highly formulaic Patterned texts are relatively easy to segment. This segmentation results in the identification of three structural elements in the most verbose texts. Shorter texts could be abbreviations (mnemonics) or in some cases demonstrable subsets of longer texts (Segments). Some of the short texts are stand-alone statements with noun+number combinations discussed in Chapter 4. It seems likely that the Complex texts are either a very different subject matter or more heavily syllabic spellings (of foreign words?). The Dholavira signboard and the texts containing that toponym makes it clear that affixes change when a word moves from medial to initial positions. The implication of this morphological fact is that the Indus verb is terminal (when present). The Indus language uses a S-O-V or O-S-V syntactic pattern. These patterns are not necessarily fixed to just one pattern. It is common that word order is somewhat flexible in many languages. Further, we know from Classic Maya books and Cuneiform texts that verbs are not always necessary for short texts. Examples of noun+number constructions are common in all writing systems where economically important items are listed (Wells 2011).

We cannot hope to decipher the Indus script without a detailed examination of the corpus in terms of temporal, geographic and artifactual characteristics. The corpus as it stands is a work in progress. The publication of new texts is unlikely to change the analysis given here, unless these texts are from new artifact types and significantly longer than those currently known. What is presented here is an analysis based on the bulk of Indus texts (4794). Care has been taken to identify unprovenanced artifacts and to avoid basing analysis on them. There are certainly some fakes in the corpus, although they are difficult to identify. The strategy here is to base the analysis on complete texts from known locations and to use damaged and unprovenanced texts as supplemental data. We lack chronological control over most of the texts and so issues of temporal change remain mostly unanswered. What is offered here is the current state of this research. There are still many issues and ideas the need further development over the coming years.

There is one further text type that needs discussing, namely artifacts with multiple texts. We have seen texts on several sides of an artifact, but there are artifacts with more than one line of text.

In this text the first line of texts contains two typical seal texts: ⊍𝕏𝕊𝕏𝕏 and ⊍⊕𝕏 combining as follows: ⊍⊕𝕏⊍𝕏𝕊𝕏𝕏. The second line is a short Complex text ⊗✝⋏⋎. These two phrases in the first line of text are both Partial Patterned texts, and both texts are IC+BC+TM structure. So this seal contains three distinct elements and within each are the necessary signs to form three sentences. It can be argued that the texts on the various sides of artifacts are unrelated. In these cases this argument cannot be made.

The longest Indus text on a single surface is M-0314 (Figure 3.39). It consists of three lines, with each line being a different type of texts.

It is certain that these signs are meant to be read together. As this artifact is unique in the corpus and late chronologically (1900-2000 BC), it can be seen as an oddity.

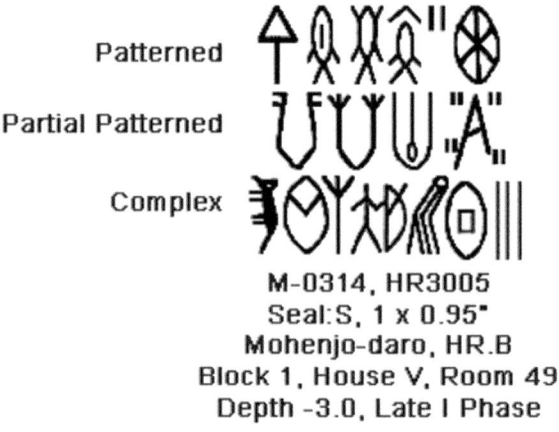

FIGURE 3.39 THE LONGEST INDUS TEXT ON A SINGLE SURFACE (M-0314).

Chapter 4

Tablets, Pots and the Volumetric System of Harappa

The Indus script presents special problems to decipherment, which have been discussed in detail elsewhere (Parpola 1994, Possehl 1996, Wells 2011). In summary it can be said that the inscriptions read from right to left, the texts are mostly short (mean = 5 signs), there is no Rosetta Stone style bilingual, our understanding of the use of the artifact is conjectural and the corpus of Indus inscriptions is now dated (Mahadevan 1977). All other aspects of the Indus script-- language, mechanics, subject matter and even the sign list-- are still open to argument.

There can be little doubt that the script is Logo-syllabic and that basic signs are combined in fixed ways to form compound signs. Minor variations in sign design often result in specific changes in sign collocations. In the previous chapter (3), it was demonstrated that Indus texts could be classified into sub-sets with similar sign patterns, or lack of pattern.

One of these classes is the Noun+Number texts. As shown in Chapter 5 (Figure 5.2) numbers collocate preferentially with specific signs. The focus of this chapter is a subset of the Noun+Number that bear sign 700 and a stroke numeral (700+#). Other Noun+Number texts are dealt with in part in Chapter 5, but a full study is need and forthcoming.

The many obstacles to decipherment limit the approaches that can be practically applied to the decipherment of the Indus script, but do not preclude all progress in this direction. What is needed is a dataset that addresses one or more of these problems. In this chapter the problem of subject matter is addressed independently of root language. To a lesser degree this chapter addresses the issue of artifact use. It is posited here that Indus artifacts had several discrete uses, and that artifacts of the same type (seals, tablets, tags, etc.) need not have a single unified function. Further, a specific artifact might be used in several ways during its use life. The corpus of Indus texts likely addresses several topics. This chapter concludes that one topic of the Indus inscriptions is economic, and related to the volumetric system in use primarily at the ancient Indus site of Harappa.

This chapter is aimed at exploring the relationship between artifacts with a specific cluster of signs in the Indus script (hereafter referred to as the V+# texts) found predominately on miniature tablets (bas relief and incised) and ceramic vessels from Harappa. For a sample of these artifacts see Figure 4.2. This relationship was first noticed in 1999 (B. Wells 1999) and it was suggested then that the V+# portion of these texts might be annotating a volumetric system in use at Harappa during the Bronze Age. Additionally, the most obvious use of bas relief and incised tablets is that they are votive offerings or rations chits (although other explanations are possible). Evidence in support of the identification of some bas relief tablets as votive offerings comes from Mohenjo-daro (M-0478, DK10337, Mackay 1938:Plate XC:23; Figure 4.1). There are four elements on this face of the artifact: a geometric design, two signs E |ᛉ|, a V+# text (V IIII), and an image of a human figure holding a pot while sitting in front of and facing a tree. Images of offerings are known from other artifacts. The most common are of an anthropomorphic figure in a tree with supplicants facing. Text b (V+# texts) consists of the volumetric marker (V) and 4 short linear strokes. Right adjacent to the V+# texts is the image of the human offering a vessel to a tree. It can be demonstrated that short strokes and long strokes have different values, with one long stroke equaling 10 units and one short stroke equals 1 unit (Wells 2011; Chapter 5). If these values are correct, then the offering is about 4 x 4.04 = 16.16 liters. The exact meaning of this iconographic element, and the others on the obverse and reverse, are unknown. The proximity of the image and the V+# in Figure 4.1 may be only coincidental, but the association can be added to the list of data that relate to the Harappa volumetric system.

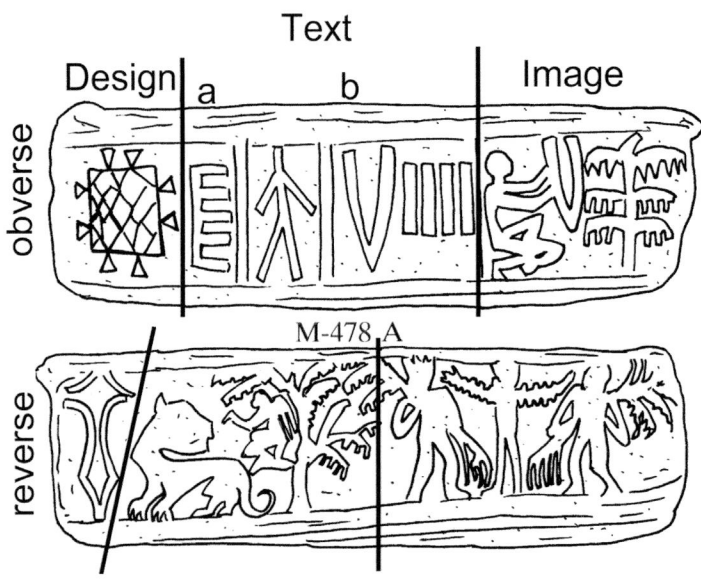

FIGURE 4.1. POSSIBLE DEPICTION OF A VIIII TREE OFFERING ON M-0478.

It has been suggested (Wells 1999) that tablets likely had several uses in antiquity depending on their design and their cultural context. This paper concludes that there is good evidence for a volumetric system in common use at Harappa during the Bronze Age (2700-1900 BC). Further, the units in this system can be estimated using complete vessels with specific texts – namely the V+# texts as shown in Figure 4.2. Long Stroke signs represent the units in the system, each standing for 40.4 liters.

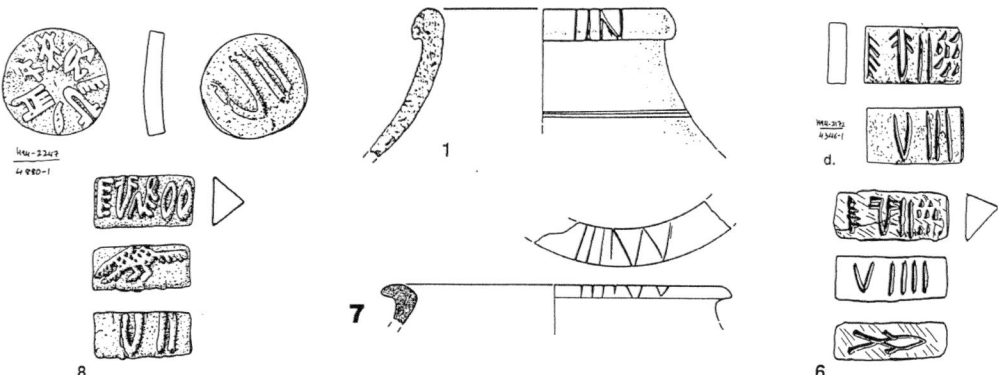

FIGURE 4.2. EXAMPLES OF ARTIFACTS BEARING V+# TEXTS. MINIATURE TABLETS (BAS RELIEF: TAB:B; INCISED: TAB:I) AND CERAMIC VESSELS.(POT:T:G). DRAWINGS COURTESY OF RICHARD MEADOW AND THE HARP PROJECT.

While the exact use of miniature tablets is unknown, it is proposed here that the V+# are annotating an underlying volumetric system, but how can this relationship be tested and what are the units of this system?

Indus Numbers

It has been suggested that the Indus number system is base 10, uses some non-stroke numeral signs and uses positional notation to express higher numerals (Wells 2011). The basic Indus number system is based on ∣ = 1 and | = 10. Whether all short signs are one system (stacked and linear) or if they represent two distinct systems is currently unclear. The special numerals) = 5, 𝍚 = 14 commonly replace for stroke signs in numeric contexts. The system has several interesting characteristics. First, some of the numbers are rare (n>5). Several numerals collocate predominately with specific non-numeric signs. This includes relatively high frequency signs such as ⩕ and ∥, which pair 57 times. Some numerals are very frequent— ‖‖ n = 231 and ⦀ n = 76. In total the number system seems uneven with several numerals dominating the system in terms of sign frequency and specific sign parings being most common. Those familiar with the Indus script will recognize ∪⌂∥ as a common noun + numeral contexts.

Numbers are found primarily on POT:T:g (213), SEAL:R (301), SEAL:S (1305), TAB:B (496), TAB:I (412), TAB:C (142), and TAG (126) artifacts. These totals contain the counts for signs 1, 2, 31, 32, and 33 they are consequently inflated by non-numeric (polyvalent) uses of these signs and by the repetitive nature of tablet texts (the TAB effect). Chapter 5 gives details of the Indus number system.

The Tablets of Harappa

In all there are 1174 tablets from Harappa. Of these 987 have at least 1 recognizable sign in the Indus Script. There are 422 miniature tablets from Harappa with V+# texts (bas

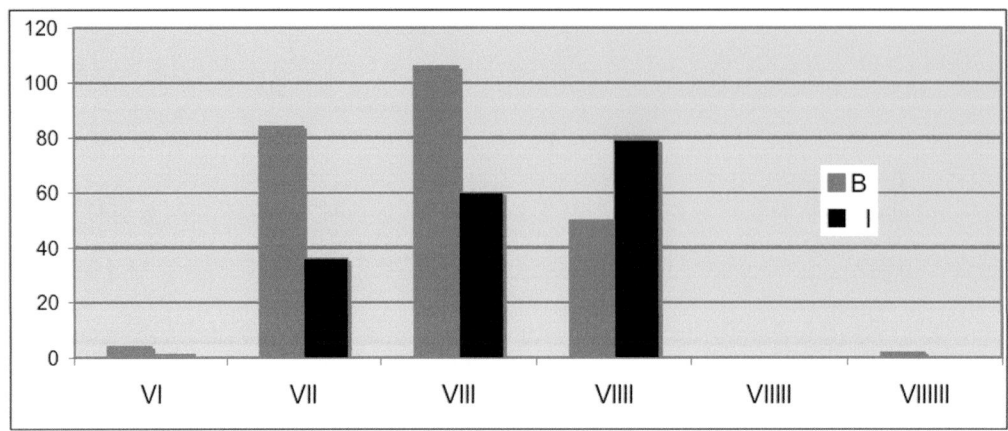

FIGURE 4.3. TABULATION OF TABLETS WITH V+# TEXTS FOUND AT HARAPPA, PAKISTAN BY TABLET TYPE AND NUMBER OF LONG STROKES (INCISED TABLETS = I, AND BAS RELIEF TABLETS = B).

relief = 246; incised = 176). These artifacts have significant differences in their V+# texts which may be marking variations in use. In Figure 4.3 the frequency of V+# texts on tablets are compared.

It is evident from this graph that there are significant differences in the V+# texts found on bas-relief (TAB:B) and incised miniature tablets (TAB:I) from Harappa. TAB:B artifacts bear sign clusters with fewer stroke-signs than do TAB:I artifacts. Whatever their uses in antiquity the basic system employs predominantly II, III and IIII either right or left of the V sign. The majority (73%) are V+# texts, while the remainder are #+V.

FIGURE 4.4. MINIATURE TABLETS WITH V+# TEXTS BY MOUND AT HARAPPA.

There is a spatial bias in the data because the largest sample comes from Mound F and Mound E/ET (Figure 4.4). TAB:I artifacts are proportionally more common from Mound F and TAB:B artifacts are more common at Mound E/ET. Further, because TAB:I artifacts have a higher frequency of Vll this sign cluster is likewise more frequent at Mound F.

It seems likely, given the details of their provenience and texts, that TAB:B and TAB:I artifacts had different uses in antiquity, but that they used an single system in their V+# texts. This analysis is very general and does not address the details of shape, sidedness, size or color. of TAB artifacts. Although these attributes are likely significant and deserve study. The goal here is to focus on the texts and defining the volumetric system as closely as possible.

The Purana Qila Pots

The question of what the V+# texts are annotation still needs to be addressed. A solution to this problem can be found in 3 complete vessels excavated by Vats (1940) from Harappa and now stored in the Purana Qila magazines in New Delhi, India. These vessels, in addition to being excavated from the same find spot at Harappa (Figure 4.5), all bear texts with long linear stroke signs and two of these have V+# texts (Figure 4.6). The two larger pots have texts that are remarkably similar in size and placement on the vessel. They give us a set of possible values in the V+# system.

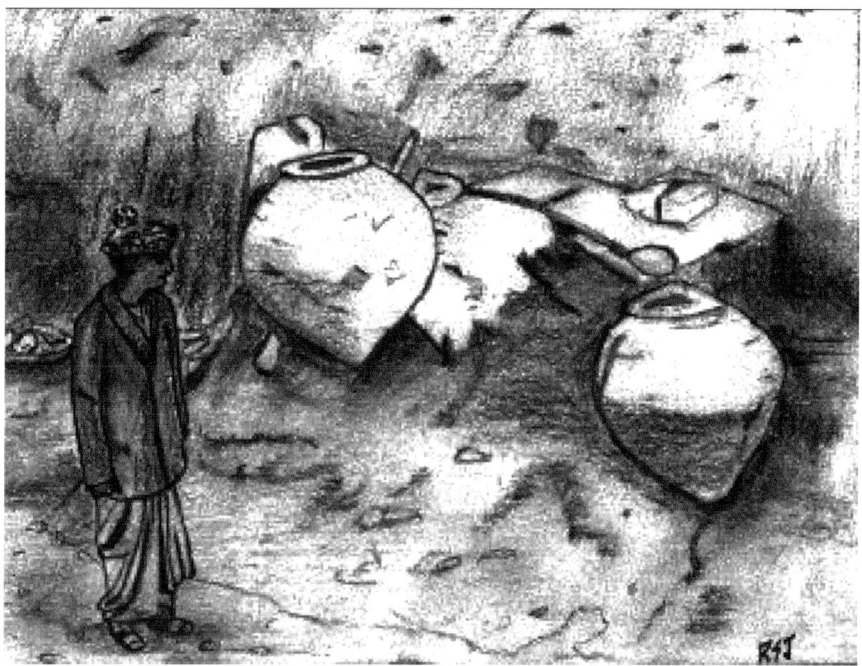

FIGURE 4.5 PURANA QILA POTS *IN SITU* AFTER VATS (1940: VOL. II, PLATE 23A).

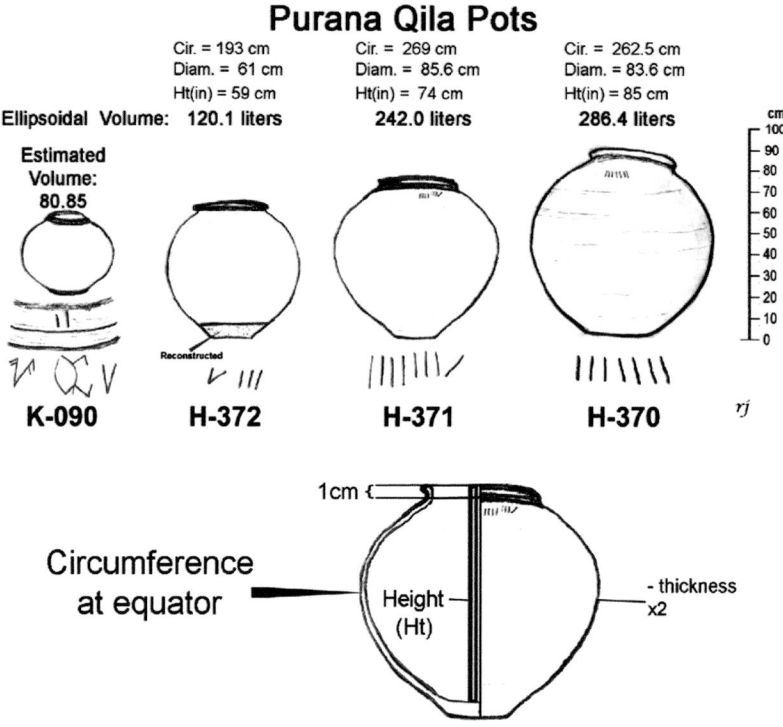

FIGURE 4.6. THE PURANA QILA POTS FROM HARAPPA WITH V+# TEXTS AND AN EXAMPLE FROM KALIBANGAN.

The volumes calculated here are close approximations to the actual volumes of these vessels. More precision in these measurements can only be attained by a full study of the pots in question. My goal here is to calculate the volume of these vessels as closely as possible without moving or photographing them (which requires special permission). Further, complicating these calculations are variations resulting from the manufacturing process.

We still have no idea what is being measured, but grains, milk, water and other economical important commodities are all possibilities. The use of tablets with V+# texts implies a high level of organization and complexity equal to that of other Bronze Age cultures. Examples of the volumetric system are far more common at Harappa. This fact points to a significant difference between Indus sites and artifact types. If this difference is bureaucratic, religious or managerial (any or all of these) is unknown. The volumetric system outlined in Table 4.2 is simple and standardized with the basic unit of about 40.4 liters. It is unlikely that this system was used to measure precious items, as the smallest unit in the system is more than 40 liters. The majority of V+# text are found at Harappa, and so the system may not be in common use over the entire Indus area. In fact, of all TAB:B artifacts 71% come from Harappa and all but 4 TAB:I artifacts as well. Of V+# texts 98% are from Harappa, with all non-Harappa examples listed in Figure 4.7.

We do not know the precision with which these pots were made. Variations in the thickness of the walls, the precise shape and size, and the level to which these pots were intended to be filled *in situ*, are all unknown. It seems likely that even the most precise measurements will still have minor inconsistencies between vessels. Difference between actual and intended volumes likely increases with vessel sizeThe clearest text is from H-372, which is inscribed with VIII. On a visit to Purana Qila in 2009 I was given the opportunity (by the Archaeological Survey of India) to measure these vessels. A close examination revealed some interesting facts about this vessel and its photograph. First, the photograph in the CISI (Joshi and Parpola 1987) has been altered. More specifically it had been trimmed along its base to remove the wooden stand it rests in from the photo. This alteration makes measurements of the vessel using this photo inaccurate. It was placed in a wooden stand because the base of the vessel had been damaged and no pressure could be placed on the base without risk of further damage. Therefore, it was placed in a stand, which supported it 6-8 cm above its base. The calculations in the following discussion are based on measurements of the vessels and not of their photographs (Table 4.1).

A careful measurement of the circumferences, inside heights and mouth widths of these vessels is summarized in Table 4.1 as follows:

ID	# strokes	circumference outside [cm]	estimated thickness [cm]	horizontal radius inside [cm]	inside height [cm]	rim [cm]	adjusted height [cm]	vertical radius inside [cm]
H-372	3	193	1	29.72	64	1	63	31.5
H-371	6	269	2	40.81	74	1	73	36.5
H-370	7	262.5	2	39.78	85	1	84	42

Results:

ID	# strokes	spherical volume [litre]	ellipsoidal volume [litre]	spherical volumetric unit [litre]	ellipsoidal volumetric unit [litre]	error of spherical unit [litre]	error of ellipsoidal unit [litre]
H-372	3	120.1	116.5	40.0	38.8	0.4	1.5
H-371	6	242.0	254.7	40.3	42.4	0.1	-2.1
H-370	7	286.4	278.4	40.9	39.8	-0.5	0.6
mean of one unit (l):				40.4	40.4		

TABLE 4.1. MEASUREMENTS OF THE PURANA QILA VESSELS WITH RADIUS AND VOLUME CALCULATIONS SHOWING VI ≈ 40.4 LITERS.

Because the interior of all three vessels are ellipsoidal we can calculate the approximate volume of these vessels using the following formula (1):

Vol = 4/3 x π x Rh x Rh x Rv   (1)

Where, Rh= horizontal radius and Rv = vertical radius and pi is 3.1415. The radii need to be decreased by the thickness of the vessel wall (≈1 cm x2), and the inside height radius needs to be adjusted about the same amount to subtract the height of the vessels mouth (1 cm) (Table 4.1). The adjusted radii can be used in formula 1 to calculate a good approximation of the volume of the vessel. The volume in cm^3 can be converted into liters by multiplying by 0.001. This value can then be used to calculate the value of VI (with the exception of the examples using short strokes) by dividing by the number of strokes on the vessel.

To begin with the volumes of the Purana Qila pots can be used to estimate VI = 40.4 liters. Using this relationship we can estimate the values for VIIIIII (6) and for IIIIIII (7) as 242.6 and 283.0 liters respectively. The estimates differ from the observed by 0.6 for H-371 and 3.41 (1.2 %) for H-370. The average of the estimates of unit values based on each vessel is given in Table 4.2 (Grand Mean). The volumetric system is estimated three times, once for each vessel. The grand mean averages these three estimates with the hope that this will minimize the variations in vessel volume resulting from the manufacturing process.

There is a whole ceramic vessel from Kalibangan (Figure 4.6, K-090) that may fit the Harappan volumetric system. It has an unusual text with two strokes on the rim and three sign on the body (Figure 4.6). The text on the body of the vessel contains V in the initial position. If this is intended to be VII, then we can estimate the volume of this vessel to be ≈ 81 liters. Using formula (1) we can calculate the radius of this vessel to be 16.4 cm. A scale is given with the photo, but the units of the scale are unknown. We can say that if this vessel is in the Harappan volumetric system, then the scale increments should be 5 cm. If so then the measured radius is ≈ 16 cm, which matches the estimate of 16.4 cm very well. As in the case of the Purana Qila pots, a full study

Pot Id.	H-372	H-371	H-370	Grand Mean	errors in liters from mean	H-372	H-371	H-370
# Strokes	3	6	7			3	6	7
V I	40.0	40.3	40.9	40.4		-0.39	-0.09	0.49
V II	80.1	80.7	81.8	80.9		-0.79	-0.19	0.97
V III	**120.1**	121.0	122.7	121.3		-1.18	-0.28	1.46
V IIII	160.1	161.3	163.7	161.7		-1.57	-0.37	1.95
V IIIII	200.2	201.7	204.6	202.1		-1.97	-0.47	2.44
V IIIIII	240.2	**242.0**	245.5	242.6		-2.36	-0.56	2.92
IIIIIII	280.2	282.3	**286.4**	283.0		-2.76	-0.66	3.41

TABLE 4.2. SUMMARY OF THE ESTIMATED UNITS OF THE HARAPPA VOLUMETRIC SYSTEM. ERRORS ARE GIVEN IN LITERSIN LITERS. ERRORS NEVER EXCEEDS 2% OF THE VESSELS VOLUME.

Mohenjo-daro

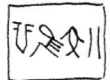
M-0511k DK4143 MacKay Plate XCIII:5 TAB:C
Mohenjo-daro, DK.G. Block 6, House II, Room 7
Depth -11.7 feet, Intermediate I Phase

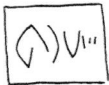
M-0512 DK3962 MacKay Plate XCIII:6 TAB:C
Mohenjo-daro, DK.G. Block 6, House II, Room 10
Depth -10 feet, Intermediate I Phase

 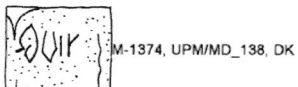 M-1374, UPM/MD_138, DK

M-1588, Mohenjo-daro

DK6861, Seal:S
DK.G, Long Lane, Depth BD -18.4

M-1425 DK11677. TAB:B
Mohenjo-daro, DK.G

M0478. DK10337 MacKay Plate XC:23
Mohenjo-daro DK.G Block 15, House II
Room 12. Depth -2.2 feet, LATE I

M-0479, DK10078
Mohenjo-dato DK.G
M-0480 DK11618
Mohenjo-daro DK.G

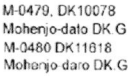
M-2104. VS875, Ivory Rod
Mphenjo-daro VS.A, Block 4,
House XXVII, Room 70, Depth -12'

M-0500, DK7810. SEAL:C
Mohejo-daro, DK.G(S), Block 7,
House V. Room 54, Depth -18.1'

DK6550, Seal:S
Mohenjo-daro, DK.G (S), Block 12,
House V, Room 96, Depth-13.5
Intermediate II Phase

Kalibangan

K-077. KLB2 21425
A HARAPPA STYLE TAB:B

K-068, KLB 19527
HARAPPA-STYLE TAB:B

FIGURE 4.7 ALL NON-HARAPPAN EXAMPLES OF V+# TEXTS.

by a ceramicist is needed. The possibility of K-090 being a trade-ware from Harappa needs to be explored. It seems unlikely that the contents of K-090 could be determined archaeologically, but one could postulate that it was ≈ 81 liters of . This connection has important implications for the decipherment of Indus writing and bears directly the topic of subject matter.

Conclusion

In the case of the volumetric system identified in this chapter and elsewhere (Wells 1999, 2006 and 2011), the level of exchange seems to be too large scale for a nuclear household (40-250 liters). The excavators of Mohenjo-daro used a "Block" and "House" designations to describe architectural associations (Marshall 1931 and Mackay 1938). These architectural features could more accurately be described as group compounds and activity areas. The situation at Harappa, while parallel, had something unique in the form of V+# texts. The scale of the volumetric system annotated in the inscriptions of Harappa needs to be considered in terms of its archaeological context, in that the Purana Qila pots are from the same find spot. If we take the whole lot together they represent ≈ 647 liters of an unknown number of commodities. This volume seems in line with settlement pattern of Mohenjo-daro, which I interpret as extended family compounds. Many of these compounds can be demonstrated to have craft specialization areas (pottery, copper-working, bead making, stoneware bangle production, etc.). For unknown reasons Harappa requires a more formal mechanism of exchange in the form of V+# texts.

It seems likely that there is a social mechanism involving redistribution of volumetric commodities and uses miniature tablets. Note too that incised tablets (TAB:I) are somewhat later chronologically than bas relief tablets (Tab:B). As both types of tablets use primarily VI (40.4 liters) through VIIII (161.7 liters) they may be annotating the same commodities, but in Figure 4.4 they have different distributions, with the V+# texts on TAB:I artifacts listing, on average, larger amounts. Only the smallest of the Purana Qila pots (VIII) is in the normal range of values found on miniature tablets. The two larger pots are about twice the size of the tablet texts. One possibility is that the smaller vessel held the same contents as annotated by TAB artifacts from Harappa. The two larger pots, once filled, could not be moved. It may be that they were meant to filled *in situ*.

The number of signs and the details of sign distribution suggests the Indus script is a logo-syllabic system (Wells 2011). Signs are constructed using a well-defined system that employs the addition of design elements and the conflation of signs to form new signs with unique characteristics. Syntagmatic and paradigmatic models can be constructed for most texts (Wells 2011; Chapter 3). Recent research (Fuls, Appendix II) has shown that many signs have preferred locations in text (i.e. initial, terminal, etc). Some sign clusters are more common than others and these sign clusters likewise have locational preferences. These non-random and consistent distributions allow the analysis of sign relations and leads to the identification of sign+number pairings, including V+# texts. This paring is common in all ancient scripts and the signs accompanying the numbers are invariably nouns (i.e. things being counted).

In most cases the identification of the noun can only be conjectural. In the case of V+# texts we can say with some confidence that V stands for a standard volumetric unit. The Indus number system is well known (Wells 2011; Chapter 5). That study showed that there are four types of numerals used in the Indus script: Long-linear, short-linear, short-stacked stroke signs and special numerals. This study also showed that some numerals (especially !, ", |, || and |||) are polyvalent (have more than one value). It is the sign's context that determines the value and function of the numerals. There are examples of polyvalent numerals from Cuneiform and Classic Maya writing (among others). From the cuneiform corpus there are many examples of worker categories being represented by a numeral sign, and examples of the value of numerals changing depending on the context and associated noun.

Proto-Cueiform employs 60 numerals in at least 13 discrete groups, and Proto-Elamite uses 14 numerals in at least 5 groups (Damerow and Englund 1989:74–5). In both cases the system being employed is understood from the context of the texts. That is, by which noun they are associated with. Proto-Sumerian and Proto-Elamite both employed more complex systems of numerals involving not only different systems of measurement, but also different values for the same numeric signs (Nissen et al. 1993:28-9). In Proto-Cuneiform texts for example, when measuring cereals the numeral ▷ has a value of 60, but a value of 300 when used in texts measuring surfaces (fields). In the case of Classic Maya text the numeral for two can be used to signal syllable doubling (^{2}ka-wa = ka-ka-wa = Kakaw(a) = 'cocao') and the numeral for 6 (*WAK*) is used for its homophone *WAK* = 'to raise-up'.

The major conclusion of this chapter is that the Bronze Age Harappans used a volumetric system with a basic unit of ≈40 liters, which is represented by VI in the Indus script. There are examples of V+# texts from two other sites, these are rare and represent only a small fraction of the corpus of V+# texts. V+# texts from ceramics are far less common than examples from miniature tablets, with only four examples of complete vessels in all. More examples are of complete ceramic vessels with V+# texts are needed to verify this system. The Kalibangan pot (Figure 4.5) is not a perfect test of the system for two reasons. First, the texts is in two-parts with the V and # components in different locations on the vessel. Second, the size of the scale is unknown. The radius of this vessel (16.4 cm) is calculated assuming that the two strokes and V sign inscribed on K-090 are indicating VII and are meant to be read together.

We can say that the numbers used on TAB:I and TAB:B artifacts are different in magnitude, with the TAB:I artifact texts having more strokes than TAB:B artifact texts. This could point to a difference in function. This is an interesting point as the TAB:B artifacts require a good deal more effort to manufacture and contain iconographic elements not present on TAB:I artifacts.

Finally, the volumetric system defined in this chapter does not require knowledge of the Indus language. Further, the system is not pan-Indus, but rather restricted in use. The differences in the magnitudes found on bas relief and incised tablets suggests that these artifacts had different uses but use the same volumetric system. The existence of the volumetric system on tablets suggests in theis case that at least some of the subject matter of the Indus inscriptions is economic.

Chapter 5

Numerals in the Indus Script and their Uses

Numerals in Indus texts are difficult to identify beyond the obvious stroke signs. The stroke signs themselves have complex distributions and some must certainly be polyvalent. Regardless of confounding circumstances many signs can be seen to function as numerals counting specific objects. In this chapter I will define the forms and distributions of Indus stroke numerals and argue for the inclusion of four non-stroke signs in the numeral class of signs based on their distributions.

In the following discussion two lines of evidence will be followed: (1) the comparison of Indus texts to other ancient texts for the purposes of assessing correspondences in form and content; (2) the contexts of the stroke (and other) numerals found in Indus texts. These two lines of evidence allow the definition of 30 stroke numerals and four non-stroke sign numerals. Further, the polyvalent values of key numeral signs will be discussed. Before discussing this material it is necessary to define more exactly some of the terms of reference:

Numeral: *a symbol that stands for one or more numbers.* For example, in Proto-Cuneiform texts the numeral | that normally has a value of 10 when counting discrete objects, takes a value of 18 when used to measure fields, and a value of 6 with dry

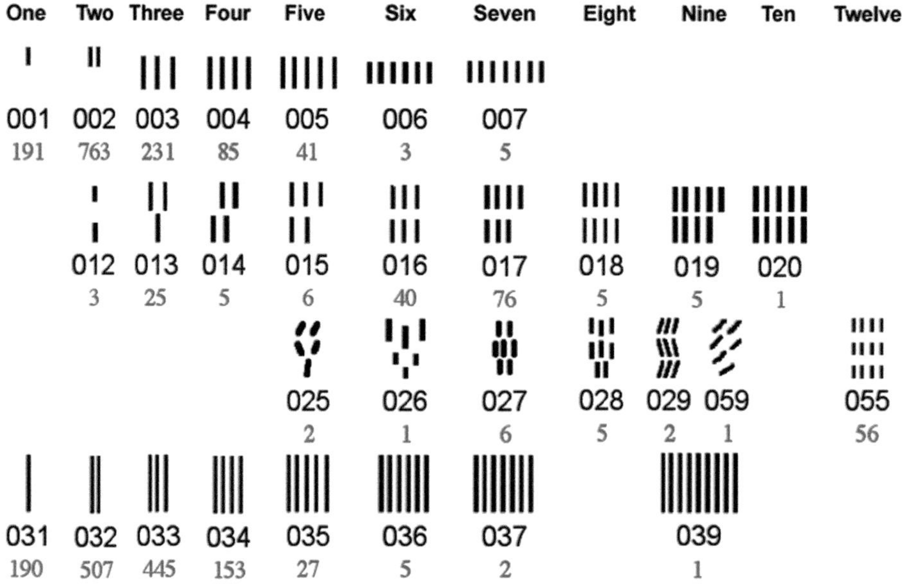

FIGURE 5.1. BASIC INDUS SCRIPT STROKE NUMERALS

measures of cereal. Therefore, | is the numeral and 6, 10 and 18 are the numbers it stands for depending on the context (Nissen et al. 1993:131-2).

Stroke sign: *a specific set of signs comprised of one or more short or long strokes* (Figure 5.1).

Figure 5.1 includes all basic stroke numerals, although there are 13 signs omitted from this figure because they are marked, enclosed or doubled. These signs occur in unique or non-numeric contexts and will be the subject of future research. Together the omitted signs occur in 45 texts, while the basic stroke numerals are found in 2727 texts.

Numerals In Other Ancient Scripts

What is the importance of identifying Indus numbers? Understanding the Indus system of numbers and the volumetric system (Chapter 4), brings us one step closer to being able to reconstruct the Indus systems of exchange and production. Combined with archaeological data we can say with some certainty that some seals and tablets had functions related to trade, rationing, storage and the cycle of production. A secondary

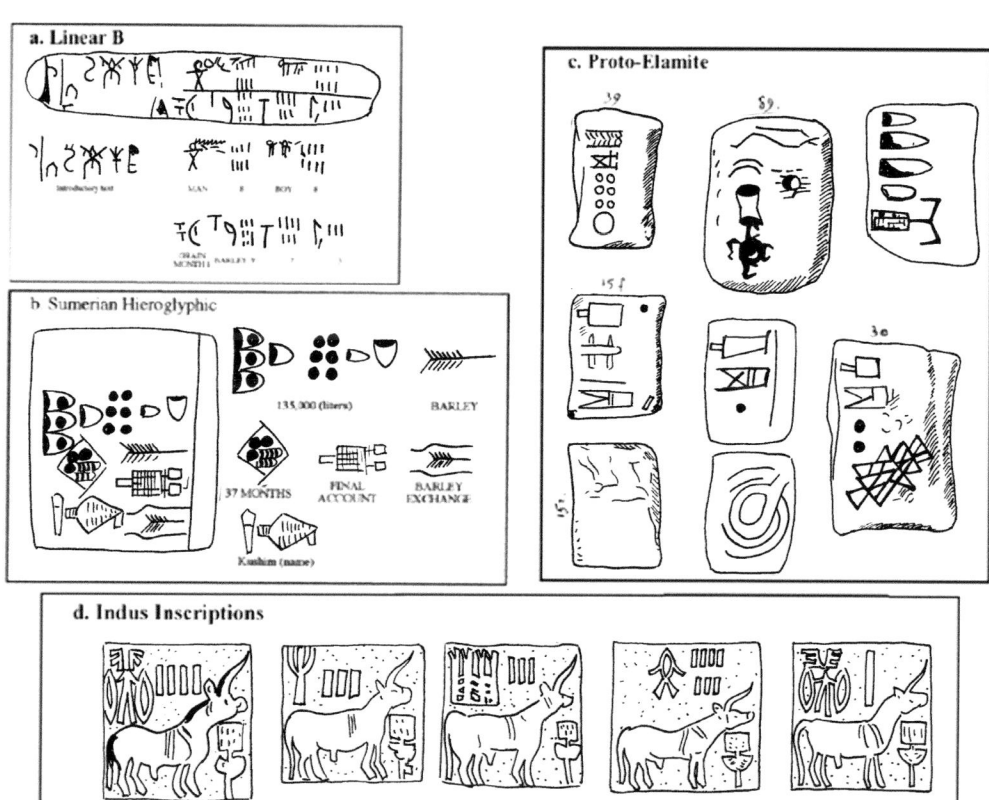

FIGURE 5.2. ECONOMIC TEXTS FROM THREE ANCIENT WRITING SYSTEMS COMPARED TO THE INDUS SCRIPT DEMONSTRATING A COMMON NOUN + NUMBER STRUCTURE.

result is that the base of the number system (8, 10 or 12) can help with the identification of the language of the Indus script. Also important is the fact 2727 text contain numerals. This is a significant proportion of the corpus (56%).

We know from other ancient logo-syllabic writing systems that economic texts are common (i.e. Proto-Cuneiform, Cuneiform, Proto-Elamite and Linear B). In these systems the numbers do not stand alone, but as counts (adjectives) of various items (nouns). In Figure 5.2 several of these texts are compared.

Linear B (Figure 5.2a) and Proto-Sumerian (Figure 5.2b) have been deciphered and the contents of their texts is known. The pattern of number plus noun is repeated in these ancient scripts in economic contexts. This pattern is obvious in the Indus script as well (Figure 5.2d). While we may not know the values of the numerals nor the nouns they associate with, we can say with confidence that they are numerals and nouns.

Epigraphic Issues

Other important epigraphic topics not yet discussed in this chapter are sign polyvalence, allographic variations and homophones. These aspects of ancient writing are well attested in all logo-syllabic scripts. Polyvalence is when a sign can stand for several words or concepts. For example, in Classic Maya writing ⬚ is the phonetic sign *ku*. In a cartouche ⬚ reads *KAWAK*, a day name in the 260 days calendar. Doubled ⬚ it reads both *pih* a phonetic sign and *PIH* a period of 144,000 days in the Long Count calendar. It can also have a value of TUUN (360 days) ⬚ when collocating with a *ni* phonetic complement, or have a reading of *JA'AB* (365 days) ⬚ depending on its contexts in the text.

A related problem arises in cuneiform texts with homophones. For example, in the fully developed cuneiform system the sound *gu* can be expressed using 14 different signs—all with different meanings: ⬚ *gu* = 'flax', ⬚ *gu$_2$* = 'neck', ⬚ *gu$_3$* = 'voice', and ⬚ *gu$_4$* = 'ox' etc. This is further complicated by the fact that ⬚ *gu$_3$* not only means 'voice' but also 'tooth' and 'mouth' (i.e. it is polyvalent). Again the exact reading of ⬚ *gu$_3$* depends on its context in the inscription.

As we know from Classic Maya writing, a single sound can be represented by signs with completely different designs (allographic variation). For example, the first person pronoun *U* can be represented by 13 different signs without changing its sound value or meaning. These phenomenon are not limited to Classic Maya writing.

These three factors can serve to confuse sign values. The confusion can only be controlled for by careful analysis of sign contexts on both the paradigmatic and syntagmatic levels. While confounding factors exist in ancient writing systems, we cannot be certain their type nor extent in the Indus system of writing. One goal of this research is to identify the ways in which numerals signs are used in the Indus inscriptions.

Short Linear Stroke Numerals

In their numeric contexts (see Chapter 3) these numerals consist of one to seven short strokes normally in the middle register of the inscription. Vertical positioning can vary according to the available space. These numerals collocate preferentially with specific signs (Table 5.1). Table 5.1 does not list every occurrence of signs left adjacent to short linear stroke numerals, but rather only those signs that are most commonly found with numeral signs.

Sign No.	Freq.	Graph	151	156	154	158	220	231	233	235	240	390	405	407/9	520	740	700	705/6	575	585
	Freq.		80	103	38	34	443	82	182	231	331	243	112	134	282	1696	565	286	72	58
1	191	'					2	1	3	5	3					1	1		6	1
2	763	"			2	1	22	12	17	31	71			1		1	1		5	
3	231	III			35		17	1	1			20	2			1	3			
4	85	IIII			1		3					16	6	14					8	1
5	41	IIIII			2							7	3	4					3	
6	3	IIIIII																		
7	5	IIIIIII														3				

TABLE 5.1. RIGHT-ADJACENT COLLOCATIONS OF SHORT-LINEAR STROKE SIGNS (SHADED CELLS HAVE A FREQUENCY >4).

Certain signs (156, the "fish" signs, 390, 405 and 407/9) collocate frequently with Short Linear Stroke signs, and other related signs. Conversely, they do not occur with signs 151 or 585 (and rarely with 154, 158, 520 and 575), although these signs do collocate with other types of numbers. Sign 003 has the widest set of collocations of this class of numeral.

There are some confounding factors at work with relation to the very high frequency of "fish" signs with signs 001 and 002. As outlined in Chapter 3 these two signs often function as Initial Cluster Terminal Markers. As the "fish" signs often follow Initial Clusters, the location of these signs right adjacent to "fish" signs is coincidental and is not a numeric context. Conversely, the collocation of sign 003 and 156 (n=35) are all numeric contexts.

Sign 006 occurs three times. In two of these contexts they are found on copper tools, and in one case on a square seal as follows: 740(2) 752(3) 006(1) 503(2) 236(4) 806(2) 2(1) 31(1) 502(3). This seems to be a numeric context. In the two inscriptions on copper tools, sign 006 occurs solo and left adjacent to sign 740. Short linear strokes signs are inefficient in their use of horizontal space and that may be the reason that the maximum value is 7.

Short Stacked Stroke Signs

One set of short stacked stroke numerals consist of two to ten short strokes arranged in two rows (Figure 5.1). Another set ranges from five to nine and twelve strokes and are arranged in three straight or staggered rows. Of this second set only sign 055 will be discussed later under the heading of *Special Numerals*.

The two row short-stacked numerals have a very restricted distribution (Table 5.2). Comparing Tables 5.1 and 5.2 it can be seen that the collocations of linear and stacked short-stroke signs are very different, arguing that they are different numeral sets. Further, judging by its contexts, sign 012 may not always be a numeral. With the possible exception of K-059 the same can be said for sign 013. This does not hold true for signs 014 through 019, which have many numeric contexts. Sign 020 remains a mystery as there is only one example and it is a solo-sign on a ceramic vessel.

High frequency collocations of sign 017 with both 575 and 585 points to a special relationship between these signs. As signs 575 and 585 are both limited in their associations to 017, the possibility that they are related functionally needs further study.

Sign No.	Freq.	Graph	151	156	154	158	220	231	233	235	240	390	405	407/9	520	740	700	705/6	575	585
			80	103	38	34	443	82	182	231	331	243	112	134	282	1696	565	286	72	58
12	3																			
13	25																			
14	5						1										1			
15	6											1								
16	40						12					10	1	3		2				
17	76						1					4	2	1		9			13	27
18	5											1	1							
19	5												1			1				
20	1																			

TABLE 5.2. RIGHT-ADJACENT COLLOCATIONS OF SHORT STACKED STROKE SIGNS (SHADED CELLS HAVE A FREQUENCY >4).

It is also worth noting that only 016 occurs with any significant frequency with signs 220, and 390. The main feature of Table 5.2 is the restricted nature of the distributions of signs and numerals, especially the lack of any collocations of signs 151, 156, 154 and 158 with any short-stacked stroke numerals.

Long Linear Stroke Signs

Long linear stroke signs consist of eight numerals counting from 1 to 9 with the eight-stroke numeral unattested. This group of numerals has a wide range of distributions, especially 031-033. The distributions of these three signs can only be explained through polyvalence.

For example, signs 031 and 032 (Figure 5.3) occur in the same texts in numeric, possible numeric and non-numeric contexts.Figure 5.3 makes it clear that sign 031 and 032 have both numeric and non-numeric (syllabic) contexts. The numeric functions of the long stroke signs are related to those of the other stoke signs (compare Tables 5.1, 5.2 and 5.3) in a general way. There is, however, one important difference—long stroke sign collocate right adjacent to sign 700 on tablets from Harappa.

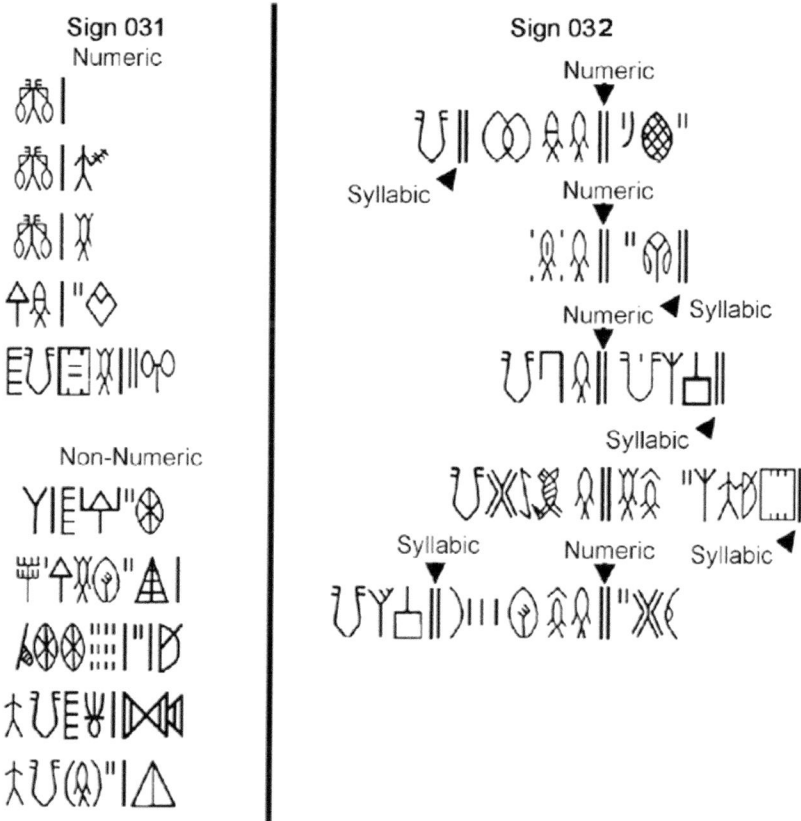

FIGURE 5.3. CONTEXTS OF SIGNS 031 AND 032 WITH NUMERIC SYLLABIC EXAMPLES

Sign No.	Freq.	Graph	151 / 80	156 / 103	154 / 38	158 / 34	220 / 443	231 / 82	233 / 182	235 / 231	240 / 331	390 / 243	405 / 112	407/9 / 134	520 / 282	740 / 1696	700 / 565	705/6 / 286	575 / 72	585 / 58	Other	Total
31	190	|	3		9		3		1		9				3	4	3	5			61	101
32	507	||					57						2	2	8	1	52	87	2		140	351
33	445	|||	3			1	2			3					15	2	137			4	104	271
34	153	||||					1				2						105				6	114
35	27	|||||										1	1		7						8	17
36	5	||||||															2				2	4
37	2	|||||||																				
39	1	|||||||||																				

TABLE 5.3. RIGHT ADJACENT COLLOCATIONS OF LONG LINEAR STROKE SIGNS (SHADED CELLS HAVE A FREQUENCY OF FIVE OR MORE).

High frequency sign collocations can be the result of the abundance of certain artifact types at a site. Tablets that have repeating text tend to elevate the frequency of signs that occur on them. The presence of large numbers of bas-relief and incised tablets at Harappa, and the high frequency of signs 700 + # pairings are with signs 32-34. This is not a result of coincidence, but rather a recognizable pattern. In fact, bas-relief and especially incised tablets very frequently contain these sign sequences and are repeated on ceramic vessels from Harappa. Larger vessels are marked with increasing magnitudes of long linear stroke signs (Figure 5.4). The details of this relationship were given in Chapter 4.

I have posited in Chapter 4 that these sign sequences (Sign 700 + #) are various values in the Indus volumetric system. In Table 5.3 the strong preferential collocation of sign 700 and signs 034 (87), 033 (137) and 032 (105) is clear. What is also clear is that these signs have other contexts that comprise even larger proportions of signs 032 and 033. Some of these contexts are numeric (i.e. "fish" signs and "phytomorphic" signs) and some are not (signs 520 and 740).

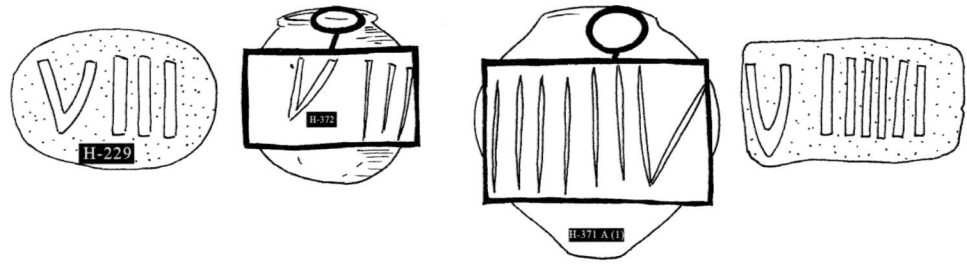

FIGURE 5.4. INSCRIBED CERAMICS WITH MATCHING INSCRIPTIONS TO TABLETS (FROM HARAPPA).

In summary, long linear stroke signs (especially 031, 032 and 033) have numeric and non-numeric functions. Other numerals of this class are more restricted to numerical uses (034, 035 and 036). Signs 037 and 039 are found in low frequencies on pot-sherds and their exact uses are unknown.

Special Numerals

There is some evidence that other signs may have numeric values. The case for adding these signs to the list of Indus number is summarized in the following discussion.

Fish Signs and Numbers

As discussed by Bonta (1995) there is good evidence indicating that some signs with a sign graph resembling fish are metrological units, most likely weights. The association of fish signs with numerals is easily demonstrable (Figure 5.5).

The close association of "fish" signs (especially sign 220) and numeral signs (Figure 5.5, left) is obvious. This association has led Bonta (pers. com. 2003) to suggest that signs location right adjacent to sign 220 may also have numeric values. This suggestion leads to the tentative identification of sign 415 as a numeral. It collocates right adjacent to sign 220, 82 times and with "fish" signs as a group 95 times. It has what seem to be non-numeric contexts, most significantly ⋃⋀| (Figure 3.25). Again, polyvalence seems the best explanation for these varying contexts. The association of numerals to sign 740 keeps open the possibility that sign 415 could be functioning as a numeral in this context as well (Figure 5.6).

It would seem from Figure 5.6 that many types of numerals can locate right adjacent to 740. It is possible, for the sake of brevity, that the Bonded Cluster is omitted because the meaning is known either from the physical appearance or social context. Less likely is the possibility that in these contexts the numerals are the bonded clusters (i.e. used for their syllabic values).

FIGURE 5.5. ASSOCIATIONS OF "FISH" SIGNS AND NUMERAL SIGNS.

74   The Archaeology and Epigraphy of Indus Writing

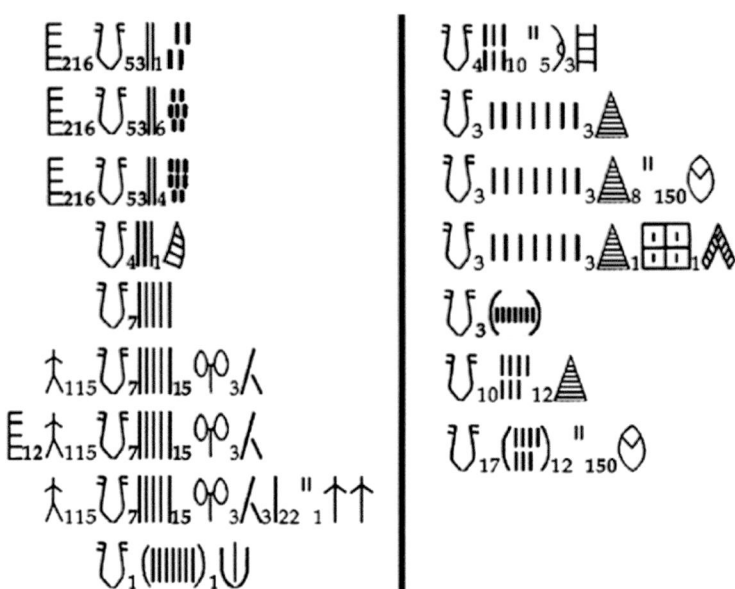

Figure 5.6. Numeral signs associated with sign 740. Numbers between sign graphs indicate the frequency of sign pairings.

Sign 900 and the Number 5

One possible special numeral is sign 900). Care should be taken not to confuse) with),)), or)(. These signs require separate consideration. The evidence that 900 is a numeral, in at least some of its occurrences, comes from two sources – the specifics of a single context and the general behavior of the sign.

One sign sequence that is very informative (because of its replacement sets) is ⋃ ⩘ (signs 740/585) which is often preceded by the numeral ⦀ (sign 017). In at least one case ⦀ is replaced by)" in H-472: ⋃⩘)"⊛.

This would suggest that) has a value equal to 5. Unfortunately, the contexts of ⩘⦀ are not that simple. In one example ⋃⩘⦀) occurs. But note the sign order: in the)" example sign 900 is adjacent to ⋃⩘, but in the other example it is separated by ⦀ from the terminal signs ⋃⩘. These contexts raise the possibility that ⋃⩘ comes in quantities of ⦀, ⦀), and)", suggesting that) stands for the number 5 (perhaps when space is lacking). Alternately, ⦀) and)". Could be examples of positional notation.

Numerals in the Indus Script and their Uses   75

The) sign is often found associated with clusters of numerals. Two such examples are: ⟨symbols⟩ (H-141) in the cluster ‖)III; and ⟨symbols⟩ (H-589) in the cluster)IIIII ‖‖. These are not the only examples of) in close association with clusters of numerals, there are many such examples (n = 38). In these contexts) does seem to be functioning as a numeral.

If the argument that in some examples of) it is a numeral are accepted, then the following inventory of positional numerals can be added to sequences of stroke numerals (Figure 5.7).

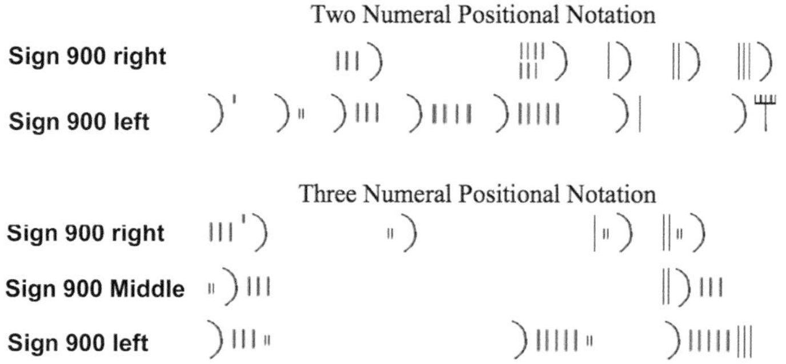

Two Numeral Positional Notation

Sign 900 right   III)   IIII) I) I) ‖)
Sign 900 left   )')")III)IIII)IIIII)|)†

Three Numeral Positional Notation

Sign 900 right   III')   ") |") ‖")
Sign 900 Middle   ")III   ‖)III
Sign 900 left   )III"   )IIIII"   )IIIII‖

FIGURE 5.7 EXAMPLES OF SIGN 900 AS A NUMERAL IN POSITIONAL NOTATION

Notice the)IIIII (i.e. 5+5) makes no sense unless the position of the numbers changes the numeral values (i.e. 5 + 5x10 = 55). As with Roman numerals, the sequencing may control whether the numeral is additive or subtractive.

These patterns are similar to the ones for numerals found else where in Indus texts, and this suggests that in these contexts) is functioning as part of a set of numerals. The evidence for) as a numeral is persuasive because it is based on many contexts and replacement sets.

Evidence for Sign 055 as a Numeral

The final *Special Numeral* is ⁞⁞⁞⁞ (sign 055). It is included under this heading because it occurs in a wide variety of contexts, and because the numeral for 11 is not attested, which has the effect of isolating this sign from the rest of the system of Indus numerals.

A brief review of the texts containing ⁞⁞⁞⁞ demonstrates the wide variety of contexts it can be found in, some numerical and some not (Figure 5.8).

One interesting result that comes out of the analysis of ⁞⁞⁞⁞ (sign 055) is that Indus sign clusters occur in different orders and locations within a given text, both in relation to

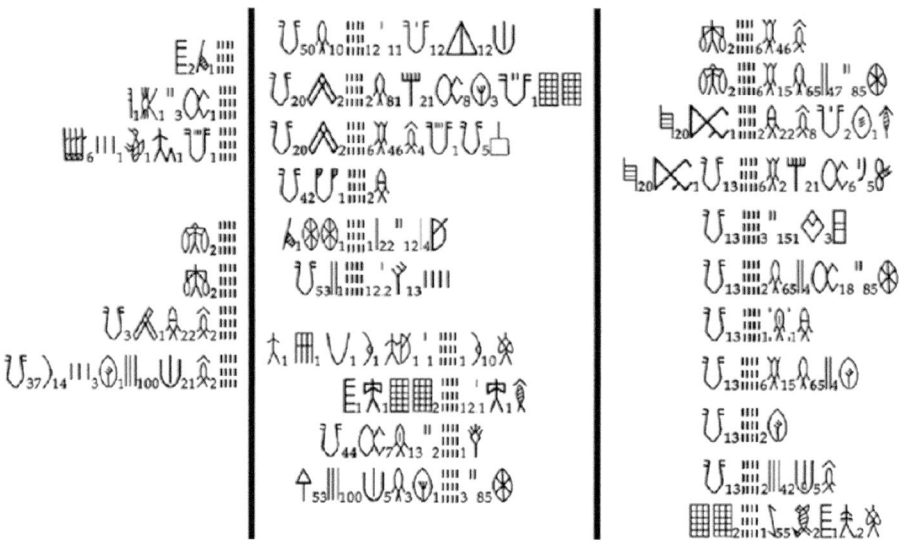

FIGURE 5.8. VARIOUS CONTEXTS OF SIGN 055

each other and to 055. This implies a certain amount of flexibility in sign order. This pattern is similar to the placement of sign clusters in economic texts from other ancient scripts where lists of items are often enumerated. Because of its distribution sign 055 is also a good candidate for a number sign with a polyvalent syllabic or semantic value.

Summary

It can be seen from the preceding discussion that the use of Indus numerals is complicated, as they are in most ancient scripts. What the forgoing discussion makes clear is that there are significant similarities between the patterns of usage of numerals in ancient economic texts and the patterns of usage in some Indus texts. These similarities strongly suggest that at least some Indus texts contain numerical information. Some Indus texts (H-25) have several counts of items recorded in a single text, and some of these counts employ positional notation. While the case for special numerals has been made for four signs, they are obviously not all equal in terms of contextual evidence. The arguments by Bonta (1995) strongly suggest that sign 415 is a numeral in some contexts. It has a special affinity for sign 220 as does sign 032.

Three distinct types of stroke signs have been defined and shown to associate with specific signs unique to each set of numerals. The use of sign 900 for the number 5 may be a strategy to save space or to avoid confusion in positional notation. While many uncertainties remain with regard to the exact values of numerals, the existence of noun + # sign clusters make the existence of a number system a certain.

Chapter 6

Proto-Dravidian and the Indus Script

Introduction

This chapter examines the Indus inscriptions for clues to the root language and specifically the match between these texts and the reconstructions of proto-Dravidian (pDr). The details of pDr morphology outlined here rely heavily on the work of McAlpin (1981). The morphological characteristics of pDr are very complex. What is offered here is an overview of the patterns of pDr morphology. A general description of the morphology of pDr is given, followed by comparisons to the structures defined in Chapter 3 and the examples of readings given elsewhere (Wells 2011). The goal of these comparisons is to discover if the Indus texts can be interpreted as pDr, or if the divergence between what is known about pDr and the structure of the Indus texts is too great. This chapter begins with an overview of pDr syntax and morphology. This is followed by examples from the corpus of Indus texts, which are analyzed in comparison to pDr. This chapter attempts to begin with the identification of sign meaning from their contexts and then to examine how these signs might read in pDr.

In this chapter the reference numbers for the Dravidian Etomological Dictionary are the "old" numbers (Burrow and Emeneau, 1961). An apology is also due to linguists for the lack of proper characters for retroflex consonants, as the font for these characters is not available to me. I believe the data as given is clear enough for our purposes here.

Indus and proto-Dravidian Syntax

I have previously proposed that the Indus script is verb initial (Wells 2011). This conclusion was based on the distribution on stroke signs. It was assumed at that time that all stroke sign have a unitary numeric function. This assumption was based on research undertaken in 2006 (Wells 2006) and lead to the conclusion that Indus syntax was VOS. Improvements in the online database and analytical software has lead to a different conclusion based on the concept of polyvalence –that signs can have more than one semantic value. In the case of Indus stroke signs the most obvious case is sign 033 |||, that has context that can only be interpreted as a word building function: ⇑ ||| ∪ (Chapter 3) and a use as a numeral ∨ ||| (Chapter 4). These concepts are dealt with in detail in Chapters 3-5.

In Chapter 3 it was shown that Indus texts are organized into three basic sets of sign clusters, which can only be adequately explained as SOV/OSV syntactic elements. As subjects and objects are nominal, the third element must be a verb. The texts related to the Dholavira signboard demonstrate that the first and second positions are related (SO/OS) and therefore through a process of elimination the third position must be the verb. It is important to realize that these texts are not ambiguous, nor do they depend on an assumed root language. Additionally, we can say that in the Dholavira signboard text the place name is medial: ⟦glyphs⟧. The meaning of the other elements in this and the other texts with this sign string (i.e. ⟦glyphs⟧) are discussed later in this chapter. The point made in Chapter 3 was that when it is medial this sign cluster ⟦glyph⟧ ends with sign 821 ⟦glyph⟧, and when it is initial it ends with sign 002. That is, affixing of the stem (⟦glyph⟧) changes with it position in the texts. It is possible for nouns and verbs to have the same stem (farm vs. farming). However, a place name cannot be used in this way. This leads to the conclusion that the verb must be terminal in Indus texts. This conclusion is made independent of any assumption as to root language. The fact that Dravidian syntax is verb terminal allows the possibility that the language of the Indus texts is proto-Dravidian (pDr). Further evidence for this is given in this chapter.

Proto-Dravidian Morphology

Dravidian languages have two main classes of words, nouns and verbs. Adjectives are limited to numbers and some basic colors. Nouns and verbs share some aspect of morphology.

The Dravidian root is generally monosyllabic and bi-consonantal. It takes the form (C)V(C). The normal Dravidian stem (i.e. root + augments) is bi-syllabic and tri-consonantal: CVCVC (McAlpin 1981:26). This can be expressed in a logo-syllabic system with two (root+augment) or three signs (spelled syllabically).

The root's general form is, $^1C_0^1\ ^1V_2^2\ ^2C_0^2$, where: $^{pos}C_{min}^{max}$ pos = position, max = maximum frequency and min = minimum frequency. But, because of tense-lax patterning, only three forms are possible:

(A) $^1C_0^1\ ^1V_2^2\ ^2C_1^1$
(B) $^1C_0^1\ ^1V_2^2\ ^2C_0^1$
(C) $^1C_0^1\ ^1V_1^1\ ^2C_2^2$

Primary Augment + $^2V_1^1\ ^3C_0^2$

The primary augments are added to the roots. This is the simplest form of derivation. For example, in Tamil *tuk(u)* 'to be fit, proper' and *takai* 'fitness, grace, beauty, to be beautiful'.

Typical Dravidian words have an agglutinative structure (i.e. grammatical elements accumulate to the end of the root), and fit the following pattern:

ROOT + (augment(s)) + MEDIAL + ENDING

Except for clitics and a few other stray forms, pDr has only two form classes, nouns and verbs. Nouns and verbs have distinct morphologies (McAlpin 1981:30).

Nouns

Noun morphology (noun modifying noun and denominal noun derivation), differs from verb morphology and derivation. Verb modifying nouns and deverbal noun derivation likewise have their own forms. There are many examples of mixed forms (i.e. verbal nouns with tense). Noun morphology can also invade the verbal system (i.e. appellatives and infinitives). Nouns and verbs can share roots. For example, in Tamil *malar* 'blossom' (noun) and 'to bloom' (verb). These roots become either nouns or verbs in their morphology.

McAlpin (1981:32) tells us: "the typical Dravidian noun is agglutinative, tends to be well defined at its end, and is often ambiguous in its morphology in the middle." The Dravidian noun can be summarized as follows:

ROOT (+derivational augment(s)) (+morphological augment(s)) + CASE (+postpositions)

Elements in brackets are optional. The root and case endings tend to be well defined.

The noun root (which is monosyllabic) takes the form (C)V(C). Every possible form of an augment (-V(C)C) is attested except *-Vrr.

Case endings can take the following forms: ∅, -V, -VC, -VCV or -(C)CV. Derivational augments normally take the form VC, while postpositions can take a variety of forms (Commonly -V(C)C). Nouns can be marked for gender. PDr used masculine vs. non-masculine in the singular and human vs. non-human in the plural as follows:

Sm -*an*/*-anre*
Sn *-ay*, *-i*, *-e*
Ph *-ar*
Pn *-am*/*-an*.

Male occupations and kin terminology use *-anre*, while female kin, animals and general neuters use *-ay* and *-i*.

The simplest form of the Dravidian noun is V-∅ (i.e. *a* 'cow, ox'; Tamil). The process of agglutination results in the following example: *ay* 'cowherd caste'; *ay* + *an* (Sm) = *ayan* 'male cowherd'. The basic difference between a case ending and a postposition is that: "a case ending cannot be separated from its noun by a clitic while a postposition can be" (McAlpin 1981:35). Otherwise the distinction between these items is arbitrary. Most other morphological components (augments, postpositions and clitics) are agglutinative and consist of -V, -VC, (C)CV and -VCV. They mark cases, singular, plural and gender or can be augments, as discussed above.

Clitics are grammatical morphemes that follow nouns and verbs to indicate:

Inclusion in a group	um
Exclusion from a group	-e
Isolated emphatic uniqueness	*tan* ('only, just')
Interrogation	-o and -um

Clitics can be used conjunctively. For example:

avanum avalum 'he and she' (i.e. –um)
avana avala 'he or she' (i.e. -a)

Clitics are also used as proforms as possessive markers. Clitics can also mark possession. These items are variants of the personal pronouns and are procliticts (prefixes). These forms in pDr were *y- my, *n- your, and *t- his, her. McAlpin (1981:38-9) gives the following example:

*ay	Mother
*yay	my mother
*nay	your mother
*tay	his/her mother

In addition to these elements nouns can also take a variety of pronouns, either personal or appellative. They are proforms. Personal pronouns are restricted to 1st and 2nd person and 3rd person resumptive. Dravidian pronouns indicate 3 persons and 2 numbers (singular and plural). Personal pronouns take the form CVC, with possession marked with C- proclitics. Third person appellative and deictic-interrogatives (except 3sm *-anre) are either -VC or -CV, with the deictics distinguished by initial *a'- glottal. Clitics also play a role in the construction of Dravidian nouns and can take a variety of forms (*-uN inclusion in a group etc., where N represents a glottal stop).

Noun Derivation

Derivational augments take the form: $^2V^1_0\ ^3C^3_0$ and attach to the monosyllabic root. Deverbal derivation and rederivation are common in Dravidian languages. For example in Tamil:

nil   'to stand, stop

nilai   'to become fixed or established'
nilaiyam   'situation, institution'

The third person masculine singular in proto-Dravidian is –*anre*. For example, *oruvanre* 'one man'. The neuter formative in pDr is -*o'* (where ' is a glottal stop). It is typical of neuter nouns, nominal derivatives. For example in Tamil *kal* 'to steal' becomes *kallan* 'thief'. The non-masculine in pDr is *-i*.

In pDr both *-ay* and -*i* refer to female kin, animals and general neuters. For example:

att-ay	'fathers sister'	[VCC-V]
akk-ay	'elder sister'	[VCC-V]
kapp-ay	'frog'	[CVCC-V]
yat(t)-ay	'ram'	[CVCC-V]
cukk-ay	'star'	[CVCC-V]
col-ay	'flower'	[CVC-V]
puk-ay	'smoke'	[CVC-V]
koy-i	'sheep'	[CVC-V]
kev-i	'ear'	[CVC-V]

A related pDr non-masculine formative is *-may*. For example: *onrumay* 'oneness, *karumay* 'blackness' and *irumay* 'twoness'. There are other non-masculine formative (i.e. *-te*). All of these words could be written in a logo-syllabic script with 2-3 signs, which is about what is found in Indus sign clusters (see Chapter 3).

Medials

Medials are monosyllabic and used in the construction of both nouns and verbs. Their morphology is complex and often no specific meaning can be attached to them. For nouns, medials consist of morphological augments and plural markers, but these are often missing.

The noun base consists of the stem + augments. Cases are added to the Base to complete the formation of nouns. The nomative is unmarked.

Verbs

McAlpin (1981:41) tells us: "The structure of the typical Dravidian verb is a complex combination of agglutination and inflection." Verbs can take one of two simple formats:

1) Verb Stem +Medial + Ending
2) Verb Stem + unitary medio-ending

Verb bases have a complex interaction with medials. Following the verb base all morphology is agglutinative. The past tense is achieved by adding a past medial to the verb stem, as are the present and the future. The imperative is formed by inserting a set of vowels (usually *u*) between the verb stem and the future or present medials. For both nouns and verbs, medials take the form $^2V^1_1\, ^3C^2_0$. The vowel must be *a, i,* or *u*. The medial is added to the verb root, which takes the form $^1C^1_0\, ^1V^1_0\, ^2C^1_1$ and combine to form the verb stem.

Augment to the Verb Root

There are several types of augments to the verb root: Primary augments take the form $^2V^1_1\, ^3C^2_0$ with the following possible combinations: Vr_1, Vr_2, Vl_2, Vl and Vz. Special augments take the form $^3V^1_0\, ^4C^2_0$. Note that this augment is optional. Secondary augments also occur but rarely. The pDr verb also uses medials to mark tense, aspect and mode with each having its own set of medials.

Finite Verbs

In Dravidian languages finite verb morphology can be summarized as follows:

Verbal Stem + Medial + Personal Ending

Personal endings of the typical Dravidian verbs closely parallel the personal pronouns and appellatives of the language. For proto-Dravidian the personal endings can be summarized as follows:

1st person singular	*-en
1st person exclusive	*-em
1st person inclusive	*-am
2nd person singular	*-ay/i
2nd person plural	*-ir
3rd person singular masc.	*-anre
3rd person singular non-masc.	*-(a)te
3rd person plural human	*-ar
3rd person plural non-human	*-av

Summary

The morphology of (proto-) Dravidian verbs is far more complex than the simple, formulaic summary given here. A more complex description would not be helpful, as it would interject into the analysis more details than can be readily compared to the analysis in Chapter 3.

What have these general morphological patterns revealed about the structure and morphology of Dravidian words is that all Dravidian nouns and verbs share a basic agglutinative structure.

While formulaic descriptions of both nouns and verbs do not define the whole morphological system, it does give us some indication of what pDr might look like if it were expressed by a logo-syllabic writing system. Noun stems can be expressed as logograph (Root) + syllable (Augments) + syllable (Case) + syllable (Clitics and Postpositions). That is, 2 or more signs. For verbs, the Stem + Medial + Ending needs 3 or more signs.

If the Indus inscriptions are written in proto-Dravidian then they should reflect the linguistic structure outlined above. It is important to avoid the pitfall of identifying the sign values based on the appearance of the sign graph. Signs found in a specific context must make sense in terms of pDr syntax and morphology. Note too that most writing systems have special spelling rules, often for bevity.

Proto-Dravidian Numbers

The pDr number system is described by McAlpin (1981:40-1) as follows:

> They are among the few forms that have anything looking like an adjective in Proto-Dravidian. An invariant compounding base is readily reconstructable for one through eight… These compounding bases are used to give the higher numerical bases—tens, hundreds, and thousands… The Dravidian number system emphatically functions in base ten. However, there are remnants of a base eight system… The compounding bases stop at eight. The root for eight *en is the same as the root for count and number (DED 678).

Several numbers are also identical to morphological elements (Table 6.1). This is evidence for one possible source of polyvalence in the Indus script. That is, there is no point in inventing a new syllabic sign if the value already exists in the script as a numeral. Nine is a problem being literally 10-1 (*onpate*). Table 6.1 summarizes the pDr number system.

We now have a general understanding of proto-Dravidian syntax and morphology, but how does this information compare to what is known about the Indus texts? This exploration is the subject of the following section.

	Compounding		Nouns	
	Base	Variant	Human	Neuter
1	or	oru, or	oruvanre (m)	
			orutti (f)	
	on			onre
	ol			
	okka	okkanre		
2	ir	iru	iruvar	iranta
3	mu(N)	mu, muC	muvar	munre
4	nal	nan		nalke
5	cayN	cayn		caynte
6	care	care		care
7	ez	ezu		eze
8				entte
9				onpate
	tol	ton		
10	pate	patin, pan		patte
100	nure	nurre		nure

TABLE 6.1 THE PROTO-DRAVIDIAN NUMBER SYSTEM.

Identification of Some Indus Signs

The Indus script has been extensively studied in the last 90 years. The obstacles to decipherment are many, yet given the right circumstances some progress can be made in testing the various root languages proposed. In this section I will make two assumptions: 1) There are some circumstances where the imagery and the signs found on Indus artifacts can be related; 2) The root language of the Indus script is proto-Dravidian. The first assumption raises the possibility that images and texts can (but do not in every case) form replacement sets or be referencing each other. The second assumption can be tested by the results of the analysis presented here.

This epigraphic exercise is aimed at testing whether or not the patterns of sign use and the reading derived from the comparison of signs, imagery and archaeological context fit the proto-Dravidian model. If so we are one step closer to decipherment. To expect a full decipherment of all Indus signs is unrealistic, but the reading of a few signs supports the assumption that the root language is proto-Dravidian, if these readings fit the syntax and morphological patterns of proto-Dravidian.

It is likewise prudent to remember that in all likelihood there was more than one language spoken by the Indus people during the Bronze Age. Whether or not these languages are also expressed in the Indus inscriptions is unknown.

Copper tablet from Mohenjo-daro

There is a set of Indus inscriptions where signs and images replace for each other on copper tablets from Mohenjo-daro. These copper wafers are engraved on both sides. The reverse bears a text and the obverse bears either an image or an additional text (Wells 2011). One subset of 16 copper tablets bears the inscription: ꓬ ꓦ ꓩ ⊛ ꓲꓲꓲ ꓴ ꓮ. Fourteen of these tablets have a picture of a hare browsing grass on the reverse, while two examples bear the sign 753 (Figure 6.1).

This co-occurrence raises the possibility that has the meaning of 'hare'. Sign 820 occasionally functions as a terminal sign (n = 10; see Chapter 3), while sign 752 occurs as a separate sign in 37 inscriptions in the pair . That is to say that needs a complementary sign left adjacent and is never found in a terminal position. Any potential decipherment must make sense of and the occurrences of its component parts. That is, the word for hare in the proposed language should consist of two parts,

  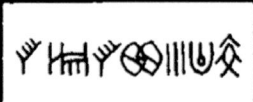 

FIGURE 6.1 COPPER TABLET ARTIFACTS FROM MOHENJO-DARO WITH THE 'HARE EATING GRASS' REPLACEMENT SET.

Proto-Dravidian and the Indus Script

with one component ⊕ capable of occurring initially (113), medially (23) and terminally (10). The identification of ⋓ = 'hare' is independent of the root language of the script. The assumption of proto-Dravidian as the root language is arbitrary and its eventual acceptance or rejection is dependent on the degree of fit of the following analysis.

If we make the assumption that the root language is an early (reconstructed proto) form of Dravidian (ca 2000 to 3000 BC), then there are two possible words with the meaning 'hare' *mual/mucal* and *ceviyan*.

While several attempts at using *mual/mucal* (DED 4071) remained unproductive, using *ceviyan* (DED 1645a) produced some interesting results. Normally, linguists would prefer *mual/mucal* as it and its cognates are far more wide spread in the family of Dravidian languages (Wells 2011). The bisection of *mual* into ⋃ = *mu* and ⊕ = *al* seems a good fit to the expectations of a syllabic spelling. Attempts to make sense of this reading, in terms of the morphology and syntax of proto-Dravidian was unproductive. As will be shown in the following discussion ⊕ should be both a common nominal ending and a logograph capable of occupying the initial position in a phrase or sentence.

DED 1645a lists *ceviyan* = 'hare' (Ta/Ma) (*keviyan*, PD). If ⋓ reads *keviyan*, then its component parts likely read ⋃ = *kevi* (ear) and = ⊕ *yan*. This fits the expectations raised above, as ⊕ can be both terminal and initial and *yan* can be both a pronoun (initial) and a common nominal ending (terminal) (Figure 6.2).

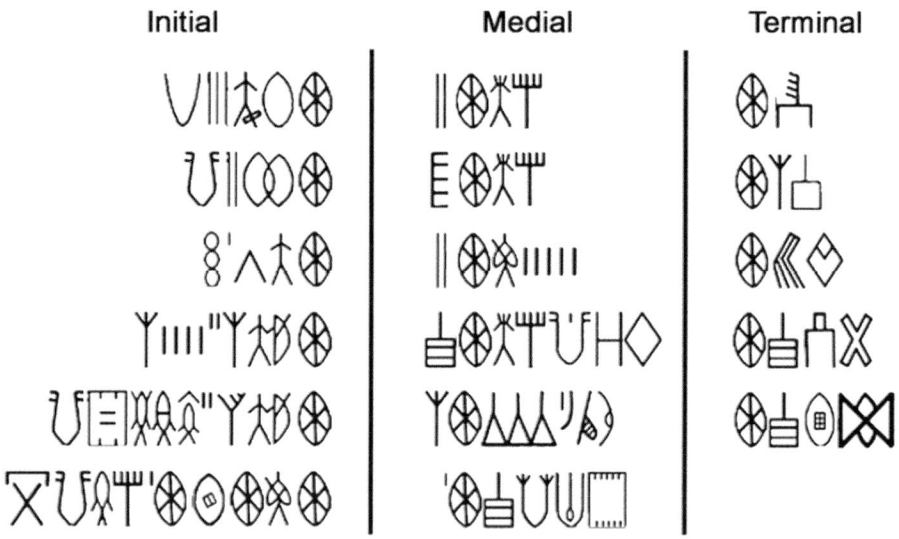

FIGURE 6.2. SOME EXAMPLES OF SIGN 820 IN VARIOUS CONTEXTS.

What is clear from Figure 6.2 is that sign 820 occurs terminally in short (Segment) texts without multiple syntactic elements, or in one example a complex texts. The following text ![sign] demonstrates that ![sign] is an initial cluster.

The contexts given above show sign 820 in initial, medial and terminal contexts. Figure 6.3 Shows sign 820 is a terminal marker.

Where sign 740 is identified as a terminal (verbal) cluster and the same bonded cluster ![sign] is affixed with sign 820 in addition to other signs. This rare occurrence is the derivation of a noun from a verbal stem as described in the discussion of Dravidian morphology.

For example in Tamil:

nil   'to stand, stop
nilai   'to become fixed or established'
nilaiyam 'situation, institution'

Figure 6.4 shows the distribution of sign 820 in various types of texts. What is clear from this figure is that, in text with well-understood syntax, sign 820 is always part of an initial cluster. It is found in terminal contexts only in complex and segment (with one element of syntax) texts. The exception being given in Figure 6.3.

Positional analysis of sign 820 (Figure 6.4) demonstrates that in Pattern texts it is always part of an initial cluster. This fits well with its identification as *yan*, the 1st person personal pronoun 'I'. In Single Segment texts it is Initial and terminal as expected for

FIGURE 6.3 CONTEXTS OF 740 AND 820 USING THE SAME BONDED CLUSTER.

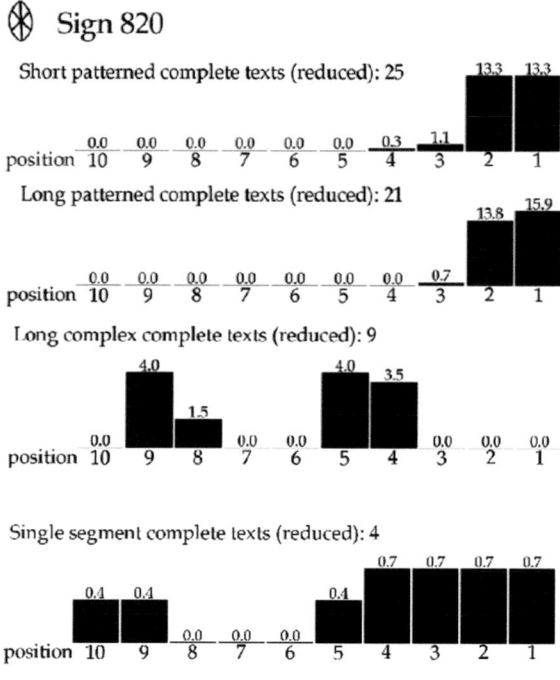

FIGURE 6.4 POSITIONAL ANALYSIS OF SIGN 820 IN PATTERNED, LONG COMPLEX AND SHORT SEGMENT TEXTS TEXTS.

texts with a single syntactic element. So sign 820 has a wide range of contexts in keeping with its identification as *yan*.

This leaves a value of **kevi* = 'ears' for ⋃. While the sign graph is suggestive of ears, its reading of **kevi* = 'ear' result from the bisection of **keviyan* and not the shape of its sign graph.

Sign 752 ⋃ occurs in 44 inscriptions (M-d=37, Har=7). It is important to note that 27 of the Mohenjo-daro texts are from mold-made tablets (i.e. bas relief). In several cases it has a numeral preceding and ⋃ following, as in the examples in Figure 6.5.

Given the suggestion of **keviyan* = 'hare' we can also expect that ⋃⋃ will form a word with **kevi* as its stem followed by some sign with the functional equivalent of ⋃ in its terminal use as a verb ending. There is a match in the DED 2265 *cevvai* (Ta) = 'correctness, fitness, accuracy, straightness, evenness, smoothness, sound condition as of mind, body' (**kevvay*). M-30 (Figure 6.6) would then read (right to left) as showing in Figure 6.3. The gloss from DED 2265 makes sense in this case with the meaning 'correctness and accuracy'. Note that in Tamil that *yan* is a typical ending for animal names and the names of castes, while **-ay* is common ending for verbs (2nd person singular).

88   THE ARCHAEOLOGY AND EPIGRAPHY OF INDUS WRITING

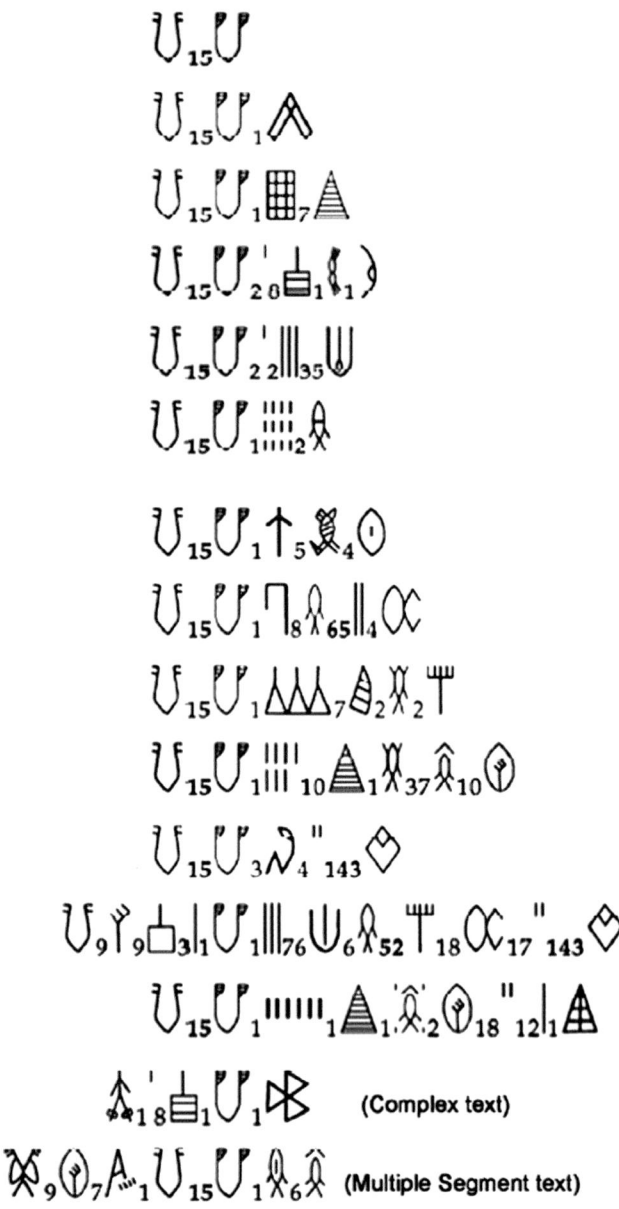

FIGURE 6.5. SOME EXAMPLES OF 740 AND 752 PAIRING IN TEXTS.

The *kevvay reading would give ⵁ a value of *–*ay* accusative case (McAlpin, 1981:122; DED(s) 2830), 2nd person singular, a word for 'cow' (DED(s) 283), and PDr for 'mother' (McAlpin, 1981:122). ⵁ = -*ay* meets the expectation that this sign should be a verbal ending (2nd person singular *-*ay*/*i*). The pattern that emerges is one where word stems and case endings combine to form words with case ending following the

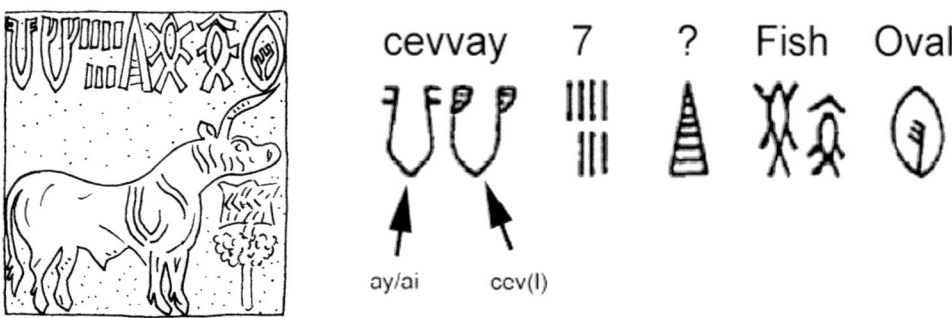

FIGURE 6.6. POSSIBLE READING OF M-30.

FIGURE 6.7. BAS-RELIEF MINIATURE TABLET H-182 WITH DRUMMER AND TIGER.

stem. The problem of texts without stems remains. This pattern matches the syntax of Dravidian languages and supports the assumption that proto-Dravidian is the language of the Indus script.

Bas-relief Tablets from Harappa

One example of patterns matching proto-Dravidian is not enough to make a convincing case. For more evidence we turn to a miniature tablet inscription found on H-182 (Figure 6.7).

As we have seen there is good evidence that ∪ may read *-*ay* and be functioning as a case ending and syllabic sign. McAlpin (1981:42) reconstructs **ir* as the proto-Dravidian numeral 'two' (possibly ‖ an/or ‖). The bas-relief tablet inscription found on H-182 combines both these elements, perhaps reading *-*iray* meaning 'anyone who is great or devine' (DED 448). Another meaning of *iray* is 'prey/food' (C. Subramanian pers.com. 2012). This may be a play on words.

The value of ⟨⟩ is unknown, but both the accompanying picture of a drummer and its graphic design, suggest that a reading meaning 'drum' or 'drummer' is likely. The only word for 'drum' in the Dravidian Etymological Dictionary which meets the expectations outlined above is DED 3319 *parai* (Ta) 'drum, a measure of capacities'; *para* (Ma) 'drum, a rice measure, disk, circle'; *pare* (Ka and Kod) 'drum' (a large double headed drum beaten by Mede); *par* (KO. and TO.) 'drum'. The root *par* 'drum' and the affixes *-iray* may read *pariray* 'great drummer' (DED not attested). In this example the stem + ending pattern is repeated. The *parai* (Ta) ' a measure of capacities' seems to fit well with some of the texts in which sign 840 is found as the following texts show:

3 Measures $\bigcup_{15} \bigotimes_{11} \overset{||}{|}$

13 Measures $\bigcup_{15} \bigotimes_{11} \overset{||}{|}_2 \overset{||}{|}_{22} \overset{||}{|}_{130} \bigotimes$

The two texts read thus far fit the syntactic pattern expected for proto-Dravidian writing. The terminal signs and word stem signs forming a consistent morphological pattern that is common to all Dravidian languages, but there are other texts that also fit this pattern?

The Dholavira signboard, revisited

As described in Chapter 3 the Dholavira signboard consists of a series of steatite blocks arranged to form 30 cm high signs that were attached to a wooden backing. It has a relatively long text containing 10 signs (Figure 6.5). From the order of the signs we know the sign fell face down and therefore the image in Figure 6.8 has been reversed to maintain the right to left reading order of Indus texts.

FIGURE 6.8. THE DHOLAVIRA SIGNBOARD WITH PHOTO REVERSED TO REFLECT READING ORDER (COURTESY OF RAJESH RAO).

I have posited (Wells 2011) that some part of this sign sequence would be the site's locative (place name). But which signs? Whatever signs form the locative might reasonably be expected to occur elsewhere in the corpus of inscriptions. This is in fact exactly what happens (Figure 6.6). The sign sequence ⟨signs⟩ is repeated on 5 artifacts. The sequence has two elements: ⟨signs⟩ and ⟨signs⟩. This is known because ⟨signs⟩ occurs without ⟨signs⟩ and visa versa. The identities of the other signs: ⟨signs⟩ and the terminal sign ⟨sign⟩ are not as clear, but there placement suggests that ⟨sign⟩ is a word sign, either a syllabic cluster (⟨sign⟩ + ⟨sign⟩) or a logograph (i.e. isolated at the end of the text), and ⟨signs⟩ is a separate introductory phrase. The sign sequence ⟨signs⟩ may be 3 syllabic signs spelling Dholavira's ancient name (Kotada?), but this assertion is highly speculative.

What Figure 6.9 shows is the internal structure of the Dholavira signboard text.

All examples of the Dholavira toponym come from Mohenjo-daro. The three examples found etched on copper/bronze implements (IMPL in Figure 6.10) are from a copper hoard excavated in the DK.G area, and their texts are identical. DK10551 also comes from the DK.G area but from a later period. The final text M-1384 has an unknown

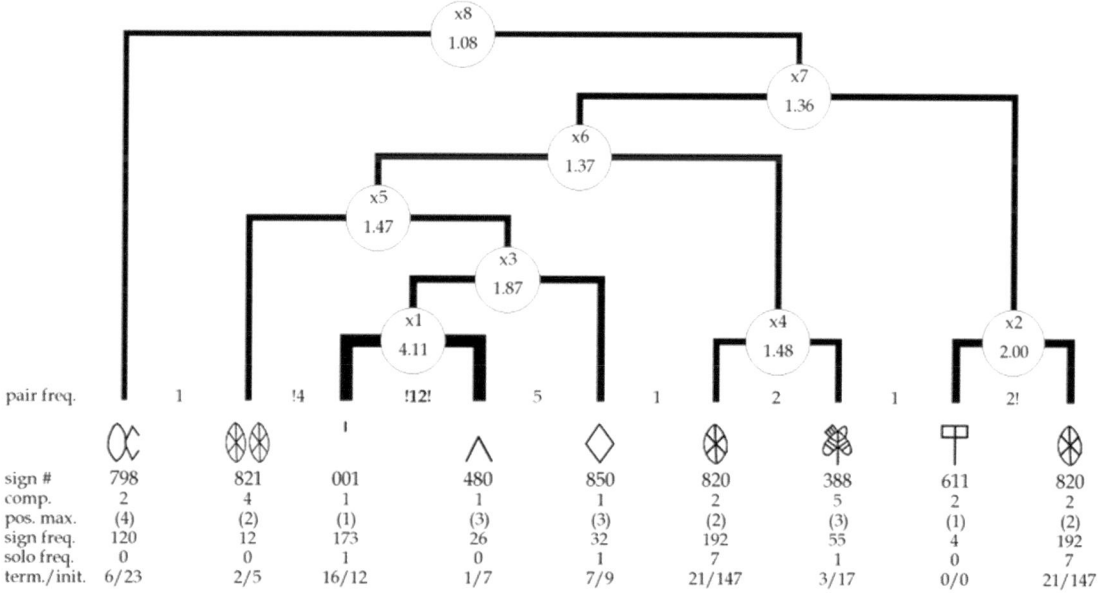

FIGURE 6.9. SEGMENTATION TREE FOR THE DHOLAVIRA SIGNBOARD

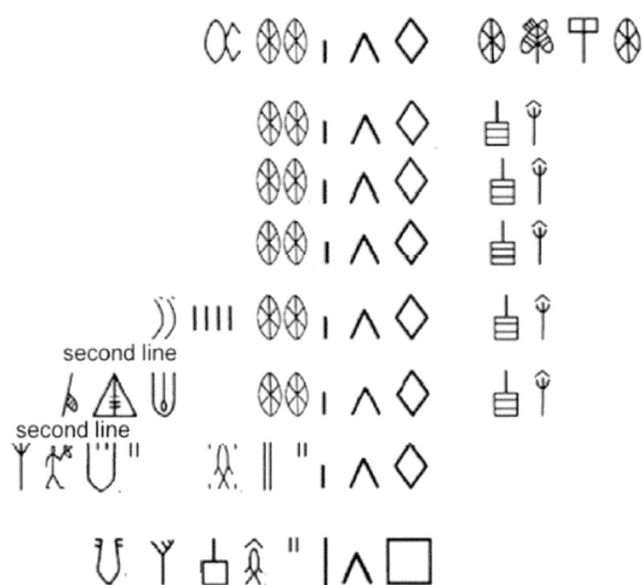

FIGURE 6.10. OTHER TEXT CONTAINING THE DHOLAVIRA TOPONYM (ALSO SEE FIGURE 3.37).

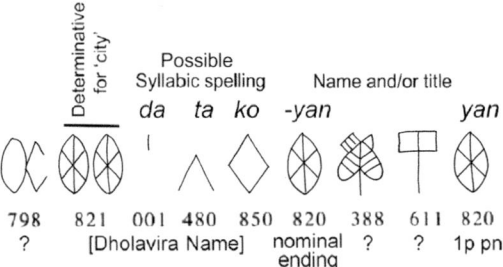

FIGURE 6.11. SUGGESTED READINGS FOR DHOLAVIRA SIGNBOARD SIGNS.

provenience. What all of these texts share is the Dholavira toponym and the sign pair. One possible meaning of this sign pair is "copper/bronze tool". I make this suggestion because the texts are found most commonly on copper/bronze tools and because the tag gives a count of items, which suggests the existence of objects to be counted. Since all other signs are accounted for (i.e. the toponym) it seems probable that what is being counted on M-1384 are copper/bronze tools from Dholavira. These two signs never collocate outside this context.

We can take the readings developed so far and apply them to the Dholavira signboard. The majority of the signs can be assigned values that make sense in terms of their contexts and the constraints of proto-Dravidian syntax and morphological rules (Figure 6.11).

It is suggested here that sign 821, in the Dholavira signboard contexts, has a meaning of 'city', either as a determinative or as a word. Some possibilities are:

752 *Ta.* ūr village, town, city.
808 *Ta. eyil* fortress, wall, fortification, city, town
3568 *Ta. nakar* house, abode, mansion, temple, palace, town, city.
4112 *Ta. pāri* temple; town, city, town of an agricultural tract, hermitage;

Any of these is possible. Which of these, if any, are the correct gloss cannot be known, but *eyil* seems the best choice given the fact that Dholavira is a walled city made of cut stone.

One verification of the sign 821 reading as 'city' has been pointed out by Andreas Fuls (pers. com. 2011; Figure 6.12). He notes that the sign combination of 861+740 matches the imagery of a cow (740=**ay*='cow') and the person in front of a structure, which may be a pictographic toponym (861 = city), seem to fit the readings developed so far.

This evidence does not bring us any closer to a reading for sign 861, but does reinforce the association of this sign with important places.

Whatever sign 821 reads it is used in a variety of contexts (Figure 6.13). While *eyil-ay* or *eyil-i* (i.e. collocating with sign 740) is not attested, this is not a nullification of the reading, as we really do not have a firm reading for sign 821.

Another interesting feature of the Dholavira signboard is the final sign, 798 (Figure 6.13). It should be a logograph because the structural analysis (Figure 6.9) shows that

FIGURE 6.12. H-176 WITH THE SIGN SEQUENCE 861+740 READING 'COW AT THE CITY'.

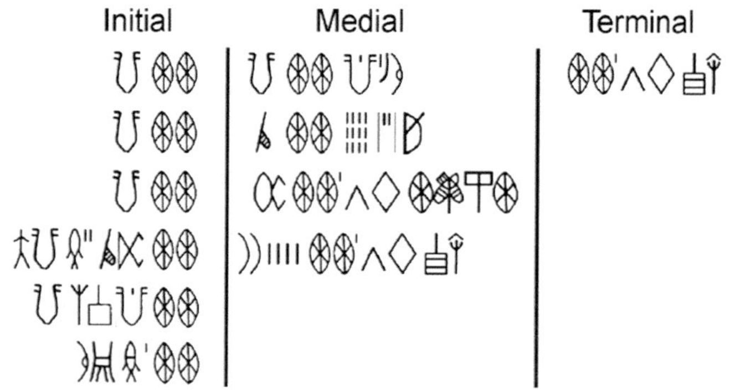

FIGURE 6.13. EXAMPLES OF THE VARIOUS CONTEXTS OF SIGN 821.

94 THE ARCHAEOLOGY AND EPIGRAPHY OF INDUS WRITING

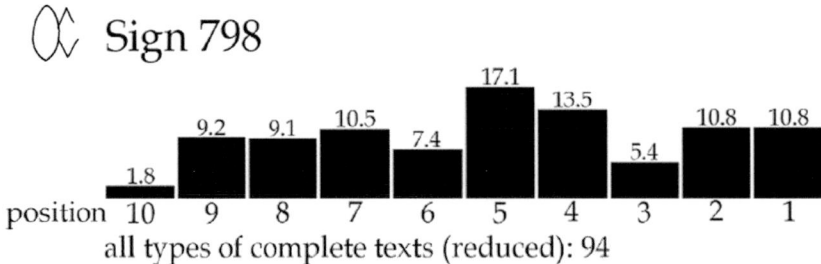

FIGURE 6.14. THE DISTRIBUTION OF SIGN 798 IN ALL COMPLETE TEXT IN WHICH IT OCCURS.

it is isolated at the end of this text. But its distribution (Figure 6.14) suggests that it is not bound by syntax and therefore should be a syllabic sign. I can be suggested with some confidence that it must be a syllabic sign that also has meaning as a stand-alone monosyllabic word in pDr (like 740 = *ay* = 'cow' etc.).

The distribution of this sign shows that it occurs in every zone of the texts. This distribution leads to the conclusion that it is most likely a monosyllabic word sign, also used as a syllable. It must be a word sign because it is isolated at the end of the toponym, but is used in every zone and in a variety of contexts as a word building sign.

The Mohenjo-daro bangle pot

Seals have a variety of functions. They were used minimally in trade, administrative control, and in the cycle of production. This is evident from the uses to which they have

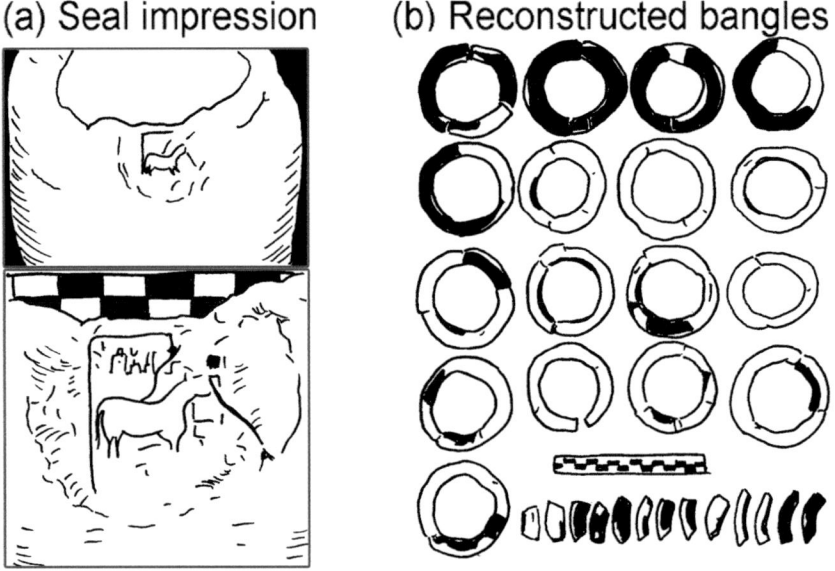

FIGURE 6.15. THE MOHENJO-DARO BANGLE POT WITH SEAL IMPRESSION AND RECONSTRUCTED BANGELS FOR FRAGMENTS FOUND IN THE VESSEL.

been put. For example, Jansen and Urban (1985) excavated a pot used for firing stoneware bangles with a purple glaze (Figure 6.15). There were actually several pots that had been over-fired and discarded in antiquity. Within one pot were fragments of bangles (82) some used in the arrangement and closure assembly, and the majority coated with indigo glaze for firing. These fragments can be used in the reconstruction of the bangles to be fired, between 15 and 20 (Figure 6.15). The seal is a typical square intaglio seal with a bull in profile and ritual standard as are commonly found at all Indus Sites.

The text of the seal impression is badly eroded on the upper right corner. The first two signs can be reconstructed with some confidence from the remaining fragments (Figure 6.16). The medial and terminal sections are both clearly legible. I would offer a reading for the medial signs as follows: 10 + 7 = 17. The number closely matches the number of reconstructed indigo bangles, and implies the seal impression is being used at the end of the manufacturing process to control the quantity of items in the pot. This makes sense in that, as the pots are of uniform size, the seal can be reused for several firings. When exhausted it can be replace. The text's number makes clear that the Indus system of numbers uses positional notation and is being used to count relatively small quantities.

As for the text, it has one interesting feature (Figure 6.16). We know from the readings of ꓴ that the last sign reads *ai*. We can guess that the sign between the number and ꓴ might be the word for firing or kiln. The word for kiln in Tamil (DED 2233) is *cullai* = 'potters kiln, furnace' (*kullay* in PD). This makes sense given -*ai* (*-ay*) ending. Here *ai* may be functioning as a phonetic complement, suggesting that sign 575 ⊓ may be polyvalent (Figure 6.16). The phonetic complement *ai* identifies it as *cullai* to avoid confusion with other values of ⊓. A review of the contexts of ⊓ (n=70; Figure 6.18) reveals that in about half of these texts ⊓ are initial. The other contexts are similar to the Bangle Pot text, suggesting at least two values for ⊓.

The positional analysis in Figure 6.17 indicates a wide range of contexts for sign 575. In Figure 6.18 give a wide variety of these contexts.

Figure 6.18 lists many of the contexts of sign 575. It is clear from these contexts that this sign has several collocations, especially important are its many pairings with sign 740 forming the *cullai* context as defined above. It has been suggested that in this case sign 740 may be functioning as a phonetic complement, but this is not the only possibility.

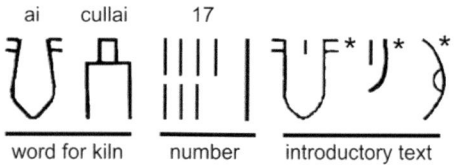

Figure 6.16. The Mohenjo-daro bangle pot text.

96 THE ARCHAEOLOGY AND EPIGRAPHY OF INDUS WRITING

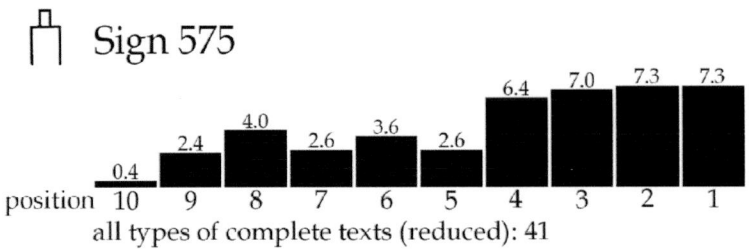

FIGURE 6.17. EVIDENCE FOR 575 AS A SYLLABLE SIGN.

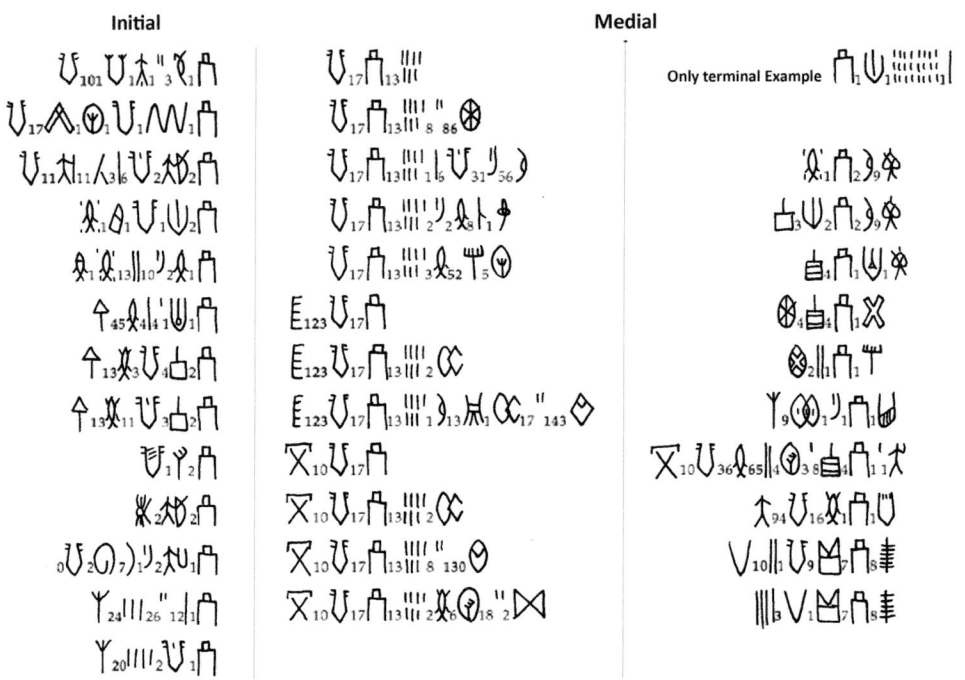

FIGURE 6.18. VARIOUS CONTEXTS OF SIGN 575.

As sign 575 is likely a logograph representing a kiln, the use of 740 as a phonetic complement is redundant and wasteful of space in a medium in which space is precious. An alternative explanation is that 740 is serving a derivational function changing the noun to a verb (i.e. 'kilned'). It may be that this addition is necessary to make sense of the post-terminal signs that are added in many of the texts. Note too that in the only terminal context of sign 575 (i.e. with 740 omitted) it might be intended as a noun. In initial context sign 575 may have a polyvalent value as a word-building element.

Pictures and sign correspondences

There is one further example of signs and iconography, which resemble one another — M-1919. In this case no readings result, but there are graphic similarities between the shape of the signs and the images in the graphic field (Figure 6.19).

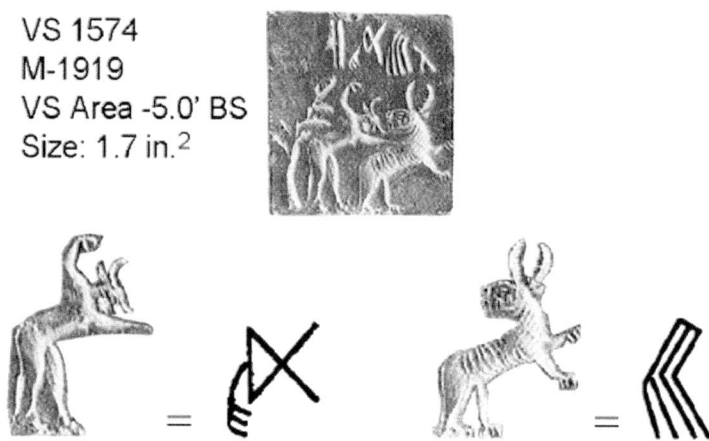

FIGURE 6.19 POSSIBLE RELATIONSHIP BETWEEN SIGNS AND IMAGES ON M-1919.

Sign 532 and sign 297 are positioned in such a way as to resemble the position of the graphic element and several of their features are repeated in the image field. It is proposed here that sign 532 is a logograph for the anthropomorphic figure and that sign 297 represents the horned tiger, or perhaps just 'tiger' generically. The bull/man pictured in the image may be a god or a human in ritual costume. The image may represent a myth or a religious rite.

Summary

The readings presented in this chapter have begun with a simple replacement of a sign for an image on copper tablets from Mohenjo-daro. These readings are compared to proto-Dravidian syntax and morphology to test the underlying assumption that this is the root language. The readings of the various texts have lead to the tentative identification of 13 signs (Figure 6.20). Seven of these are independent of the root language.

The readings presented in this chapter are not intended to be a definitive demonstration of a proto-Dravidian root language for the Indus script, but rather to demonstrate the high probability of it. One reading can be a coincidence, but when the assumption of proto-Dravidian becomes productive and result in the identification of words and place names it must be considered a serious possibility.

This is not to say that other possibilities should not also be considered. I propose that, while it seems highly probable that the root language of the Indus script is proto-Dravidian, we should keep open the possibility that there were several languages spoken in the Indus valley and that these languages may also have texts representing them in the Indus corpus of inscriptions. Finally, the purpose of this chapter is to present some ideas regarding the relationship between the texts, imagery and possible root language of the

Sign Graph	Sign Number	Reading	DED Number	Meaning
	763	*keviyan	1645	hare
	752	*kevi	1645	ear
	820	*yan	4335	I', Common noun ending
	740	*-ay	2830	cow, mother, Singular Neutral noun ending, Female kin term ending, 2nd person singular verb ending
	032	*-ir	McAlpin 1981:42	Two, 2nd person plural verb ending. duality
	840	*parai	3319	drum, a rice measure
	850	ko?		syllabic ko?
	489	ta?		syllabic ta?
	001	da?		syllabic da
	391/595	none		logographs for copper and impliment
	821			determinative for city
	575	*kullay	2233	potters' kiln, furnace

FIGURE 6.20. PROPOSED VALUES FOR SOME INDUS SIGNS.

Indus script. My hope is that these ideas will create discussion among, and attract the critique of, Dravidianist and epigraphers interested in Indus writing.

Given the readings of the signs listed in this chapter (Figure 6.20) and the syntax of proto-Dravidian, we can say that some of these signs are being used as endings for verbs (Figure 6.21).

		Singular	Possible sign	Plural	Possible sign
1st person		*-ēn		*-ēm	
2nd person		*-i / *-āy		*-īr	
3rd person		Masculine		Non-Masculine	
		*-anrə		*-(V)tə	
		Human		Neutral	
		*-ār		*-av	

FIGURE 6.21 PROTO-DRAVIDIAN VERB ENDINGS AND ASSOCIATED SIGNS

Of the associations given in Figure 6.21 the 2nd person are the clearest. We know from the structural analysis given in Chapter 3 that they are TMs, and the values assigned to signs 740 (*-*ay*) and 032 (*-*ir*) are found in terminal contexts in Dravidian languages.

Because there is only one TM with two signs and only one bi-syllabic ending, 526/550 pair (*-*anre*) seems the logical choice for the 3rd person masculine. As we have both 2nd person endings and the 3rd person masculine, it seems a logical extension of this pattern to assign the other common TM (sign 520) to the 3rd person non-masculine (*-*(V)te*). The rest of the terminal markers are unidentified.

In addition to endings (TMs), proto-Dravidian nouns and verbs use clitics and postpositions in an agglutinative way. While we cannot know which signs are which morphological elements, we can say that post-terminal signs are the best candidates for these items (clitics and postpositions): 090 ↟, 400 E, 621 ⊞, 622 ⊟ and 679 ✕. As for the identity of signs 001, 002 and 060, no identification has yet been made, but they are likely related to noun morphology, perhaps names or titles.

This chapter has attempted to link what is know about proto-Dravidian morphology and syntax to the patterns of sign distribution in the Indus corpus. The resulting readings of signs fit these patterns. There are still many signs left unread and several of the proposed readings, especially 526/550 and 820, need verification. The assumption of the root language as proto-Dravidian has been productive, but it falls to linguists and students of South Asian languages to test and critique these results.

Appendix I

Automated Segmentation Of Indus Texts

Andreas Fuls

Acknowledgments

Many thanks to Bryan K. Wells and Chandrasekhar Subramanian for the corrections and suggestions to an earlier version of this Appendix.

About the Author

Dr. rer. nat. Andreas Fuls
Berlin Institute of Technology
Department for Geodesy and Geoinformation Science
Sekr. H12
Straße des 17. Juni 135
D-10623 Berlin
Germany
email: andreas.fuls@tu-berlin.de

homepage:
http://www.archaeoastronomie.de/
http://www.gis.tu-berlin.de/menue/mitarbeiter/andreas_fuls/parameter/en/

Segmentation of Texts

The segmentation of texts will separate longer sign sequences into smaller units by determining morphological boundaries and bounded sign clusters within each text. After the segmentation process the results must be evaluated by comparing the segmentation trees with results derived from paradigmatic cluster analysis, structural analysis and the positional analysis of signs. The goal is, to determine meaningful units (e.g. syntactic elements).

Previous Methods

Several methods have been proposed and applied to segment Indus texts into smaller units. Most methods use statistical behaviour of signs, counting frequencies of signs and sign pairs. None of the previous attempts has distinguished between different text classes. Instead, past analysis has placed all texts together without consideration of differences in archaeological or linguistic variations in their contexts. As known from other writing systems, the context has a great influence on sign frequency, in that each context has a specific sign inventory. For example, economic texts have a higher frequency of numerals than does poetry. In organized urban context economic texts can be repeticous in content (i.e. Chapter 4).

Harris Approach

Parpola (1994) applies the Harris approach to Indus inscriptions. Each text is compared to similar sign sequences and their frequency starting from left and right of a text. The method requires a huge amount of similar texts not available for the Indus writing system. A detailed description of this approach is given by Parpola (1994:98-99).

The method only works for a huge corpus of texts. This means that for Indus texts only patterned texts (which have a high frequency of similar texts) can be analysed by the Harris approach. The lack of detail in the Parpola sign list undermines this analysis as much as the mixing of text types.

Comparative Method

Bonta (1995:17) suggests the comparative method, which compares similar sign sequences to determine morphological boundaries within the sequences. It is similar to the Harris approach, but does not account for the frequency of sign pairs as in the Harris approach.

Korvink's Method

Michael Korvink (2006) combines three methods to split Indus texts into smaller units. These are

a. Paired combinations
b. Strong and weak bounds
c. Process of elimination

Korvink (2006:6-7) distinguishes between weak, medium, and strong combinations of sign pairs (bounded sign pairs) depending on the pair frequency and the frequency of each sign. He gives several examples of strong bounded sign pairs like 100-415 (pair *40x*, sign 415 *132x* / sign 100 *105x*), but did not offer an objective measurement of the strength. Another drawback is the sign list on which his analysis is based (Mahadevan 1977). Mahadevan has a much reduced sign list of 387 signs, thereby lumping graphically similar signs together. This sign list was criticized by Wells (2011 and Chapter 2). Wells uses a similar method to Korvink, but relies on epigraphic sources (Kelley 1973) for a methodology. Both Korvink and Wells achieved similar results regarding initial sign pairs, terminal markers and bounded clusters.

In this Appendix (I) we will introduce a formula to measure the strength of bounded sign sequences for pairs, triplets, etc. (discussed below in section *Bounded Sign Pair*).

Process of Elimination

Korvink (2006:7) uses a process of elimination method, which is similar to the comparative method. The only difference is that the process of elimination is an iterative process, which starts from both text ends. After identifying typical initial and terminal signs, longer sign sequences can be reduced by eliminating known sign clusters in initial and terminal position. This step leaves the medial signs.

In a next step the medial signs are separated by identifying:

1. Signs that belong to the same group and appear together in the same text position (i.e. fish signs, numerical sign)/
2. Single signs with their own meaning (sign 741, 742, 745).
3. Bounded Clusters with a strong paired combination.

The process of elimination can be summarized as follows:

Determine Initial Marker
Determine Terminal Marker
Define groups of sign that are used together
Determine meaningful single signs
Determine bounded sign clusters
Segmentation of texts

The process of elimination also includes complete solo signs and sign pairs, which represent most likely a unit of meaning.

For a hypothetical example of the sign sequence A-B-C-D-E-F-G the result might look as follows (in this example the reading direction is from left to right).

FIGURE AI.1 SEGMENTATION OF H-026 AFTER KORVINK (2006:68)

This method only works for patterned text with typical initial and terminal markers, bounded clusters and known sign groups like fish signs and numerical signs. No pattern can be recognized by the process of elimination for complex text or text parts with low frequency sign sequences.

Z-Score Method

Sinha *et al* (2010) developed a segmentation method using z-scores. It is based solely on the frequency of sign pairs. This is efficient for bounded clusters, but does not consider repetitive sign sequences in Indus texts.

The resulting segmentation trees can be compared to the results from structural analysis (Wells 2011). The conclusion is, that the frequency of signs and sign pairs is influenced by many different factors and we need to consider other parameters as well. If the Indus script is mostly logographic, then each sign can be a separate word.

A simple example will illustrate the problem of multifunctional sign usage. In the following list of English sentences each English word or morpheme can be replaced by one sign code:

English sentence	Code of morphems
Bob-play-s-with-the-blue-ball.	001-002-003-004-005-006-007
Bob-s-ball-is-blue.	001-003-007-008-006
The-ball-of-John-is-green.	005-007-009-010-008-011
Bob-play-s-foot-ball.	001-002-003-012-007
John-and-Bob-play-ing-foot-ball.	010-013-001-002-014-012-007

The words "foot-ball" and "play-ing" might be represented each by a composition of two signs each (code 012-007 and 002-014). Also the word "play-s" is a root + suffix. The high frequency of the sign pair "Bob-play" (code 001-002 with frequency of 3)

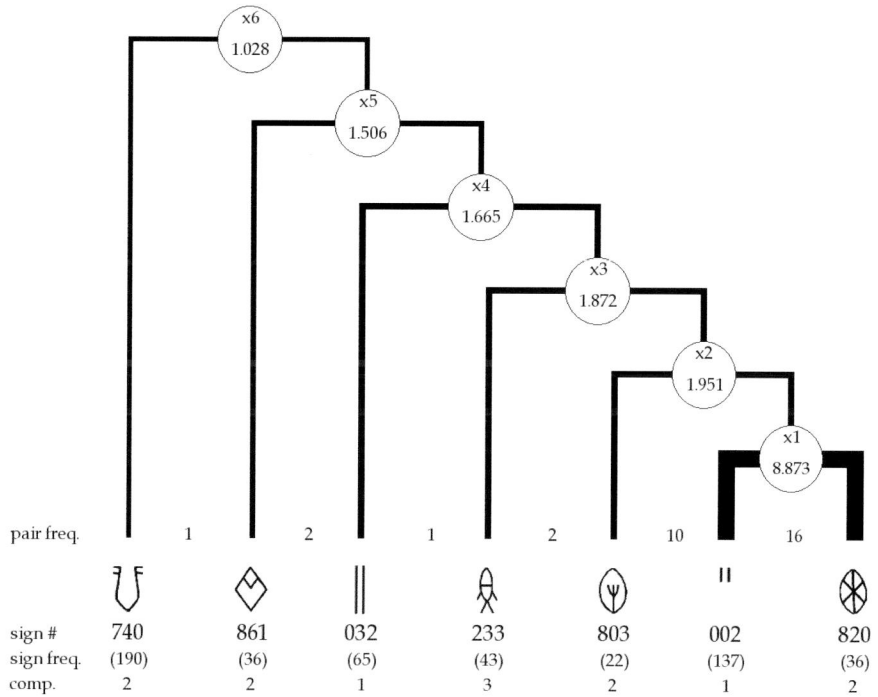

FIGURE AI.2 SEGMENTATION TREE USING THE Z-SCORE METHOD (SINHA ET AL., 2011)

does not correlate with the syntactic relationship, since they belong to two different phrases, the noun phrase and the verb phrase. Additionally, the sign for the suffix "s" (code 003) would be used as a genitive case marker of nouns as well as a verbal ending of 3rd person singular. Therefore, multifunctional sign usage as well as polyvalent signs creates a problem in pure statistical methods, which based solely on sign frequency.

The segmentation tree in Figure AI.2 shows, that method 3, which is based solely on sign frequency, does not work for sign sequences with a low frequency signs. The same text will be segmented by applying the Multivariate Segmentation Method in the discussion that follows (see Figure AI.5).

Multivariate Segmentation Method

Previous methods discussed here are based mainly on the frequency of signs and sign sequences. Because there are many short texts that are often segments of longer texts, and because signs or sign pairs are used solo or in initial or terminal positions in short texts, these well defined segments can be used to search for morphological boundaries within longer texts. The combination of these parameters leads to a multivariate segmentation method. Each parameter used in the multivariate segmentation method will be described in detail before discussing the method.

Parameter of the Multivariate Segmentation Method

During the Multivariate Segmentation method the frequency count of signs and sign pairs based on a reduced text corpus, where identical texts from the same site and artefact type are reduced to a frequency of 1. This minimizes the effect of many duplicates, especially from tablets.

Solo sign

A solo text (with one sign) can be considered as a complete unit of information (i). Therefore, the connectivity to the neighbouring signs is decreased by NPS(i). NPS(i) depends on the number of peaks in the sign position histogram, which indicates the number of possible grammatical functions of the sign in different syntactic text positions. The factor is calculated by the formula [1]:

$$NPS(i) = 1/HP \qquad [1]$$

where, HP is the number of peaks in the positional sign histogram. This factor allows signs with one grammatical function and polyvalent signs to be distinguished from each other. At the present solo sign frequency and the number of positional peaks is not used in the process of segmentation but is given in the output as additional information for each sign. This supports the manual interpretation of segmentation trees and allows candidates of logograms and syllables to be distinguished.

Initial sign

Any sign (i) in initial position starts a unit of information, thus there is a morphological boundary before the sign. For this reason there can be assumed a morphological boundary within a text before that sign, but only if the terminal frequency of the sign is smaller than the initial frequency. In this case, the connectivity to the preceding sign is decreased by NPI(i) as follows [2]:

NPI(i) = log(initial frequency of sign i) / log(total frequency of sign i) [2]

The logarithmic scaling emphasizes differences of low frequency signs and reduces the influence in differences of high frequency signs. For example, if the total sign frequency is 100 the influence on the connectivity factor NPI increases by 0.15 for initial sign frequency increasing from 10% to 20%, but only by 0.03 from 80% to 90%. This means, that an initial sign frequency of 80% or 90% of the total sign frequency has almost the same influence on the connectivity to the preceding sign. But for a low initial frequency sign with 10% or 20%, the connectivity varies by 0.15 or 15%. If the total frequency of a sign is small (e.g. n<10) there must be relatively more initial signs to have the same influence as high frequent signs. Figure AI.3 also shows, that a sign frequency of one has no effect (NPI=0).

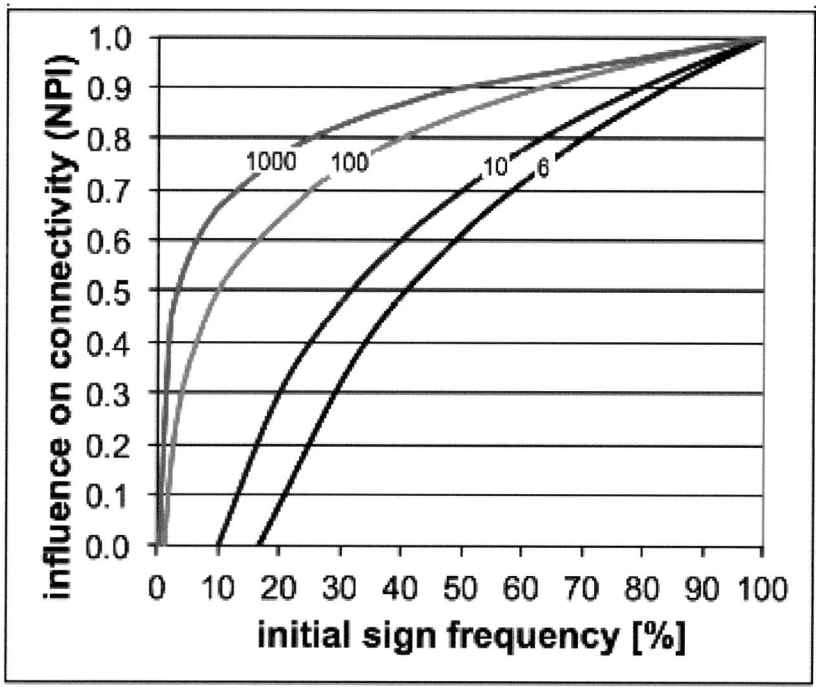

FIGURE AI.3 LOGARITHMIC INFLUENCE OF INITIAL SIGN FREQUENCY (GIVEN AS PERCENTAGE OF TOTAL FREQUENCY) ON THE CONNECTIVITY.

The logarithmic formula is derived from information theory. It compares the self-information of a sign being initial to the maximum self-information of the sign.

Terminal sign

A morphological boundary can also be assumed after a sign that appears in terminal position. If the initial frequency is smaller than the terminal frequency of the sign, the connectivity to the following sign is decreased by NPT(i) [3]:

NPT(i) = log(terminal frequency of sign i) / log(total frequency of sign i) [3]

The formula compares the self-information of a sign defined as I=log(frequency) to the self-information of the sign being terminal.

Sign complexity

Signs with one or more infixed sign or element represent a complex unit of meaning. Therefore, they could be treated as a bounded sequence of signs with the highest connectivity between the internal signs and a low connectivity to the neighbouring signs. At present sign complexity is not used in the segmentation process, but the number of sign components for each sign as well as the sum and the mean value of sign components is listed in the output to identify compact information.

Bounded sign pair

A sign pair (i,j) with a sign pair frequency f(i,j) and individual sign frequencies f(i) and f(j) has a probability of [4]:

P(i,j) = f(i,j)/ f(i) x f(i,j)/ f(j) [4]

  = f(i,j)^2 / (f(i) x f(j)),

This is proportional to the strength of the bounded pair. The strength of a bounded pair increases with the pair frequency f(i,j) is increasing up to the smaller value of f(i) or f(j), respectively. The smaller value of f(i) and f(j) is the upper limit of the pair frequency f(i,j). Comparing the self information of the sign pair to its upper limit leads to formula [5]:

NPP(i,j)=log(pair frequency f(i,j)) / log(minimum of total sign frequency f(i),f(j)) [5]

Solo Sign Pairs

If a sign pair is used anywhere as a solo text, the strength of the bounding pair increases. For solo sign pairs NPP(i,j) is multiplied by a factor of KSP=3. In the output diagram they are marked by "!" on both sides of the sign pair frequency.

Initial sign pairs

If a sign pair i,j is not a solo pair but has a high frequency of being used in initial position the chance of a morphological boundary before the sign pair increases, but only if the previous initial or terminal pair frequency is smaller than the actual initial pair frequency, and if the frequency of sign i and j is greater than one. In this case, the connectivity to the previous sign is decreased by [6]:

NPPI(i,j)=log(pair frequency+1)/log(frequency of sign i)/log(frequency of sign j) [6]

In the output diagram an initial sign pair is marked by "!" on the right side of the sign pair frequency.

Terminal sign pair

If a sign pair i,j is not a solo pair but has a high frequency being used in terminal position the chance of a morphological boundary after the sign pair increases, but only if the following initial or terminal pair frequency is smaller than the actual initial pair frequency. In this case, the connectivity to the next sign is decreased by [7]:

NPPT(i,j)=log(pair frequency+1)/log(frequency of sign i)/log(frequency of sign j) [7]

In the output diagram a terminal sign pair is marked by "!" on the left side of the sign pair frequency.

Ratio of initial to terminal sign frequency

The symmetrical relationship of the initial and terminal sign frequency of sign pairs (i,j) has a strong influence on the strength of the sign pair. The strength can either increase or decrease as described in the following discussion.

If the initial frequency of first sign (i) is greater than its terminal frequency, and the terminal frequency of the second sign (j) is greater than the initial frequency, then the strength of the sign pair is increasing by [8]:

NIT = log(initial frequency of sign j) / log(frequency of sign j) * log(terminal frequency of sign i) / log(frequency of sign i) [8]

This means, that the strength of the sign pair increases. In contrast, if the terminal frequency of the first sign i is greater than its initial frequency, and the initial frequency of the second sign j is greater than the terminal frequency, then the strength of the sign pair is decreases by [9]):

NIT = log(terminal frequency of sign j) / log(frequency of sign j) * log(initial frequency of sign i) / log(frequency of sign i) [9]

This means that a morphological boundary falls between the two signs. The parameter is applied only if the sign frequency of both signs is greater than 6. Otherwise low frequency signs would lead to a high influence on the connectivity.

Groups of signs in a specific orders

Signs like fish signs or numerical signs often appear after each other forming a sequence of one unit of information (e.g. numerals in positional notation or fish signs in a specific order; Wells 2011). These signs belong to the same group forming one unit of information. Therefore, the connectivity between these signs should increase putting these signs together. The usage of sign groups based on previous interpretation of specific signs would manipulate the result of the segmentation process in a way that the result complies the expectation, but does not lead to new information. Therefore, specific sign groups are not used in the segmentation process, but can be used manually to evaluate the resulting trees.

Paradigmatic sign groups (NOT USED)

Signs that behave similar to the same sign neighbours form a paradigmatic sign group. If a Sign (j) belongs to a paradigmatic sign group of signs $[a_1, a_2, ... j ..., a_n]$, its connection to the neighbouring sign can be increased by a mean probability NP of paradigmatic related sign pairs. The mean probability to the neighbouring sign (x) can be calculated by [10]:

$$NP = (NP(x, a_1) + NP(x, a_2) + ... + NP(x, a_n)) / n \qquad [10]$$

Known paradigmatic sign groups are initial signs 817, 820, and 920, etc. Paradigmatic sign groups overlap with bounded sign pairs, e.g. 033-705 and 033-706. Of course, the connectivity to the neighbouring sign (x) should be increased only once. In the current analysis this parameter is not used.

The Model of Sign Connectivity

Texts with longer sign sequences are composed by attaching units of information after each other according to the syntax of the language or rules forced by context or available space. It is the goal of this method to segment texts into smaller units of information that form semantic classes of signs. The following method allows a flexible measure of connectivity between sign pairs within a text based on several parameters as described above. This means that morphological boundaries are not definite but depend on the degree of their statistical relationship. Signs that belong to the same unit of information (or grammatical text part) have a strong relationship given by a high value of connectivity. Small values of connectivity indicate a morphological boundary between two adjacent semantic units of information.

The connectivity of each sign pair is a positive real number. This means, the connectivity does not fall below zero. The only exceptions are multi-lined texts (text class 2L and 3L), where the connectivity between two lines of text is set to zero.

The process of segmentation is initialised by setting the connectivity to 1.5. During the process of segmentation the sign sequence is analysed for the parameters and thereby increase or decrease the connectivity values between signs. At the end of the process the text can be segmented into smaller units. The strength of the connection between signs is indicated by the thickness of a line. Low connectivity values have a thin line, indicating a high probability of a morphological boundary. High connectivity values have a thick line and indicate a stronger relationship between two signs falling within the same unit of information (Table AI.1).

Segmentation parameter	Effect on the connectivity		
	to previous sign	to following sign	within sign pair
Initial sign	-NPI x KI		
Terminal sign		-NPT x KT	
Initial sign pair	-NPPI x KITP		
Terminal sign pair		-NPPT x KITP	
Bounded sign pair			+NPP x KP
Solo sign pair			+NPP x KSP
Ratio of initial to terminal sign frequency: a) strong sign pair b) boundary between sign pair			a) +NIT x KIT b) –NIT x KIT

TABLE AI.1 SEGMENTATION PARAMETER AND THEIR EFFECT ON THE CONNECTIVITY BETWEEN SIGNS.

The first four parameter are analysing signs, thereby decreasing the connectivity to the previous or following sign. The last three parameter are analysing sign pairs or longer sign sequences, which increases or decreases the connectivity within the sign pair or sequence. Each parameter is multiplied by a factor to adjust the influences of the parameter on the connectivity. The sum of all segmentation parameters result in the final connectivity between each sign pair [11].

Connectivity = 1.5 - NPI x KI - NPT x KT - NPPI x KITP - NPPT x KITP

$$+ \text{NPP} \times \text{KP [or KSP]} \pm \text{NIT} \times \text{KIT} \qquad [11]$$

The multiplication factors are determined during the evaluation of resulting segmentation trees, where bounded sign pairs, initial and terminal markers, and typical sign sequences are known from previous structural analysis. This is especially known for Long Patterned (LP) texts. The multiplication factors are as follows:

```
KI = 0.2;      //-initial sign
KT = 0.2;      //-terminal sign
KP = 1.0;      //-pair frequency
KSP = 3.0;     //-solo pair factor>=1
KITP = 1.0;    //-pair found in initial or terminal position
```

110 The Archaeology and Epigraphy of Indus Writing

KIT = 1.0;   //-ratio of initial to terminal sign frequency:
a) terminal/total(second sign) x initial/total(first sign)
b) initial/total(second sign) x terminal/total(first sign)

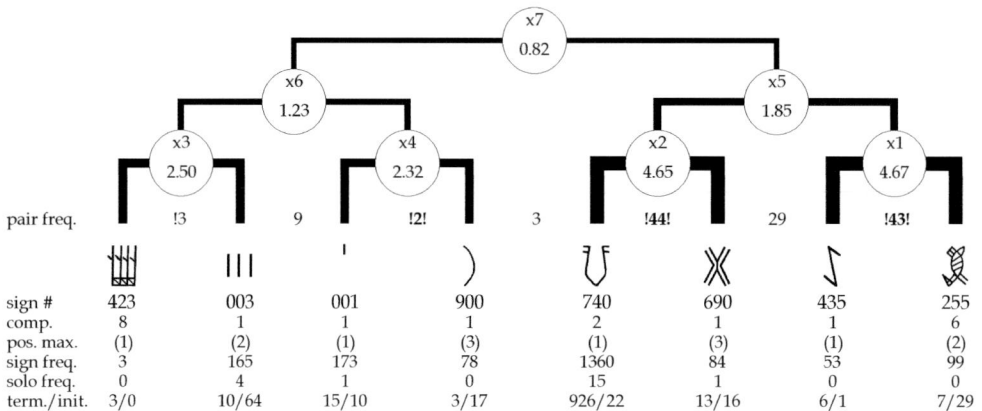

Mohenjo-daro M-0525 L982 TAB:C MS
ConnectMean 2.578 +-0.237 CompSum 21 CompMean 2.625
ID 3841 #Signs 8 tree height 3 index 0.38
Multivariante Segmentation Method developed by Andreas Fuls (TU Berlin), database by Bryan K. Wells

a

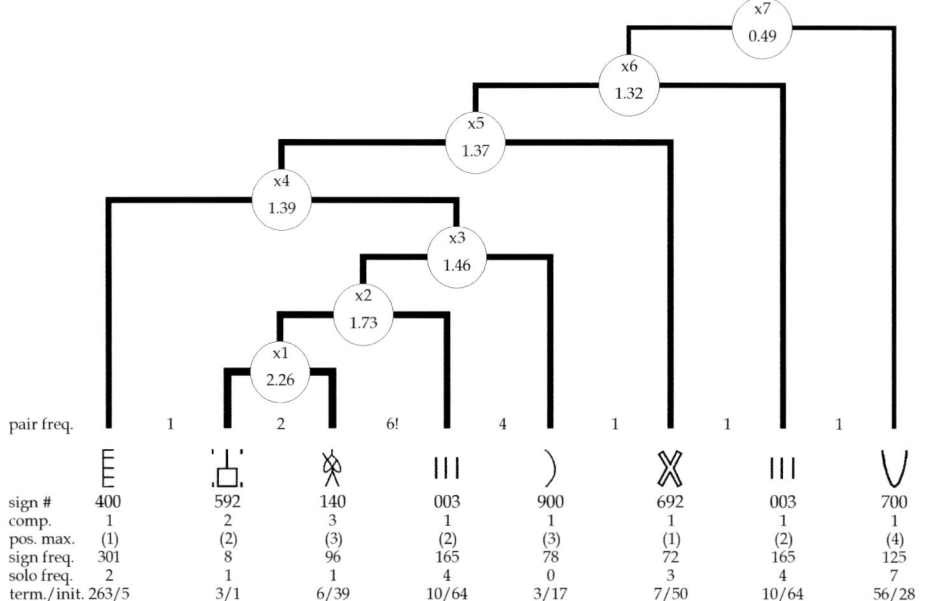

Mohenjo-daro M-0500 DK7810 SEAL:C LC
ConnectMean 1.432 +-0.098 CompSum 11 CompMean 1.375
ID 3808 #Signs 8 tree height 7 index 0.88
Multivariante Segmentation Method developed by Andreas Fuls (TU Berlin), database by Bryan K. Wells

b

Figure AI.4 Example of a) highly structured text, b) less structured text, both 8 signs long.

It is also possible to draw a segmentation tree from the connectivity values, in that a high connectivity value corresponds to a high z-score as in method 3. The process of drawing a segmentation tree starts with the highest connectivity until all signs are connected by tree branches. Every time a sign is connected to the other neighbouring sign the tree height increases. The tree height depends on the text length and the number of directly connected sign pairs. This means a small tree index indicates a well structured text and a high tree index is given for a less structured texts. If a text remains less structured, this is due to the low frequency of signs, sign pairs, and unusual sign sequences.

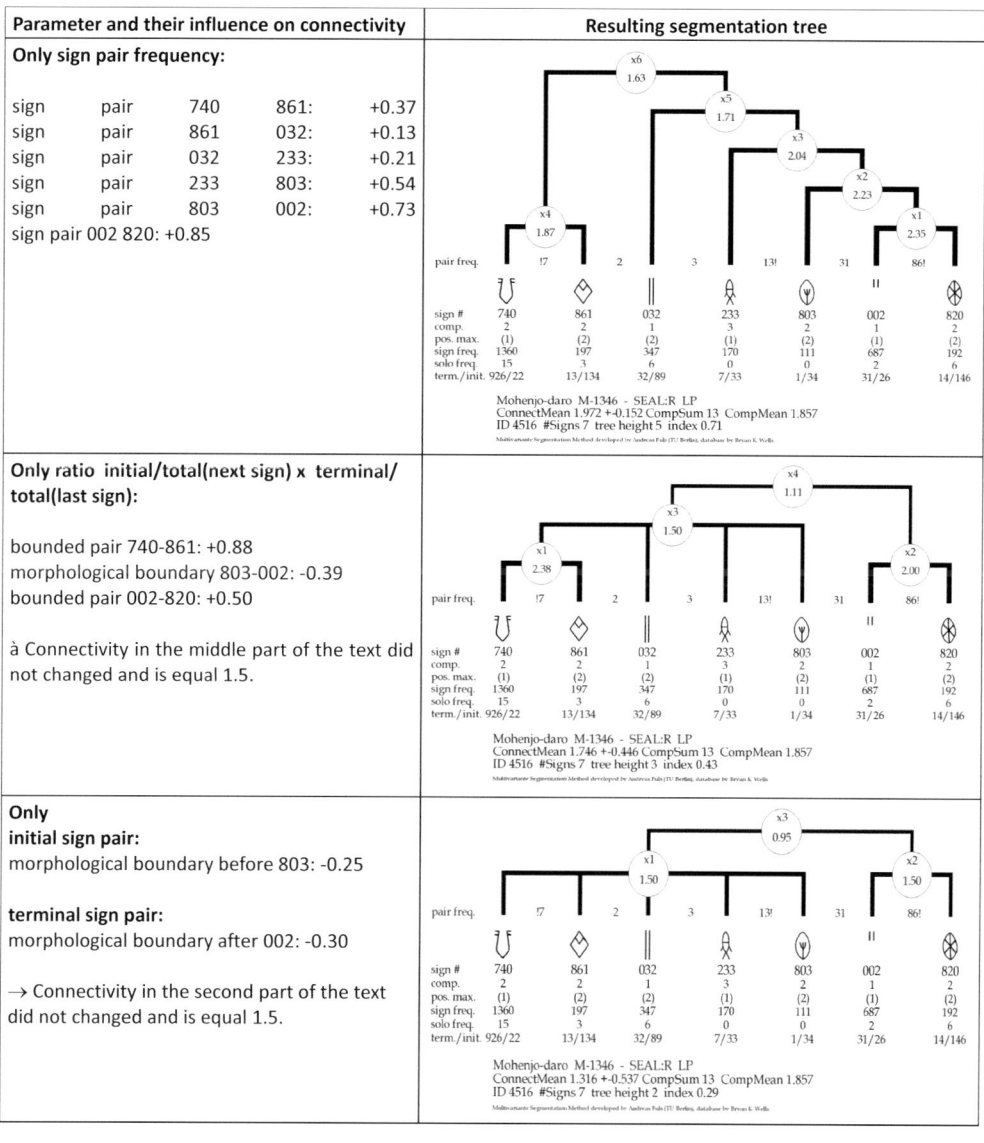

112 THE ARCHAEOLOGY AND EPIGRAPHY OF INDUS WRITING

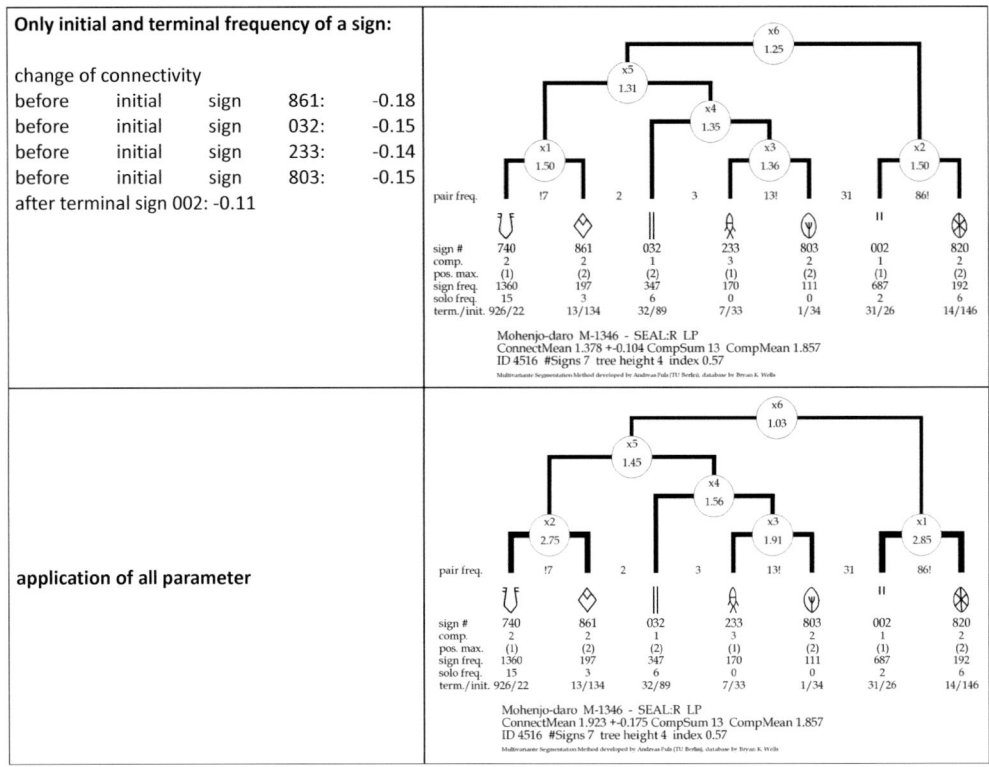

FIGURE AI.5 STEP BY STEP PROCESS OF SEGMENTATION AND FINAL MULTIVARIATE SEGMENTATION TREE

The influence of each factor is shown in the following figure (Figure AI.5), where for the same text only one parameter is used and at the end all parameter together.

Comparing the above MVS tree with the Korvink's result of the process of elimination shows that signs 740-388 are used twice as a solo pair (H-138 and M-1321). Therefore, they belong together and form one unit of information, but Korvink separates them into medial and terminal. Korvink separates sign 798 from the fish signs, but there are 21 texts starting with the sign sequence −240-798+, which means that after the initial phrase of 001-820+ a new phrase starts. The only agreement is that the second fish sign 231 belongs to the first fish sign 240. In sum, Korvink's result is partially wrong or at least not very informative.

Evaluation of Segmentation Trees

As shown in Figure AI.7 SC and LC texts have the smallest mean connectivity. This is because these texts use more unusual sign sequences unknown in other texts, and less segments. The highest mean connectivity can be seen for two V# texts with more than 2 signs and SS texts.

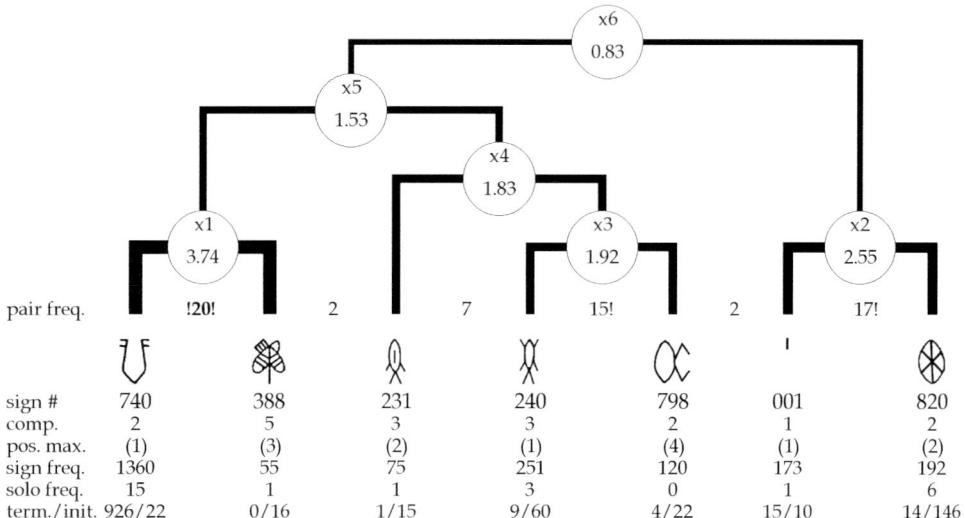

FIGURE AI.6 SEGMENTATION TREE OF H-026. COMPARE SEGMENTATION RESULTS TO FIGURE AI.1

Text classes also have different standard deviations of the mean connectivity. Small standard deviations can be found on 3L, LP and LC texts. The reason for this that the variation of the connectivity is divided by a high number of signs. This means, that the standard deviation depends on the text length.

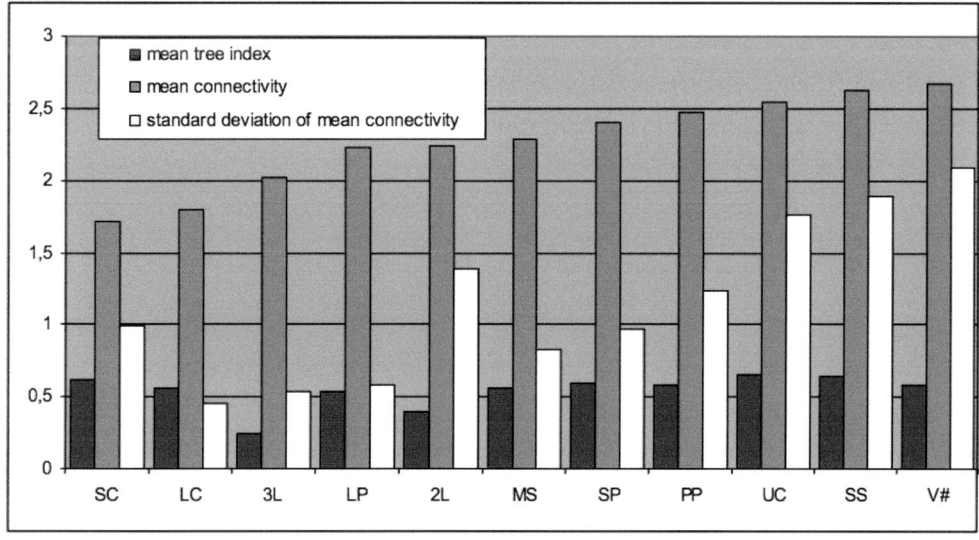

FIGURE AI.7 MEAN TREE INDEX, MEAN CONNECTIVITY AND ITS STANDARD DEVIATION FOR DIFFERENT TEXT CLASSES.

Figure AI.8 shows, that text classes can be differentiated by the mean connectivity and its standard deviation. Text classes with a low standard deviation have a connectivity vector with less variation, while a high standard deviation indicates strong sign pairings interrupted by strong morphological boundaries. This results in a great variation of the connectivity.

The relationship of the mean connectivity to its standard deviation shows a linear trend from LP, MS, SP, PP, UC, SS to V# texts. Text classes that fall outside of the linear trend are SC, LC, 3L and 2L texts.

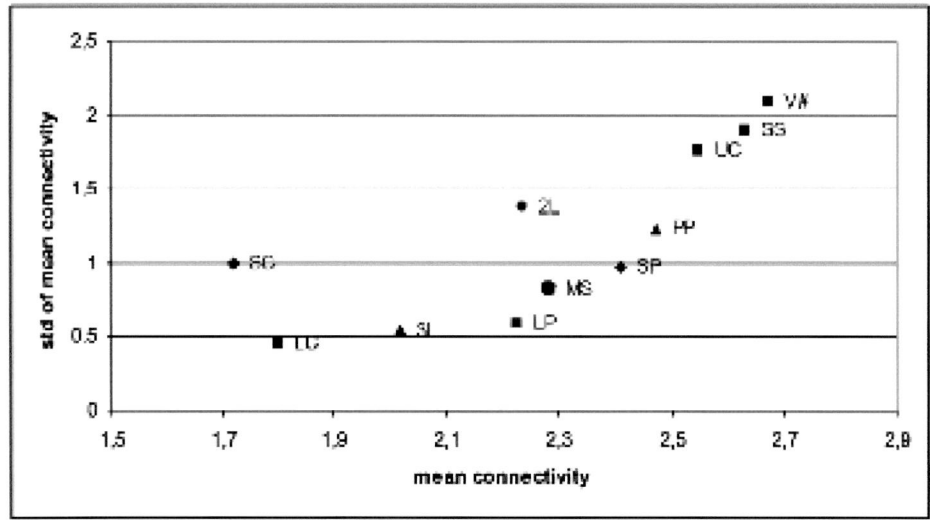

FIGURE AI.8 RELATIONSHIP OF MEAN CONNECTIVITY TO ITS STANDARD DEVIATION (STD) BY TEXT CLASS

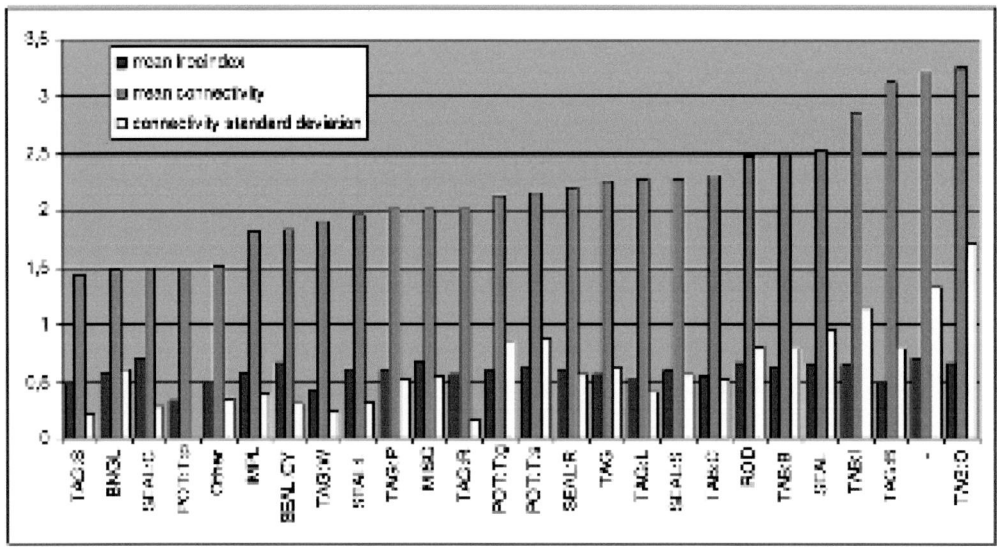

FIGURE AI.9 MEAN TREE INDEX AND MEAN CONNECTIVITY FOR DIFFERENT ARTEFACT TYPES

The diagram also indicates, that, for example, LP and MS texts have similar structures. Figure AI.9 shows, that artefact types bear different texts of different complexity and numbers of segments. There are 9 SEAL:C with a very low mean connectivity, since texts on SEAL:C are very unusual and show almost no known pattern. They are all complex texts and the highest pair frequency of all SEAL:C texts is only 7.

Self-information

The self-information of a sign is $I=-\log(f/T)$, where $f=$ absolute frequency and $T=$total frequency. It can also be written as $I=\log(T) – \log(f)$. For a frequency of $f=1$ the self-information is $I1=\log(T) – \log(1) = \log(T)$, which is the maximum self-information.

The relation of a self information to the maximum self information is [12]:

$I / I1 = (\log(T) – \log(f)) / \log(T) = 1 – (\log(f) / \log(T)) = 1 - RI.$ [12]

The ratio $I / I1$ is the relative self-information, comparable to the relative frequency or probability $p=f/T$ in statistics. If the absolute frequency (f) increases to T (f--> T), when $I / I1 --> 0$. This means adding the same information again and again until its maximum new information decreases to zero. In other words, no new information is added.

The term $RI = \log(f) / \log(T)$ can also be called relative information. If the relative information is high, the influence on connectivity is also high, and vice versa. Therefore, RI is used as a measure to add or reduce the strength of connectivity of a sign to its neighbours.

116 THE ARCHAEOLOGY AND EPIGRAPHY OF INDUS WRITING

Examples of Segmentation Trees By Text Type

Long Complex Texts

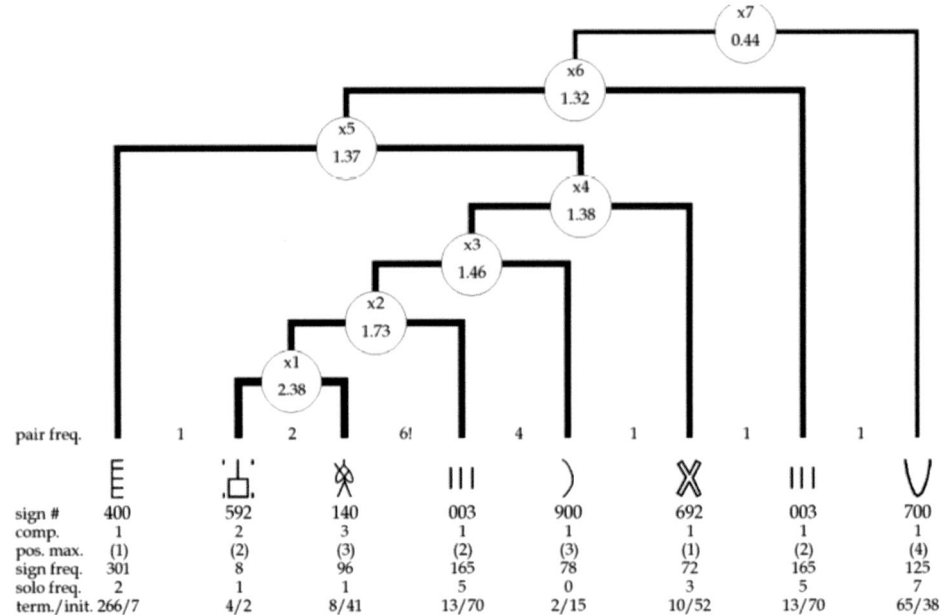

Mohenjo-daro M-0500 DK7810 SEAL:C LC
ConnectMean 1.438 +-0.270 CompSum 11 CompMean 1.375
ID 3808 #Signs 8 tree height 7 index 0.88

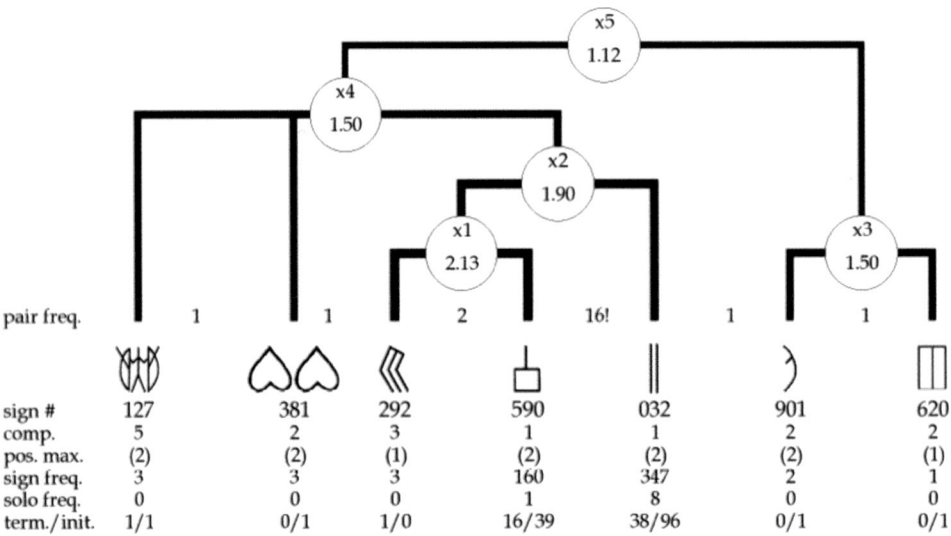

Mohenjo-daro M-1316 DK10609 SEAL:R LC
ConnectMean 1.631 +-0.532 CompSum 16 CompMean 2.286
ID 4487 #Signs 7 tree height 4 index 0.57

Long Patterned Texts

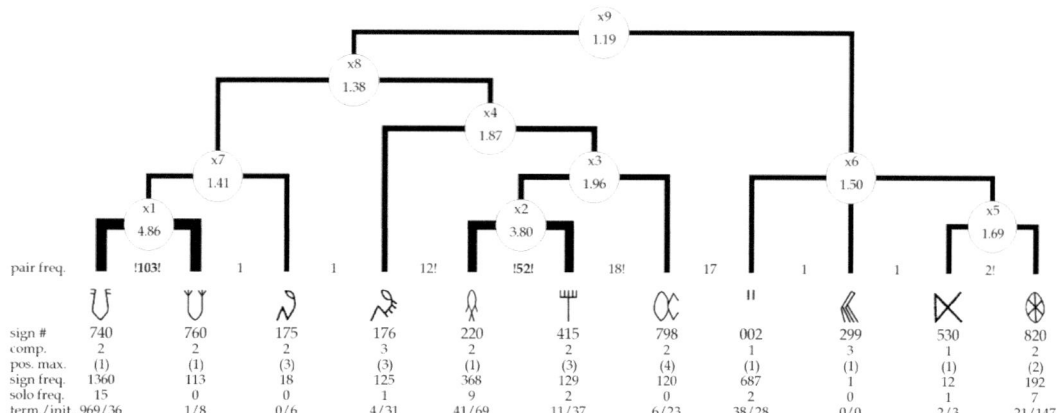

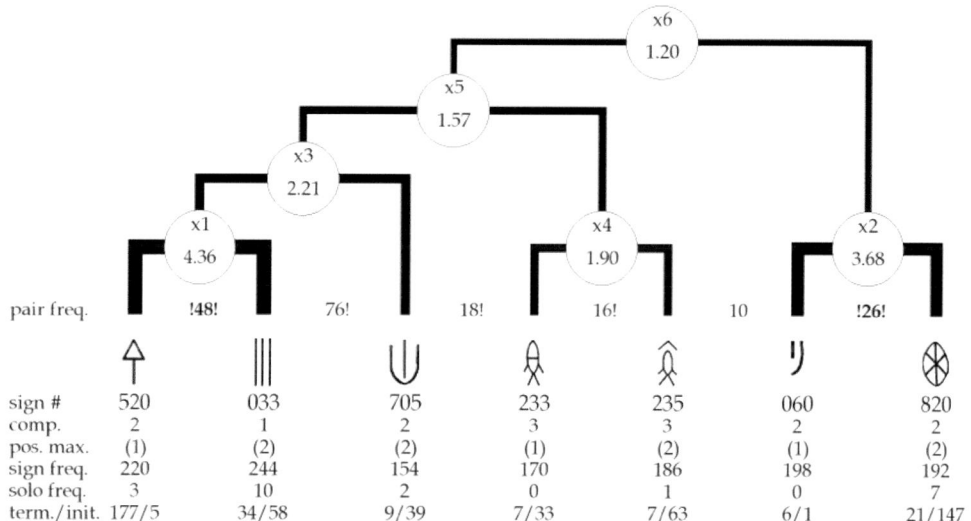

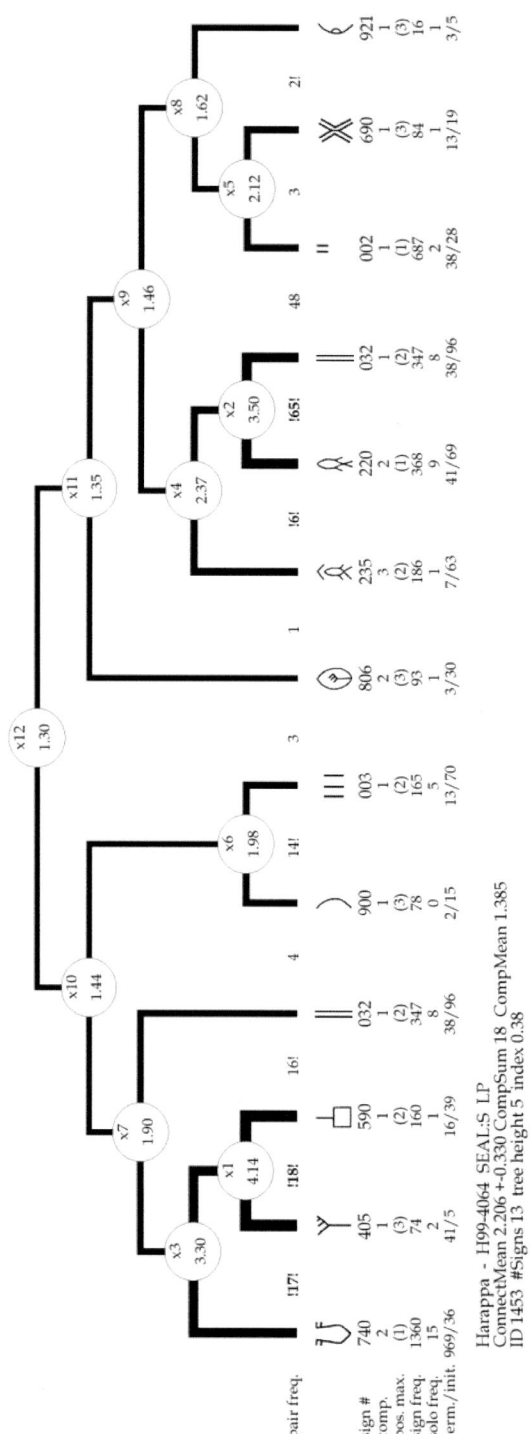

Appendix II

Positional Analysis of Indus Signs

Andreas Fuls

This research was first published in *Voprosi Epigrafiki* Vol. VII (1):253-275, 2013. In this appendix the original has been modified to standardize the terminology and formatting.

Introduction

The position of signs in the Indus inscriptions is an important factor in analysing sign function. Some signs are typically found in initial position, while other are mostly terminal, but many signs were only be classified as medial, which is not a precise description. A new method is needed to classify each sign's positional behaviour, beyond the initial, medial and terminal classification. That is, a more detailed analysis and classification of Indus sign behaviour is necessary. This method would preferably account for sign behaviour in all texts as well as for specific text classes.

The method developed here can also be used to show that graphically similar signs often differ in their preferred positional behaviour. That is, they are not allographs but distinct graphemes. The positional histograms of signs derived from different text classes indicate, that Indus signs can have more than one preferred text position depending on the content and the structure of the texts. This is important to emphasise, because previous statistical tests of Indus signs very often have put all texts together without considering of different context or text structures.

Since the beginning of the study of Indus signs they have been tabulated and distinguished by graphic form alone. This results in sign lists of 386 to 419 signs.

 Mahadevan 1977 and Parpola 1994, respectively). The question remains: *Which signs are distinct signs and which signs are allographs*? The identification of allographs is a time consuming task of searching for sign replacement patterns and requires a large text corpus. This can be done by the structure analysis (developed by Forrer (1932)) and was applied by Wells (2006, p. 67-93) to create a detailed sign list with 676 signs. This looks like a step backwards if one is looking for a condensed (Simplified) sign list. But as long as allographs cannot be clearly distinguished from distinct signs this is the most secure way of creating a sing list, especially for scripts with many low frequency signs. See Chapter 2 and Wells (2011) for more details on sign list construction.

The following research is based on an updated sign list from Wells (2006) with 695 signs (last update autumn 2010). Inscriptions are stored in the ICIT database (Interactive

Corpus of Indus Texts) with a total of 3898 inscribed artefacts (one to three sided) and 4791 texts. Of these, 3723 texts of them are complete using a total of 13556 signs. They are used as the text corpus for the following analysis of sign positions.

Many artefacts have identical texts coming from the same site and often they come from the same mould. Other duplicate texts have the same provenience. These artefacts are often incised or cooper miniature tablets. Because they are often found on tablets, the effect of duplicate texts is called the TAB effect (Wells 2006, p. 168). In the following analysis identical texts from the same artefact type coming from the same site are reduced to a frequency of 1 text, for the purposes of analysis. Otherwise they would lead to a high frequency of some signs, which do not represent the usage of signs in the Indus script. Additionally, multiple line texts are not included, since it is uncertain how to read the second or third line. The lines could be read right/left, boustrophedon or each line could represent an independent phrase (Parpola 1994, p. 64-67). This leaves 2474 complete and different texts, reducing the total number of relevant signs to 9700 signs. The mean text length for this sample is 4.01 signs. Table 1 summarizes the text lengths of the study data. They are stored in an online database of Indus texts (Fuls 2010).

To get a better idea about the Indus writing system and the fraction of logograms versus syllables, I have made a comparison of sign frequency histograms between different writing systems (logographic, syllabic, logosyllabic and alphabet with and without vowels). The result is that the Indus writing system is most similar to Proto-Sumerian cuneiform, an early stage with many logograms and about 37% to 54% syllabic. A regression line between their sign frequencies shows a strong relationship of $R^2 = 0.9986$ (Wells 2006, p. 96). Therefore, we can expect about the same fraction of syllables in the Indus script.

text length	total no. of texts	no. of texts from Mohenjo-daro	no. of texts from Harappa
1	232	80	112
2	477	163	244
3	477	195	225
4	412	188	177
5	360	212	110
6	233	148	57
7	150	107	32
8	59	41	9
9	40	24	10
10	19	11	5
11	7	6	1
12	4	3	1
13	3	2	1

TABLE AII.1. FREQUENCY OF TEXT LENGTHS IN THE REDUCED TEXT CORPUS OF COMPLETE INSCRIPTIONS WITHOUT DUPLICATES FROM THE SAME SITE OR ARTEFACT TYPE

Methods of Sign Analysis

Previous works has distinguished between initial, medial, and terminal sign position. It is well known that some signs like sign 740 are mostly located in the terminal position of texts, while others are very often in the initial position in Indus texts. The preferred sign position gives us some clues about the possible sign function(s) assuming a language with a fixed syntax. We can expect that logograms describing objects, names, or actions have a limited text position, while syllables can appear more diverse text positions. Some signs are polyvalent (Chapters 3 and 6). The distribution of a sign position can be used to evaluate possible sign functions.

Wells (2006, p. 138) classifies some signs according to their preferred text position as Initial signs (INS), Terminal Marker (TMK) and Post-Terminal Marker (PTM). He also discovered, that sign 60 appears only in position 1 to 4 (except 5 two-lined texts), which is often replaced by sign 1 or sign 2 (Wells 2006, p. 141). They are called Initial Cluster Terminal Marker (ICTM). Yadav et al. (2008, p. 9-13) analyse combinations of two to four signs in the Indus script and their frequency in solo, left, middle, and right position. Conclusions derived from high frequencies in solo, left-end or right-end position are well defined, but sign combinations in middle position can not be interpreted.

One simple approach is to label signs as being initial, medial or terminal. This results in a loss of all details concerning medial signs. In order to improve our understanding of the behaviour of medial signs is new method is developed, which gives us a more detailed impression on medial sign positions. The question is, how to classify signs that are commonly medial and how to distinguish different sign positions in the middle part of texts? Because of the different text lengths medial/middle is not a precise term. This is a reason to develop a normalized weighted sign position explained here.

Normalised Weighted Sign Position

To compare sign positions in text of different lengths, it is necessary to normalize the text length. Normalization is a process of reducing long texts and stretching short texts to a standard length. In this case, a standard text length of 10 signs is used. The normalization is linear as shown in Figure 1.

The relative sign position can be calculated as follows. The original sign position SP of a text with L signs is scaled to a normalised text length NL (e.g. NL=10).

$$MINP = int((SP - 1) \times NL/L + 1) \qquad [1]$$

$$MAXP = int(SP \times NL/L) \qquad [2]$$

Where, SP: absolute sign position; L: text length; NL: normalised text length (here NL = 10 signs); MINP: minimum of relative text position; MAXP: maximum of relative text position.

The results MINP and MAXP are rounded down to integer values in the range [1,NL]. They represent the minimum and maximum value of the relative sign position(s).

After normalisation a sign position of a short text might be counted more than once (like sign 002 falling into relative sign position 9 and 10, Figure 1). To avoid an overweighting of signs from short texts each sign position is weighted linearly to text length. This means, that signs of short texts get a lower weight than signs of longer texts. The weighting is calculated as follows:

$$W = L/NL \qquad [3]$$

Where, L: text length; NL: normalised text length; W: weight.

This means, that each sign in a text of NL signs gets a weight of 1, while longer texts have a higher precision of each sign position and get a higher weight. In contrast, shorter texts get a smaller weight, since their sign position is less precise.

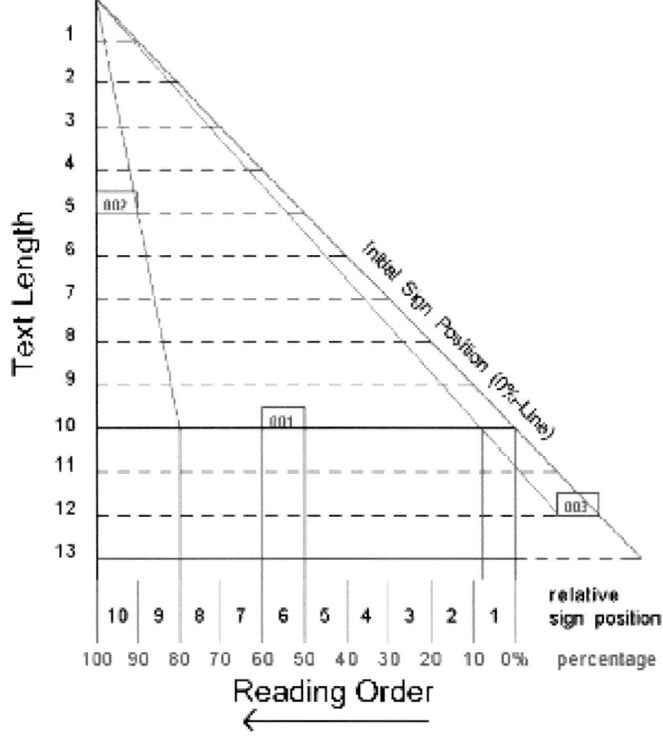

FIGURE AII.1. NORMALIZATION OF SIGN POSITIONS FOR DIFFERENT TEXT LENGTHS. SIGN 001 FALLS BETWEEN 50-60% (RELATIVE POSITION 6), SIGN 002 FALLS BETWEEN 80-100% (RELATIVE POSITION 9 OR 10), AND SIGN 003 FALLS BETWEEN 0-8.3% (RELATIVE POSITION 1). THEREBY, THE RANGE OF EACH RELATIVE SIGN POSITION (MINP UND MAXP) DEPENDS ON THE TEXT LENGTH AND IS NORMALISED TO A TEXT LENGTH OF 10 SIGNS.

Histogram

The histogram shows the frequency of sign positions for a constant number of intervals. Each interval represents a normalised sign position counting from 1 to NL. In the following discussion NL is set to 10. To calculate the histogram for each sign the weight is added to the relative sign position(s) between MINP and MAXP. For example, sign 002 from a text of length 5 has a weight of 0.5 and is counted twice, for relative sign position 9 and 10, respectively. In contrast, sign 003 from a text of length 12 has a weight of 1.2, which is added to position 1 (Figure 1).

Some signs frequently produce high values in the histogram. For visual reasons the height of the histogram is scaled to the same size or each sign, so that the histogram of rare and frequent signs can be easily compared. Only complete texts can be used to analyse sign positions, therefore, incomplete texts are omitted. Additionally, there are many duplicates of identical texts (TAB effect). Reducing them to one text results in a list of 2474 complete and different texts. This is the data used in the following analysis.

Classification of Indus Signs

Many Indus signs are already recognised as initial or terminal signs (Mahadevan 1977; Parpola 1994; Wells 2006). It can be shown that histograms of normalised weighted sign positions are useful to distinguish between common terminal and initial signs. Initial and terminal signs can easily be compared to graphically similar signs, to determine if their preferred positions are identical.

Initial signs

Initial signs are known from structural analysis (Wells 2006, p. 138; Chapter 3). Most, but not all, of their histograms conform to this pattern (Table 2, left column). Signs 690, 790, 824, 850, and 921 are graphically similar to the Initial signs 692, 817, 820, 861, and 921, respectively. But the positional frequency shows, that they locate in different positions, not exclusively initial. This confirms, that they are distinct signs despite their graphic similarity (Table 2, right column). Other signs mostly initial are signs 190, 853, 880 (Figure 2).

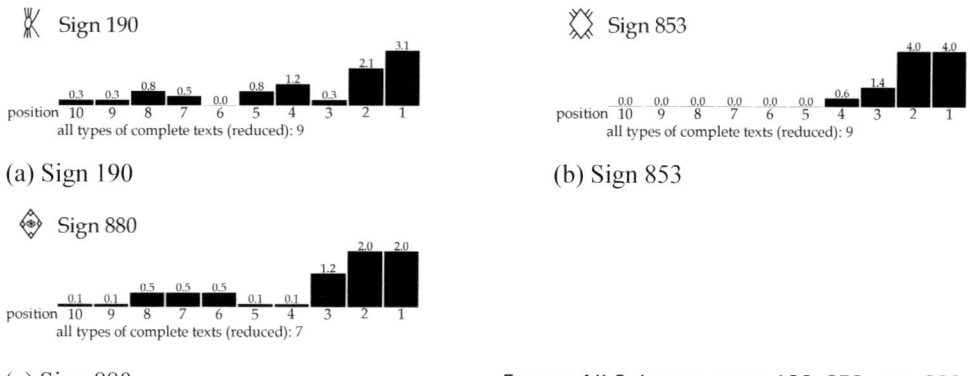

(a) Sign 190

(b) Sign 853

(c) Sign 880

FIGURE AII.2. INITIAL SIGNS 190, 853, AND 880.

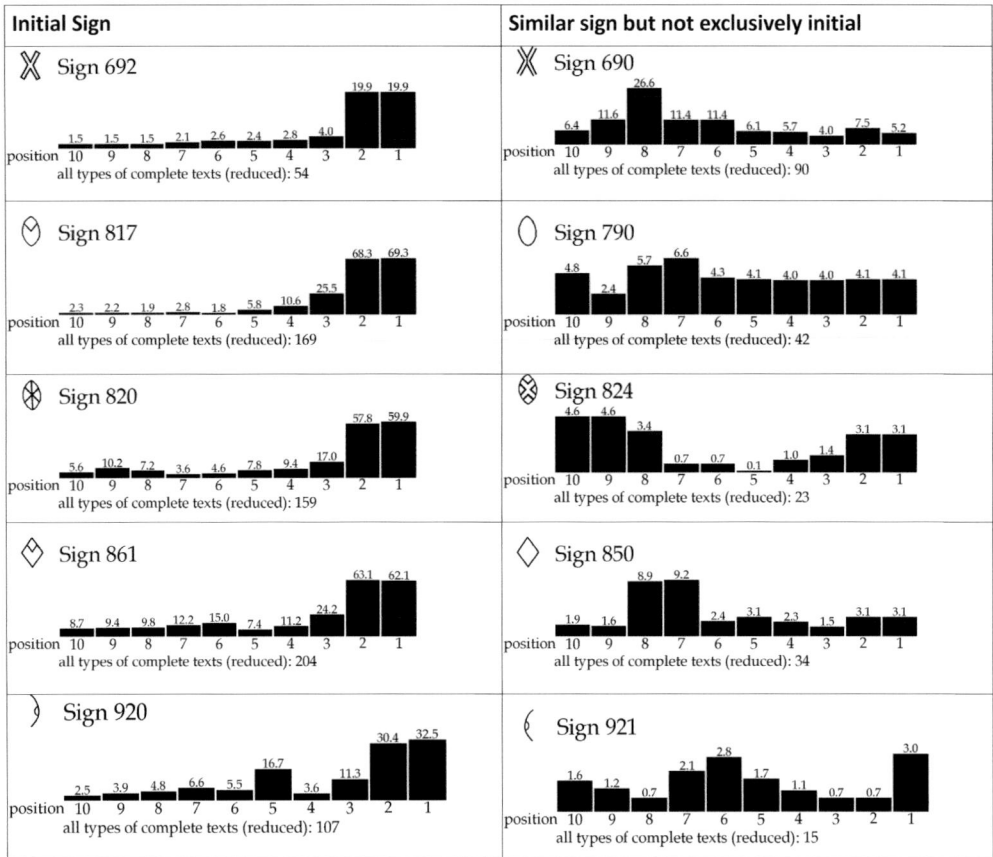

TABLE AII.2. POSITIONAL HISTOGRAMS OF INITIAL SIGN AND GRAPHICALLY SIMILAR SIGNS.

Terminal Markers

Terminal markers are discussed by Wells (2006, p. 198-200; Chapter 3). They appear often at the end of texts. About half of them show a high frequency at the left side (terminal position), but many Terminal marker have a very different distribution of positional frequency (Table 3). Sign 156 and 158 appear anywhere at the second half of text positions. Sign 741 is similar to sign 740 with a maximum at position 5 but not terminal as sign 740 is.

TABLE AII.3. POSITIONAL HISTOGRAMS OF TERMINAL MARKER AND GRAPHICALLY SIMILAR SIGNS.

Post-Terminal Signs

Post-Terminal signs are discussed by Wells (2006, p. 198-200; Chapter 3). They appear mostly at the end of texts as an affix after Terminal Markers. Post-Terminal signs are sign 090, 400, 621, and 679 (Figure 3). Other Terminal or Post-Terminal signs are sign 161, 422, and 423, but their frequency is very low.

A high frequency focused on one position might be a good indicator of a grammatical function with a restricted grammatical position (e.g. case marker).

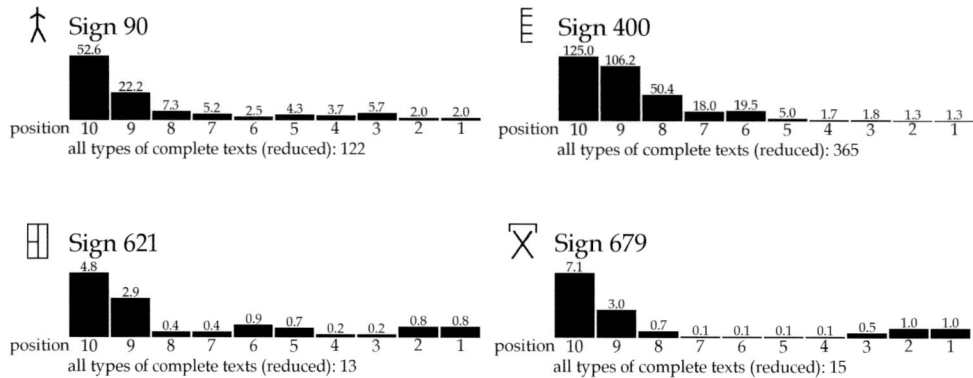

FIGURE AII.3. POSITIONAL HISTOGRAMS OF POST-TERMINAL SIGNS.

Uniform sign distributions

A uniform frequency for all positions is a good indicator of a syllable sign, since syllables are used everywhere in texts without syntactic restriction. Signs with an almost constant distribution are signs 382, 790, 832, and 892 (Figure 4).

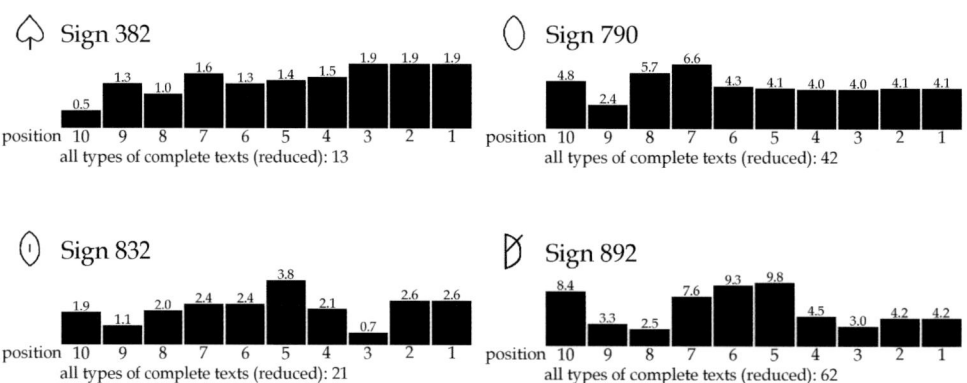

FIGURE AII.4. SIGNS WITH AN ALMOST CONSTANT POSITIONAL DISTRIBUTION.

Uniform but not initial sign distribution

Sign 368 and 595 are more or less uniform but almost never initial (Figure 5). The reason for the relatively low frequency in the initial position is unknown. It might indicate a syllabic value of a grammatical feature, which doesn't occur in initial position because the grammatical marker is always suffixed. Sign 368 is already recognized by Knorozov (1968) as a possible grammatical marker.

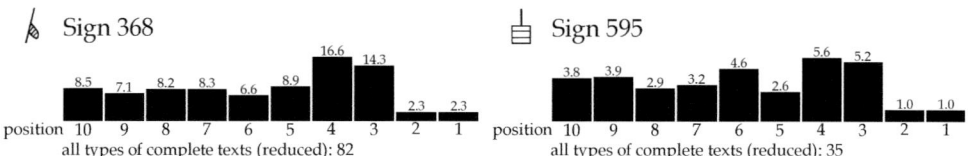

FIGURE AII.5. SIGNS WITH A CONSTANT BUT WITH LOW FREQUENCY IN THE INITIAL POSITION.

Medial sign classification

In the following sections three new classes of signs in predominantly medial position are defined. They are called Early-Medial, Mid-Medial, and Late-Medial signs.

Signs which have a maximum at positions 3 to 4 are called Early-Medial signs (Figure 6). Sign 002 and 060 are known as a marker after initial signs or initial sign clusters. As expected their preferred position is in the Early-Medial part of the text. Wells (2006) calls them, together with sign 001, Initial Cluster Terminal Markers (ICTM), since they mark the end of inital clusters.

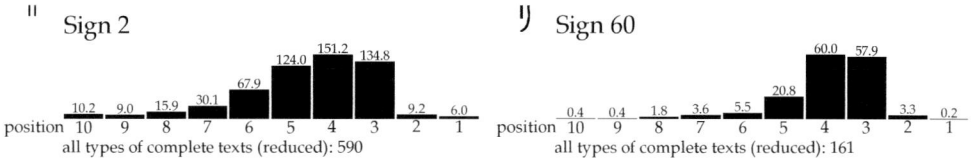

FIGURE AII.6. SIGNS WITH AN EARLY-MEDIAL POSITIONAL DISTRIBUTION.

Signs that have a maximum at positions 5 to 6 are called Mid-Medial signs. The histogram of signs 741 and 742 show a maximum at position 5 (Figure 7). Their positional behaviour differ from the typical Terminal sign 740, although they are graphically similar except for the additional stroke(s). This shows, that markings can effect the preferred sign position.

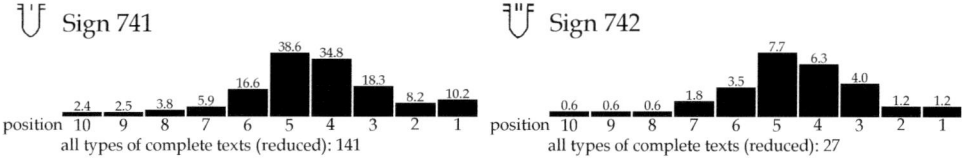

FIGURE AII.7. SIGNS 741 AND 742 HAVE A MID-MEDIAL DISTRIBUTION.

Signs that have a maximum at positions 7 to 8 are called Late-Medial signs (e.g. sign 555 and 752; Figure 8). Another Late-Medial sign is sign 590, but only in long patterned texts (see see Figure 9c).

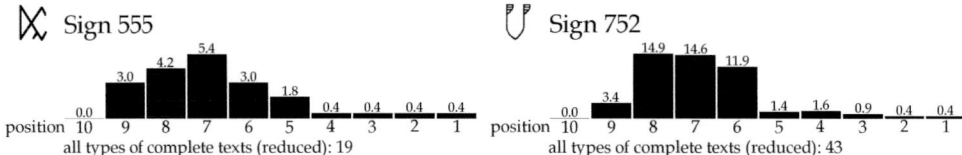

FIGURE AII.8. SIGNS WITH A LATE-MEDIAL SIGN DISTRIBUTION.

Doubled Signs

Signs can appear sometimes doubled. For example, sign 090 is doubled to form sign 091 and sign 820 doubles to form sign 821. Double signs are not coded in the inscriptions as a pair of the single sign (i.e. 090-090), but are treated as a new sign. This is because it is known from other writing systems that doubling affects the meaning of the sign. In alphabetic writing doubling a vowel often indicates a long vowel and thereby changing the meaning of the word, for example in English "red" versus "reed", and "god" versus "good". Not only vowels are doubled. In ancient Maya writing doubling the syllable *ku* results into the syllable *pi*, and doubling the logogram *IK* results into the syllable *ch'o* (Kettunen and Helmke 2009).

The analysis of the sign position allows a check of the effects of doubling in Indus writing. Sign 090 is a typical terminal sign, but sign 091 is used in any position with a maximum at initial position (Table 4). The second example is sign 820, a typically in the initial position. The doubled sign 821 is still often initial, but also frequently in late medial or terminal position.

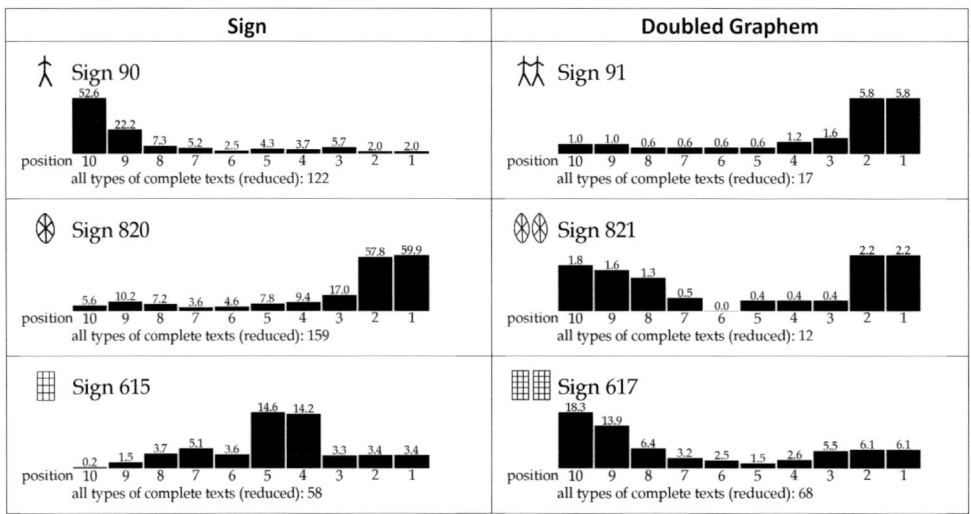

TABLE AII.4 COMPARISON OF SIGNS AND THEIR DOUBLED GRAPHEM

The last example is sign 615, which is mostly in late medial position, but can occur anywhere except in terminal position. The doubled sign 617 is mostly in terminal position, especially in single and multiple segment texts.

These examples show that doubling can have an effect on the sign's positional behaviour. Most likely this effect is due to a change in the grammatical function as a result of a different phonetic or semantic value. Therefore, a doubled sign should not be treated as twice the same basic sign but as a distinct sign (Wells 1999).

Mirroring of signs

The comparison of sign 920 to sign 921 has already shown, that mirroring of signs can change the positional histogram (Table 2). Other examples are sign 407 versus 408, or 435 versus 436 (Table 5). In contrast, sign 526 and its mirrored sign (527) have a similar positional distribution. Other mirrored signs are too rare to be analysed with confidence.

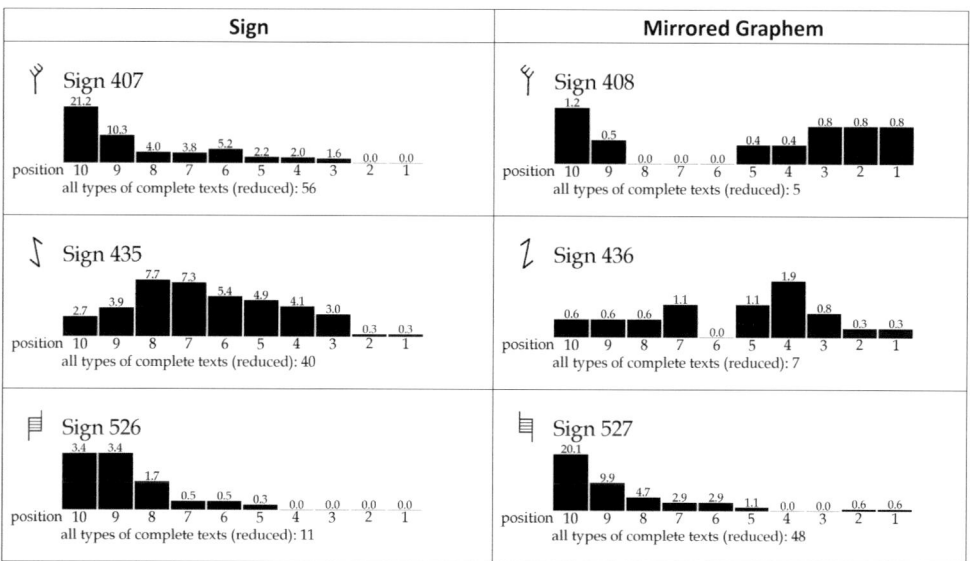

TABLE AII.5. COMPARISON OF SIGNS AND THEIR MIRRORS.

Sign Functions

Another important fact to consider is the class of texts. Text classes as defined by Wells (2006, p. 134; Chapter 3) distinguish between different text length (short or long) and typical sign pattern combinations (Fuls 2010, Table 2). In the following example signs 590 and 550 are analyzed for different text classes.

The sign 590 histogram of positional frequency for all complete texts shows a maximum at position 6 (Figure 9a). For Short Patterned texts (Figure 9b) the maximum is at about the same position (6-7). If the frequency is counted for Long Patterned texts (LP), a steep maximum at position 8 is evident (Figure 9c). For Multiple Segment texts (MS), sign 590 shows a typical behaviour of an initial sign (Figure 9d), and in Long Complex texts (LC), the positional distribution is irregular (Figure 9e). Therefore, sign 590 has different syntactic functions for different text classes, and the histogram of all text types shows the sum of the frequency curves for all text classes. This means that complex positional frequency curves are most likely a mixture of different positional frequency curves and must be analysed for different text classes separately.

Sign 550 also appears often in first position in about 46% of all complete texts (n = 82), but in all other texts the sign can occupy any sign position (Figure 10a). Its first (absolute) maximum is at position 1, but its second (local) maximum is at position 7 to 8. The second maximum at is highlighted in the histogram for Short and Partial Patterned texts (Figure 10b and c). This means that sign 550 has most likely two different functions or values depending on its context. Wells (2006, p. 152) suggest, that sign 550 is a syllabic sign, because the frequent sign pair 527-550 (n = 28) functions like one sign.

In two complete texts from Lothal (L-106 and L-229) it is used as alone, suggesting it is a logogram. At the present we do not have enough data regarding Indus syntax to determine the exact function(s), but that it has more than one function or value is certain.

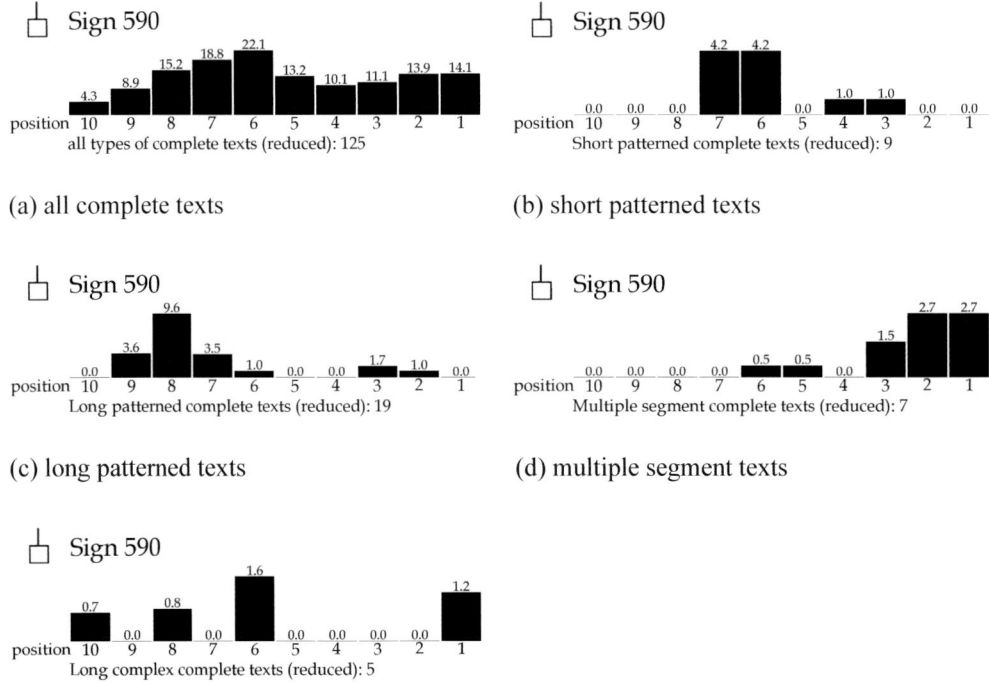

(a) all complete texts

(b) short patterned texts

(c) long patterned texts

(d) multiple segment texts

(e) long complex texts

FIGURE AII.9. HISTOGRAMS OF SIGN 590 FOR DIFFERENT TEXT CLASSES.

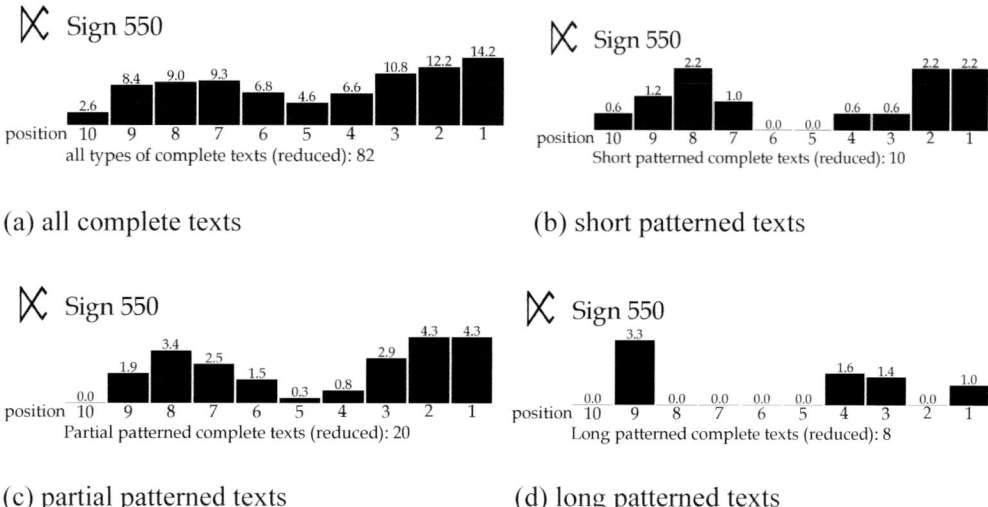

FIGURE AII.10. HISTOGRAM OF SIGN 550 WITH TWO MAXIMA AT POSITION 1 AND 8 IN VARIOUS TEXT CLASSES.

Summary

The normalized weighted sign position method summarizes texts of different length to calculate a histogram of positional sign behaviour. This method distinguishes different text lengths, in that short texts have a smaller weight then do longer texts. Positional preferences of signs can now be easily determined and it allows the identification of allographs by comparing positional histograms of similar sign graphs.

The positional analysis results in different classifications of Indus signs. Signs can be classified as Initial, Early-Medial, Mid-Medial, Late-Medial, Terminal. The histograms of Post-Terminal signs shows no difference when compared to Terminal signs, and can only be distinguished by detailed structural analysis.

The positional analysis shows, that doubling, mirroring, hatching, or marking of Indus signs can change their positional classification. Most likely this indicates a different function or semantic value of the modified signs. Signs with a similar positional distribution can now be grouped together. In each positional group signs share the same preferred text position and thereby the same syntactic position. Further analysis is needed to establish positional groups of signs with more confidence, since positional analysis highlights syntagmatic but not paradigmatic relationships of signs.

Positional analysis will help to distinguish between logograms and syllabic signs. Logograms and grammatical markers should be found in restricted syntactic positions (depending on the syntax of the Indus language), while syllables should have an almost constant positional distribution. Signs 382, 790, 832, and 892 are good candidates of syllabic signs. Many signs have a different preferred position depending on their text class. This indicates, that they can have more than one grammatical function or semantic value. Therefore, future analysis of the Indus script must differentiate between classes of texts and deal with the possibility of polyvalent signs. Each text class has specific features, for example, typical sign pattern of initial and terminal signs or text length (Wells 2011) and must be analysed separately. This is important, since previous statistical tests often analysed all Indus texts together (Yadav et al. 2008; Rao et al. 2009; Sinha et al. 2010).

The position of signs, and sign clusters, in specific texts classes are more predictable than when all text classes are combined for analysis (Figure 11). In patterned texts the positional histogram of each sign corresponds to its syntactic position. This allows the comparison of sign patterns in the more formulaic texts against those in Complex texts).

Multiple line texts are excluded in the calculation of positional histograms. The signs in multiple line texts can now be analysed to determine the reading direction and to investigate questions about the relationship of multiple lines of text to each other. Do they form a series of independent phrases or one long text?

The results of normalized sign distributions given in this Appendix have shown that there are significant differences in sign uses between the various text classes defined in Chapter 3. The reasons for this are not certain, but the most likely explanation is a shift in subject matter. Additionally, it has been show that some signs have restricted distributions (initial, medial or terminal) and other signs are in more general use. This may be indicating that some signs are logographs (restricted distributions) and others are syllabic signs (general distributions). This fact supports the conclusion in Chapter 3 that the Indus script is a logo-syllabic writing system. This system of sign position analysis is far more useful and informative than the initial, medial and terminal classification system in common use.

In Chapter 3 and 6 evidence of the syntax of Indus signs was presented. The identification of signs with restricted distributions supports the conclusion that there are three distinct sign cluster comprising full Indus texts.

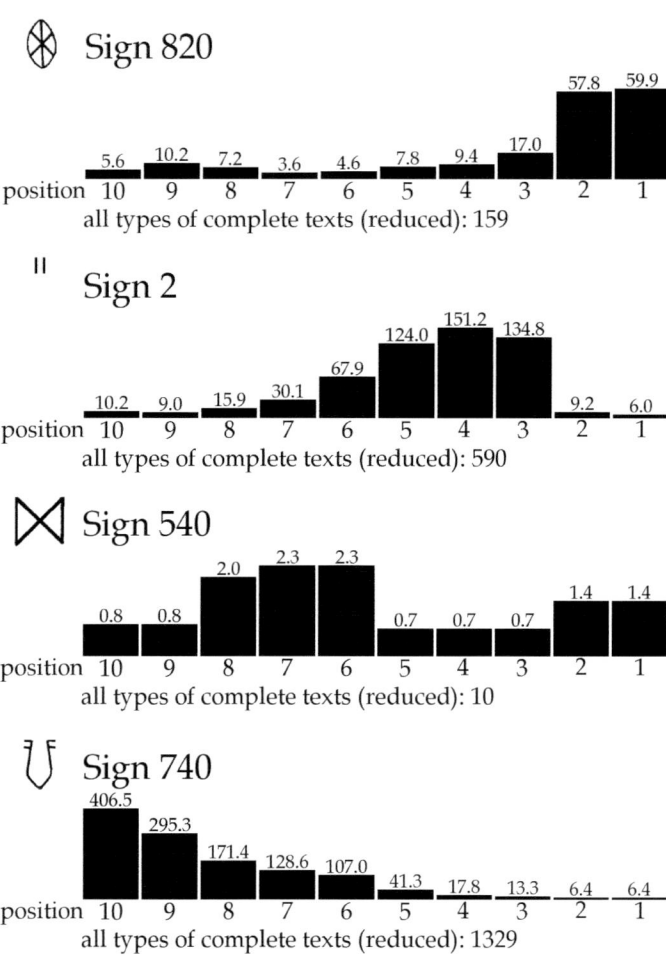

FIGURE AII.11. POSITIONAL HISTOGRAM OF SIGNS IN THE TEXT +740-540-002-820+ (SEAL M-1088). IT IS A TYPICAL EXAMPLE OF A SHORT PATTERNED TEXT WITH INITIAL CLUSTER 002-820 AND TERMINAL SIGN 740.

Appendix III

Classifying Undeciphered Writing Systems

Andreas Fuls

The purpose of this Appendix is to explore methods of measuring the similarity and differences between languages and between writing systems. Writing systems are classified as logographic, syllabic, or alphabetic, but intermediate forms are also extant. In ancient times most writing consisted of a mixture of logograms and syllables (logo-syllabic). The number of signs and their frequencies depend on the type of writing system and correlates inversely to the degree of phonetization of a specific script. In other words, fewer signs indicate greater phonetization. It can be shown that the mean word length depends on the sign distribution expressed by a linear relationship between mean word length and the exponent of a power law of the sign frequencies. The function can be applied to undeciphered writing systems to determine the mean word length by counting the frequency of the signs, and allows the classification of logographic-syllabic writing systems in greater detail than previously possible when only the number of different signs is counted.

Several ancient writing systems remain undeciphered or their proposed decipherments are controversial. For example, the decipherment of Isthmian script from Mesoamerica by Kaufman and Justeson ([1]) was severely criticized by one group of scholars ([2]). A detailed examination of this decipherment demonstrated that some aspect of the decipherment were sound, while other specific readings were conjectural (Wells n.d.). More than 60 published attempts have been made to crack the Indus script ([3]) and likewise no decipherment has been universally accepted. In some cases (Phaistos disk, proto-Biblic, etc,) only a limited number of texts are known, which reduces the chances of a successful decipherment.

One of the first steps in analysing an undeciphered writing system is the count of signs (graphemes; see Chapter 2), thereby creating a list of signs with unknown meaning and sound. While alphabetic or consonantal scripts have no more than about 36 signs, "pure" syllabic writing systems fall between 40 and 90 signs ([4]). If there are several hundred signs or more the script certainly contains many logograms. The classification of logographic-syllabic writing systems with an unknown ratio of logograms to syllables is problematic. The number of syllables depends on the language and varies between

---

[1] Justeson, John and Terrence Kaufman 1993 A Decipherment of Epi-Olmec Hieroglyphic Writing. Science, Vol. 259.
[2] Houston, Stephen D. and Michael D. Coe 2003 Has Isthmian Writing Been Deciphered? Mexicon, Vol. XXV:151-161.
[3] G. L. Possehl, *Indus Age: The Writing System*, (Univ. of Pennsylvania Press, Philadelphia, 1996).
[4] M. Coe, *Breaking the Maya Code*, (Thames and Hudson, New York, ed. 2, 1999), p. 43.

40 to 150 signs. Therefore, it is inappropriate to classify and describe the degree of phonetization of an unknown writing system using the number of different signs.

Counting the frequency of each sign gives a more precise measure of a writing system. Writing systems consisting mostly of logograms (Chinese or Proto-Sumerian) have several thousand signs, but most of them occur infrequently. In syllabic or mixed writing systems some signs are very frequent, but the majority of signs have medium to low frequencies.

George Kingsley Zipf proposed a power law in counting the frequency of words in different languages (Zipf's law). Testing Zipf's law for the frequency of signs in writing systems shows that the rank distribution of sign frequency does not fulfil a simple power law of:

$$f(r) = A/r = A*r^{-1} \tag{1}$$

where, rank = r, constant = A, and sign frequency = $f(r)$. Instead, counting the number of signs with the same frequency follows a modified power law (MPL):

$$w(r) = B*r^{G} \tag{2}$$

where, rank = r, exponent = G, constant = B, and the number of signs with the same frequency = $w(r)$ ([5]). Ranking is performed by sorting $w(r)$ in descending order. In a double-logarithmic diagram each MPL is represented as a strait line, where the slope equals the exponent G (Figure AIII.1). The exponent varies between about -2 for word counts and pure logographic writing systems, about -0.6 for pure syllabic writing systems and zero for alphabets. Logographic-syllabic writing systems like Classic Maya glyphs (G = -1.4) or Old-Assyrian cuneiform (G = -1.1) fall in between the extreme values. For Egypt Hieroglyphs (G = -1.4) the mean word length is dependent on how grammatical suffixes are treated: Counting suffixes as part of the words increases the mean word length by about 0.6 signs/word. Affixation has a great influence on word length; therefore we have to distinguish between languages with a high or low degree of affixation. It is important to realize that a highly affixed language can be represented in a logographic writing system with only one sign. Egyptian Hieroglyphic writing is a special case. The writing system gives no vowels explicitly. Instead phonetic signs represent 1, 2 or 3 consonants. Logographs are frequently used, as are determinatives. Determinatives are special signs used to classify the whole word but have no phonetic value. These aspects of ancient Egyptian writing create a more complex writing system than is found in either the strictly syllabic or Logo-syllabic systems. All ancient writing systems are unique in some way, and use special signs as markers or to clarify meaning (determinatives and phonetic compliments especially).

---
[5] S. Naranan, V. K. Balasubrahmanyan, (In: *Quantitative Linguistics*, R. Köhler, G. Altmann, R. G. Piotrowski, Ed., (Walter de Gruyter, Berlin, 2005), pp.716-738.

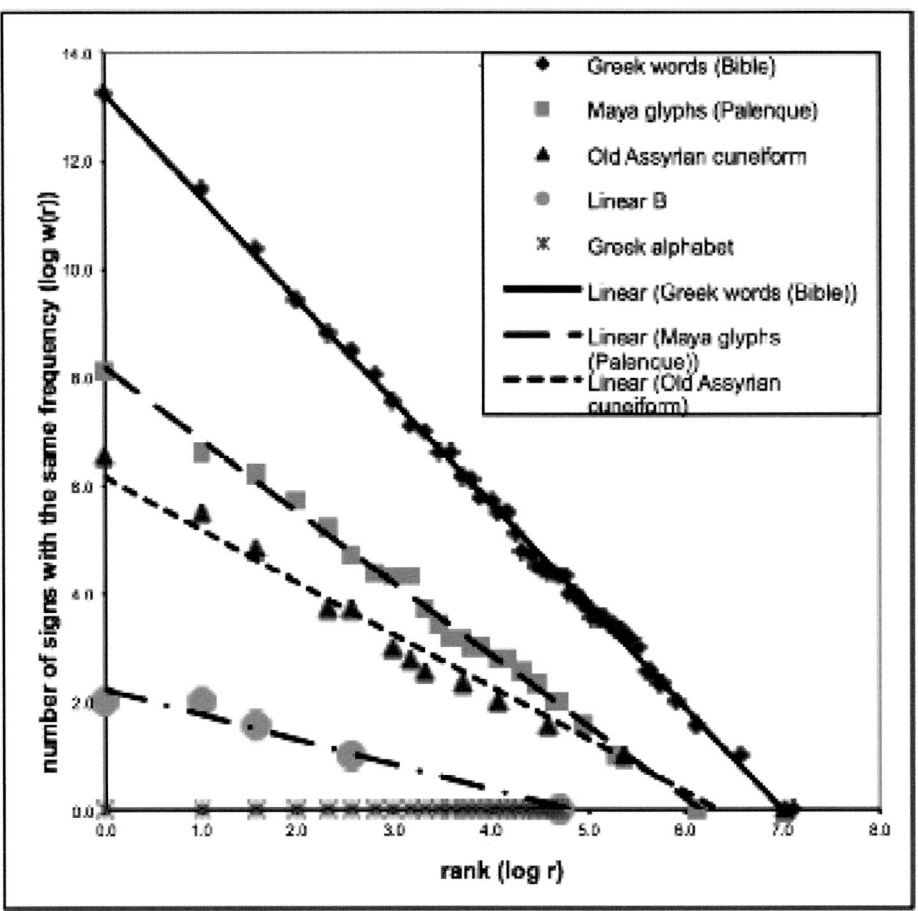

FIGURE AIII.1: RANK VERSUS NUMBER OF SIGNS WITH THE SAME FREQUENCY IN A DOUBLE-LOGARITHMIC SCALE FOR DIFFERENT WRITING SYSTEMS. THE SLOPE OF EACH LINEAR TREND EQUALS THE EXPONENT G OF EACH MPL (FORMULA 2).

Analysing the sign frequency curves of various writing systems, shows that the exponent G and the mean word length of each script is highly correlated and dependent on the degree of affixation of the language (Figure AIII.2). Each linear function allows the estimation of the mean word length (WL) by calculating:

for isolating languages and lists: $WL \approx 0.70 * G + 2.81$ (3)

for fusional languages: $WL \approx 1.97 * G + 4.71$ (4)

for polysynthetic languages: $WL \approx 2.66 * G + 6.41$ (5)

The mean word length of unknown writing systems, even if the script does not indicate any word divider, can now be estimated.

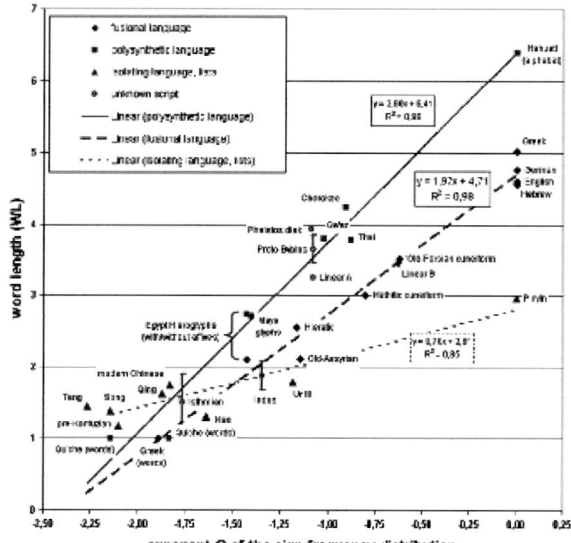

FIGURE AIII.2: RELATIONSHIP BETWEEN EXPONENT G OF SIGN FREQUENCY CURVE AND MEAN WORD LENGTH WL (FORMULA 3, 4 AND 5) FOR DIFFERENT WRITING SYSTEMS. THE LINEAR FUNCTIONS ARE BASED ON KNOWN WRITING SYSTEMS FOR POLYSYNTHETIC LANGUAGES ($R^2 = 0.98$), FUSIONAL LANGUAGES ($R^2 = 0.98$), OR ISOLATING LANGUAGES AND LISTS ($R^2 = 0.85$). DATA SOURCES: BIBLE FOR GREEK AND HEBREW ([6]), NAHUATL ([7]), QUICHE WORDS ([8]), ISTHMIAN (1,2), MAYA GLYPHS ([9]), INDUS ([10]), LINEAR A AND LINEAR B ([11], [12]), HIEROGLYPHIC EGYPTIAN TEXTS ([13]), HIERATIC EGYPTIAN TEXTS ([14]), PROTO-BYBLOS ([15]), OLD-ASSYRIAN AND UR III CUNEIFORM ([16]), HETHITIC CUNEIFORM ([17]), PERSIAN CUNEIFORM ([18]), GE´EZ ([19]), CHINESE TEXTS ([20]).

The frequency distribution of the 697 signs in the Indus script indicate an exponent G = -1.35 (Figure AIII.3). Since Indus signs are written *scriptio continua* most often without any word divider it is difficult to determine word boundaries. Therefore, it is necessary to estimate the mean word length using different methods. First, complete inscriptions

---

[6] J. Planeta, DAVAR3 version 3.0.2.319 (http://www.davar3.net/).
[7] A. J. O. Anderson, C. E. Dibble: Florentine Codex: Books 1, 3-5, (The School of American Research and The Univ. of Utah, Santa Fe/New Mexico, 1970).
[8] A. J. Christenson: *Popol Vuh Electronic Library* (Brigham Young Univ., Provo/Utah, 2007).
[9] W. M. Ringle, T. C. Smith-Stark: *A Concordance to the Inscriptions of Palenque, Chiapas, Mexico*, (Tulane Univ., New Orleans, 1996).
[10] B. Wells, Epigraphic Appoaches to Indus Writing, (Oxbow Books, Oxford, 2011).
[11] D. W. Packard: *Minoan Linear A*, (Univ. of California Press, Berkley, 1974).
[12] T. Timm, *Der Diskos von Phaistos*, (Books on Demand, Norderstedt, 2008).
[13] JSesh Hieroglyphic Editor v. 4.3 (http://jsesh.qenherkhopeshef.org/).
[14] Thesaurus Linguae Aegyptiae, (http://aaew.bbaw.de/tla/index.html).
[15] M. Dunand: *Byblia Grammata*, (Beyrouth, 1945).
[16] Cuneiform Digital Library Initiative, (http://cdli.ucla.edu/downloads.html).
[17] Hethitologie Portal Mainz, (http://www.hethport.uni-wuerzburg.de/HPM/txthetlink.php).
[18] E. A. W. Budge, *The Sculptures and Inscriptions of Darius the Great on the rock of Behistûn in Persia*, (British Museum, London, 1907).
[19] J. Tropper: *Altäthiopisch – Grammatik des Ge´ez mit Übungstexten und Glossar*, (Ugarit-Verlag, Münster, 2002).
[20] Baidu (http://baike.baidu.com)

with one or two signs might represent only one word, which would lead to a mean word length of 1.7 signs per word. Second, complete inscriptions with three or more signs have been analysed using the multivariate segmentation process (Chapter 3 and Appendix I). In order to separate sign sequences and count the number of words, a connectivity limit has to be set. This means, that sign sequences with a connectivity value greater than the limit value are taken as one word. Any sign pair with a connectivity value smaller than the limit value will be separated and belong to different words. A connectivity limit of 1.5, which is the starting value of the multivariate segmentation process, results in a mean word length of about 1.9, but a higher connectivity limit of 1.7 leads to more words and therefore to a smaller mean word length of about 1.5 signs per word. Comparing all three estimations shows, that the mean word length in Indus inscriptions falls most likely in the range between 1.5 and 1.9 signs (i.e. ≈ 1.7 ±0.2 signs).

The structural analysis in Chapter 3 would suggest a word length of 2 to 5 signs. The comparatively low mean value is influenced by the many Indus text with 1 or two sign. The problems with the Indus corpus have been detailed in Chapter 2 and elsewhere (Wells 2011). The main problem relating to word length is the lack knowledge regarding subject matter and root language. The shortest texts (1-3 signs) may be abbreviations or mnemonics, or their contexts of use may be self-explanatory. For example, a ceramic vessel containing 100 bead may only require the amount (100) if this type of vessel is only used for storing and/or transporting beads. Likewise, in the case where only beads are being traded between groups or individuals the descriptive portion of the message is unnecessary. So mean word length in the case of the Indus script can be a guide. But may not be taken out of their archaeological and epigraphic context as a precise and objective measure.

As can be seen in Figure AIII.2 Indus writing is similar to Ur III cuneiform texts with a mean word length of 1.79 signs. There are two possible explanations. First, it is indicating a language with less affixation (e.g. a fusional language). Second, the low mean word length might reflect that most Indus texts are lists of objects like Ur III cuneiform texts, which does not require a complex grammar with many affixations. In fact, many Indus texts appear to be noun+number configurations (Chapter 4 and 5).

The structural analysis in Chapter 3 identified several texts that were lists. Additionally, as Indus texts are on very small media (mostly < 1 inch^2) there is no room for verbose literary remarks. Conversely, there are many texts that are longer (6-15 signs) that do exhibit both paradigmatic and syntagmatic structures. The apparent word lengths of the syntagmatic components are 2-3 signs. Often this takes the form of a one or two sign stem followed by a one or two sign affix(s). Word length based on structural analysis is 1-4 signs, with a mean word length of 2-3 signs.

For Proto-Byblos writing the frequency distribution of 130 different signs (G = -1.1) and a mean word length of 3.65 (± 0.2) signs indicates a polysynthetic language. This is

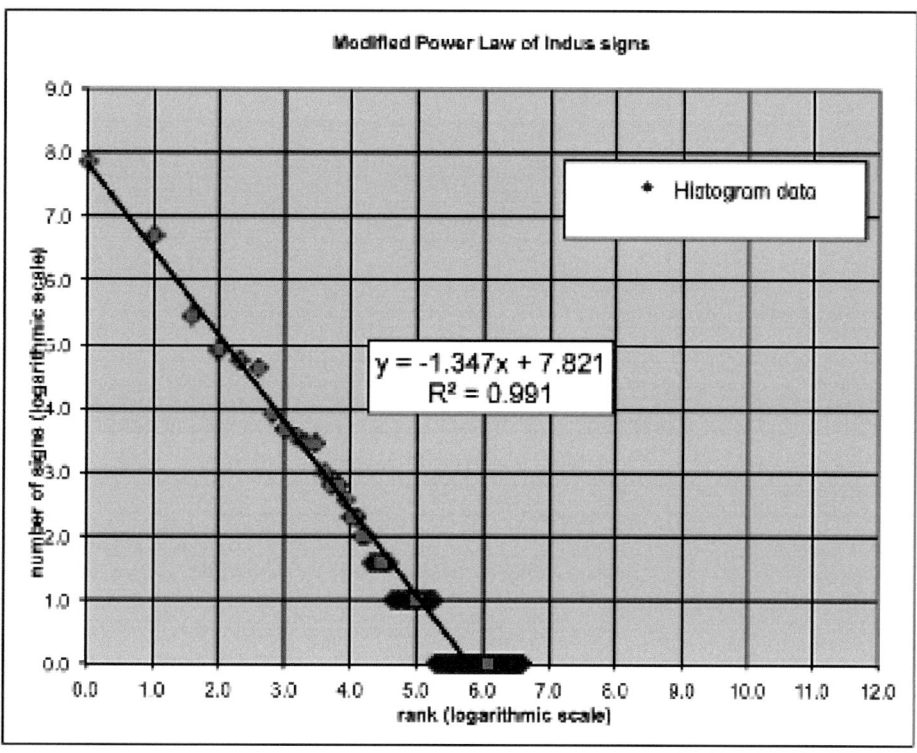

FIGURE AIII.3: MODIFIED POWER LAW (MPL) OF INDUS SIGNS RESULTS IN EXPONENT G = -1.347 (R^2 = 0.991).

in agreement with three root signs plus affixes as in Semitic languages, very similar to the Ethiopian syllabic script (Ge´ez). Proto-Byblos is likely highly phoneticized.

The frequency distribution of 211 Isthmian signs (G = -1.75) results in a mean word length between about 1.1 to 1.8, therefore most signs are logograms. Detailed structural analysis of Isthmian texts shows a patter of 2 sign words—logograph + affix. The average word length is ≈ 2 sign blocks. As with Classic Maya writing, Isthmian often conflates logographs or syllabic signs, or both, into a single glyph block. For example, the Isthmian glyph for 'day' = *jama* can be written syllabically as *ja* + *ma* (2 syllables) or logographically as JAMA. A third example gives the phonetic spelling = *ja* + *ma*, but with an affix *wu* marking the past tense (i.e. 'yesterday'). In this example the word length is one, two or three signs.

On the Phaistos disk the sign frequency curve (G = -1.1) and mean word length of 3.9 signs indicates a highly syllabic writing system for a polysynthetic language with many affixes.

A special case is Chinese writing, where the mean word length increases from pre-Confusian texts (1.2) to modern Chinese (1.75) to 3 signs/word in Pinyin. The earliest Chinese writing (Shang) is logo-syllabic and linear. The exponent G of the sign frequencies falls in the same range as for pure word counting. Early Chinese texts indicate a trend toward logo-syllabic writing from pre-Confusian to Han, which was interrupted by the orthographic standardization from Xŭ Shèn (~100 A.D.) [21]. Later texts indicate a linear trend starting with Tang and ending with modern Chinese (G = -2.3 to –1.8).

The number of signs and their frequencies depend on the type of writing system and the language. Other factors influencing the total number of signs are allographs, polyvalent signs and context. Further research is needed to define the influence of these confounding factors on the frequency distribution of signs. Further, it is desirable to determine word length and sign frequencies of other known writing systems in order to better understand the full range of epigraphic and linguistic relations. As any analysis of undeciphered scripts must be based on knowledge of both the root language and the mechanics of the writing system, the information supplied by this method is crucial to the process of decipherment.

---

[21] W.G. Boltz: Early Chinese Writing, (In: P. T. Daniels and W. Bright, The World's Writing Systems, Oxford Univ. Press, Oxford, 1996), p. 196.

Literature Cited

Binford, Lewis R. 1962. Archaeology as anthropology. In Contemporary Archaeology, ed by M. Leone, pp. 93-101. Southern Illinois University, Carbondale, USA

Bonta, Steve 1995 *Study of the Indus Valley Script*. Master of Arts, Brigham Young University 11(2):19-57

Burrow, Thomas and Murray Barnson Emeneau 1961 *A Dravidian etymological dictionary*, Clarendon Press

Forrer, Emil O. 1932 *Die hethitische Bilderschrift*. University of Chicago Press, Chicago

Fuller, Dorian Q. 2008 *Encyclopedia of Archaeology* vol. 1, pp. 756-768 Neolithic Cultures, Institute of Archaeology, University, College London

Fuls, Andreas 2009 Methoden zur Entzifferung von Schriftsystemen. Megalithos, Vol. 10, no. 3, p. 98-104

Fuls, Andreas 2010 Entwicklung einer geographisch-epigraphischen Datenbank der Indusschrift. In: Sven Weisbrich and Robert Kaden (Ed.), Entwicklerforum Geodäsie und Geoinformationstechnik 2010, p. 29–45, Shaker Verlag, Aachen

Fuls, Andreas 2012 Volumenmaße von Tongefäßen der Induskultur. In: Sven Weisbrich and Robert Kaden (Ed.), Entwicklerforum Geodäsie und Geoinformationstechnik 2011, p. 101-114, Shaker Verlag, Aachen

Jansen, Michael and G. Urban 1985 *Mohenjo-Daro: Report of the Aachen University Mission 1979-1985*. E.J. Brill, Leiden

Joshi, Jagat Pati and Asko Parpola 1987 *Corpus of Indus Seals and Inscriptions*. Suomalainen Tiedeakatemia, Helsinki

Kelley, David H. 1976 *Deciphering the Maya Script*. University of Texas Press, Austin

Kelley, David H. 1982 The Puuc in Perspective. In L. Mills (ed) *Puuc Symposium 1977*. Central Kettunen, Harri and Christophe Helmke

Kelley, David H. 2009 *Introduction to Maya Hieroglyphs*. URL: http://www.wayeb.org/download/resources/wh2009english.pdf, last access: 5.10.2010 College, Pella

Knorozov, Yuri 1968 *Brief Report on the Investigation of the Proto-Indian Texts*

Knorozov, Yuri 1970 The Formal Analysis of the Proto-Indian Texts. *Journal of Tamil Studies* II:13-28

Kober, Alice E. 1942 The American Journal of Philology, Vol. 63, No. 3, pp. 320-327. The Johns Hopkins University Press

Kober, Alice E. 1945 Evidence of Inflection in the "Chariot" Tablets from Knossos. American Journal of Archaeology, Vol. 49, No. 2, pp. 143-15. Archaeological Institute of America

Kober, Alice E. 1946 Inflection In Linear Class B: 1-Declension. *American Journal of Archaeology* 50:268-276

Kober, Alice E. 1948 The Minoan Scripts: Fact and Theory. *American Journal of Archaeology* 52:82-103

Korvink, Micheal P. 2008 The Indus Script: Positional Statistical Approach. Gilund Press

Mackay, E. J. H. 1938 *Further Excavations at Mohenjo-daro*. Munshiram Manoharlal Publishers Pvt. Ltd., Delhi

Mahadevan, Iravatham 1970 Dravidian Parallels in Proto-Indian Script. *Journal of Tamil Studies* 2:157-276

Mahadevan, Iravatham 1977 *The Indus Script, Texts Concordance and Tables.* Archaeological Survey of India, New Delhi

Mahadevan, Iravatham 1982 *Terminal Ideograms in the Indus Script.* Oxford and IBH Publishing Co, New Delhi

Mahadevan, Iravatham 1986 Dravidian Models Of Decipherment Of The Indus Script: A Case Study. *Tamil Civilization* 4:133-143

Marshall, Sir John 1931*Mohenjo-daro and the Indus Civilization.* Arthur Probsthian, London

McAlpin, David W. 1981 *Proto-Elamo-Dravidian: The Evidence and its Implications.* The American Philosophical Society, Philadelphia

Meadow, Richard H. and J. M. Kenoyer 1993 *Harappa Archaeological Research project: 1993 Excavations.* Director General of Archaeology and Museums

Meadow, Richard H. and J. M. Kenoyer 2001 *Recent Discoveries and Highlights form Excavations at Harappa: 1998-2000.* Indo Koko Kenkyu No. 22. Indian Archaeological Society, Tokyo

Meadow, Richard H., J. M. Kenoyer and Rita P. Wright 1994 *Harappa Excavation 1994.* Director General of Archaeology and Museums

Meadow, Richard H., J. M. Kenoyer and Rita P. Wright 1995 *Harappa Excavation 1995.* Director General of Archaeology and Museums

Meadow, Richard H., J. M. Kenoyer and Rita P. Wright 1996 *Harappa Excavation 1996.* Director General of Archaeology and Museums

Meadow, Richard H., J. M. Kenoyer and Rita P. Wright 1997 *Harappa Excavation 1997.* Director General of Archaeology and Museums

Meadow, Richard H., J. M. Kenoyer and Rita P. Wright 1998 *Harappa Excavation 1998.* Director General of Archaeology and Museums

Meadow, Richard H., J. M. Kenoyer and Rita P. Wright 1999 *Harappa Excavation 1999.* Director General of Archaeology and Museums

Meadow, Richard H., J. M. Kenoyer and Rita P. Wright 2001 *Harappa Excavation 2000 and 2001.* Director General of Archaeology and Museums

Nissen, Hans J., Peter Damerow and Robert K. Englund 1993 *Archaic Bookkeeping: Early Writing and Techniques of Economic Administration in the Ancient Near East.* The University of Chicago Press, London

Parpola, Asko 1970 The Indus Script Decipherment: the situation at the end of 1969. *Journal of Tamil Studies* II:89-110

Parpola, Asko 1994 *Deciphering the Indus Script.* Cambridge University Press, Cambridge

Parpola, Simo, Asko Parpola and Robert H. Brunswig, Jr. 1977 The Meluḫḫa Village: Evidence of Acculturation of Harappan Traders in Late Third Millennium Mesopotamia? *Journal of the Economic and Social History of the Orient,* Vol. 20, No. 2 (pp. 129-165)

Possehl, Gregory L. 1996 *Indus Age: The Writing System.* University Of Pennsylvania Press, Philadelphia

Rao, Rajesh P. N., Nisha Yadav, Mayank N. Vahia, Hrishikesh Joklekar, R. Adhikari, and Iravatham Mahadevan 2009 A Markov model of the Indus script. *Proceedings of the National Academy of Sciences* (PNAS), 106:13685–13690

Ratnagar, Shereen 1981 *Encounters: The Westerly Trade of the Harappan Civilization*. Oxford University Press, Delhi

Sinha, Sitabhra, Raj Kumar Pan, Nisha Yadav, Mayank Vahia and Iravatham Mahadevan, 2009 Network analysis reveals structure indicative of syntax in the corpus of undeciphered Indus civilization inscriptions, *Proceedings of the 2009 Workshop on Graph-based Methods for Natural Language Processing* Association for Computational Linguistics Stroudsburg, PA, USA Sinha, Sitabhra, Md Ashraf Izhar, Raj Kumar Pan and Bryan K. Wells

Sinha, Sitabhra, Raj Kumar Pan, Nisha Yadav, Mayank Vahia and Iravatham Mahadevan, 2011 Network analysis of a corpus of undeciphered Indus civilization inscriptions indicates yntactic organization. *Computer Speech and Language*, Volume 25 Issue 3. Academic Press Ltd. London, UK

Vats, Madho Sarup 1940 *Excavations at Harappa*. Munshiram Manoharlal Publishers Pvt. Ltd., Delhi

Wells, Bryan 1999 *An Introduction To Indus Writing*. Early Site Research Foundation, Independence

Wells, Bryan 2006 *Epigraphic Approaches to Indus Writing*. PhD Dissertation, Harvard University, Cambridge, MA

Wells, Bryan 2012 *Epigraphic Approaches To Indus Writing*. ASPR Monograph Series, Cambridge, MA. Oxbow Press.

Wooley, Leonard C. 1934 *Ur Excavations, Volume 2: The Royal Cemetery*. The Joint Expedition of the British Museum and The Museum of the University of Pennsylvania to Mesopotamia

Yadav, Nisha, M.N. Vahai, Iravatham Mahadevan, and H. Joglekar 2008 A statistical approach for pattern search in Indus writing. *International Journal of Dravidian Linguistics*, 37(1):39–52.